THE NEW
AUSTRALIAN CINEMA

THE NEW AUSTRALIAN CINEMA

Editor: Scott Murray   Associate editor: Peter Beilby

ELM TREE BOOKS/LONDON

This book was initiated by Peter Beilby and reflects a
desire to evaluate critically the renaissance of the
Australian film industry in the 1970s. Originally
conceived as a series of articles for *Cinema Papers*, the
project expanded in direction and size to its present
format.

Unless otherwise indicated, the director is named with
the film — e.g., Tim Burstall's **End Play** — and the date
of its Australian premiere is given in parentheses.

While every attempt has been made to keep this book
up-to-date and comprehensive, the completion dates of
some chapters may have prevented mention of several
features completed late in 1979.

Published in Great Britain 1980 by
Elm Tree Books/Hamish Hamilton Ltd
Garden House, 57-59 Long Acre, London WC2E 9JZ

ISBN 0241 104394

First published in Australia 1980 by
Thomas Nelson Australia Pty Limited

Produced by Cinema Papers Pty Ltd
Designer: Keith Robertson
Sub-editor: Maurice Perera
Proof-reader: Arthur Salton

Typeset in Computerset Times 11/13 pt by
Affairs Computer Typesetting

Printed by Tien Mah Litho Printing Co. (Pte) Ltd.

CONTENTS

FOREWORD

Phillip Adams

Just 10 years ago, on behalf of The Australia Council Film Committee, I wrote a report that began: "To borrow from another declaration, this Committee holds certain truths to be self-evident." It then went on to suggest that, after 60 years of cinema, an indigenous film industry might be fun.

Much to our delight, John Gorton pushed the recommendations, legislating for an Australian Film and Television Development Corporation (which subsequently metamorphosized into the Australian Film Commission) and for an Experimental Film Fund (which promptly bit the feeding hand by producing, as its first film, an anti-Vietnam documentary). The Australian Film and Television School, almost a victim of the de-Gortonizing spirit of the McMahon government, was consequently brought into being by Gough Whitlam.

For 30 years, Australian filmmaking had been as stuffed as Phar Lap. A few brave eccentrics like Cecil Holmes and Tim Burstall had battled on, only to see our cinema doors slammed in their faces. Suddenly, unbelievably, Australia was all but deafened by the cacophony of clapper boards.

The new Australian Film Industry may not rank with Egypt's Fifth Dynasty or the Italian Renaissance when mankind's cultural apotheoses have been recorded, but it has been an exhilarating time. We can now enjoy the luxury of feeling blasé about our successes, taking for granted the fact that, tonight, Australian films will be screening in up to 70 nations.

There was a conscious irony in the way I pinched that opening line from the American Declaration of Independence to open our plea to Canberra, for American cultural imperialism has undoubtedly played a major role in the death of the industry that Ken Hall and his colleagues had established. Yet cultural imperialism was only half the story — the rest was our cultural cringing, our sense of inferiority and inadequacy.

I grew up at a time when the Australian accent was never heard from a radio, a stage or a screen *unless* it was from a comedian. Indeed, when Bruce Beresford, Barry Humphries and I set out to make **The Adventures of Barry McKenzie** (1972), we couldn't find actors who could 'do' the accent. After all, unless they'd cracked it for a part in *The One Day of the Year* or *Summer of the Seventeenth Doll*, it was unlikely that a local Thespian had ever played an Australian role.

Now a new truth is held to be self-evident. Our politicians, film corporations and investors are insisting on the need for commercial success in the U.S. We are starting to make films aimed principally at that market, and are eagerly dubbing them with Los Angelean accents. Doesn't that smack of cultural imperialism and cultural cringing? Isn't that tantamount to Sid Nolan putting a stetson on one of his Kelly paintings to help it sell in Dallas or Houston?

When we re-established the Australian film industry it was a declaration of independence. We needed to hear our own accent. We wanted our voice to be heard in the world. So why the unseemly rush to become the colloquial dolls for Columbia, Warners and Fox?

Do you remember the portrait of that Sydney Yank in Phillip Noyce's **Newsfront** (1978)? Suddenly, there are a lot of those unlovely hybrids around. Beware.

INTRODUCTION

Ken G. Hall

This is an important book because it deals with a most important subject: the renaissance of the Australian film industry in the 1970s.

The revival occurred because of government financial sponsorship of film production for the first time in the history of this country. In the nine to 10 years since it began to happen, more than 130 features have been made. The bulk of them are analysed by the authors of the following contributions. But to discover why a revival was *necessary*, and how the giant step forward came about, one must look briefly at the past.

The coming of sound created a great revival of feature production in Australia in the most unlikely, and indeed completely inappropriate, period of the Great Depression at the beginning of the 1930s. We at Cinesound, who in 1931 began to put one stone upon another as the possible foundations of an industry, had an abundance of nothing to begin with. But somehow a healthy, thrusting nucleus evolved and our early films were successful beyond our wildest hopes. We made no masterpieces and essayed none. But we *did* make commercially-successful films. We had to; there was no choice. You sank or swam on your commercial success at a time when next to nobody, and governments in particular, wanted to back Australian film production — that is, until **On Our Selection** (1930) outgrossed all films, foreign or local, released in Australia up to that time.

Andrew Pike, in his thoughtful analysis ("The Past") which follows, says: "Hall's philosophy of showmanship . . . has been falsely characterized [by his critics] as anti-art and primarily concerned with the 'conning' of money from the public."

The money my early films made did not go into company coffers — or my pockets! It helped to turn a skating rink into a film studio which endured for 40 years, and to equip it with the vital necessities of filmmaking. It made future production possible. Besides, one cannot con the public for long — certainly not for nine years and 17 films.

So, I must raise again the wicked bogy of commercialism in filmmaking, knowing that it will send at least some of the aforementioned critics into paroxysms of hysterical anger. But it is a truth which, like it or not, has to be learned: *There will be no enduring film industry in this country unless it is based on commercially-successful films.*

I am no enemy of Art; I deeply admire and respect it in all its aspects. But I am suspicious of the pseudo artistic approach which is so often used as a camouflage for confused and negative thinking. Film production is a tough and highly competitive business fraught with grave risks: it is not for the immature.

Until some take their heads out of the clouds, they will not be able to see the people on earth around them. It is for these people, the multitude, and not the favored few, that films are made.

The production upsurge of the 1930s, halted by the war, regained temporary momentum in 1946 when successful films like **Smithy**, **The Overlanders** and **A Son Is Born** were released. But the apparent upbeat was really a downbeat. A grim doldrum settled over the entire local scene. Charles Chauvel made two more films in the next 10 years — the first, **Sons of Matthew** (1949), a success; the second, **Jedda** (1955), a failure. I made newsreels.

The 25-odd years from the mid-1940s to the 1970s were indeed the Dark Ages of film production in this country. The pre-war thriving industry had been effectively throttled. And perhaps because those years were so grim to look back upon, so baldly unproductive of anything worthwhile, that a small band of very dedicated people, concerned no doubt by the wasted years and the wasted talent, decided to do something about it. Their identity it seems has never been officially acknowledged, but it is highly probable that Barry Jones and Phillip Adams, in association with Dr H. C. Coombs, first sowed the seed in the mind of John Gorton, Prime Minister of the day. For bringing about something that had never been achieved in the past, all concerned, including John Gorton, deserve the highest praise.

There was an immediate flurry of preparation, cameras rolled and eventually finished prints found their way, at increasing tempo, into the theatres of the country.

After a time lapse of almost 10 years what has been achieved?

The writers of the ensuing sections have devoted themselves mainly to analyses of the quality, or otherwise, of the films under review, the artistic aspects of them and what motivated the directors and producers. All of these are very important objectives, of course. But the overwhelming question, like it or not, is the blunt: How well have we done? How successful have we been in the markets of the world?

We have not done badly, but we have to do better.

On the credit side, first-class directors have shown their creative talent and outstanding cinematographers have left their indelible marks. Able, and by now experienced, producers, designers and film editors are working in the industry.

On the commercial credit side is the fact that, this year, four Australian films, **Picnic at Hanging Rock** (1975), **The Last Wave** (1977), **Patrick** (1978) and **Mad Max** (1979), have broken sturdily into the previously impregnable American market, by far the largest — and the toughest — in the world. They have set quite remarkable box-office gross figures, but, because of inordinately high costs of theatre operation, advertising and distribution fees in the U.S., the real answer will be in how much revenue comes back to the producers in Australia. Time, as usual, will tell.

Aided by a sympathetic press, and media generally, which publishes the good news and seldom the bad, the public has an undoubted impression that the industry is thriving, striding steadily forward. But is it? Is that the feeling of all the people in the industry? Is the percentage of failure low enough to ensure the industry will survive? Are we making too many films (average about 16 a year)? Could the output be reduced to enhance quality and with greater emphasis on marketability governing choice of subject? Are we making too many bland, lacklustre, poorly-titled films which will surely become B-graded by distribution and exhibition interests?

It is not for me to answer these questions and the many more which could be asked. But the people in the industry — and the authorities controlling it — must face up to them.

I believe everybody involved is genuinely and sincerely intent on finding success, and I speak as I do only because I do not want to see the tragedy of those Dark Ages revived. I do not want to see the door slammed down again, for if that happens it may not be re-opened this century — or the next for that matter. Because the cinema, as we know it, is certain to be replaced — and soon.

1 THE PAST: boom and bust

Andrew Pike

The past, in terms of Australian feature film production, is a distant one. After a short burst of activity between 1910 and 1912, the production of feature films declined sharply and continued at a level of rarely more than 10 features a year until World War 2. Efforts to revive production after the disruptions caused by the war failed, and during the 1950s and 1960s only a few locally-made features were completed. The result was that for two decades Australians became used to seeing little but British and American films in their cinemas. This period of inactivity ended abruptly, however, in 1970; new people had come to dominate production, beliefs in the nature of a viable industry had altered, and the films being made bore little resemblance to earlier work.

This distinction between past and present is more acute than in some other film-producing countries, where continuity of production has been maintained throughout the century, and where the evolution of production techniques and philosophies has been more gradual. In contrast with the present industry, the Australian cinema before World War 2 was essentially local in content and marketing orientation. But to label that earlier cinema "local" is not to call it "narrow" or "parochial". Many early films benefited from a sense of specific location and from familiarity with specific audiences — qualities that are often missing in the cosmopolitanism of current production. Indeed, the success of past filmmakers in communicating directly with their local audiences makes their work especially relevant to the present industry in its attempt to find a viable foothold in home and overseas markets.

The most obvious single factor in the revival of production in the 1970s was the high level of government investment brought about by Prime Minister John Gorton's decision to establish a film bank and film school in 1969. Not only does the present industry rely on the availability of government finance, but also on the government to absorb its losses. Neither government investment, nor the cushioning effect of the film bank on commercial failures, was available to filmmakers before 1970. In fact, the history of production in those years is one of constant struggle to achieve financial stability in a hostile marketplace, and to break through the barriers erected by the distribution and exhibition arms of the industry.

Barriers to Production

The most common cry of producers, from the 1920s to the 1960s, was that the grip of powerful foreign production companies over the Australian distribution and exhibition trade was stifling the local industry by making Australian screens inaccessible to Australian filmmakers. But the Americans, who had begun to arrive in force towards the end of World War 1, merely perpetuated a trading environment that was already established.

As early as 1912, when feature film production was in its infancy, Australian exhibitors and distributors had begun to form alliances to establish a monopolistic control of one organization over the Australian film scene. The "combine", as it was known in the industry, traded as Australasian Films in distribution and as Union Theatres in exhibition;[1] it barely left room in the marketplace for rivals, or for films that came from outside the sources of the organization. Displaying little interest in Australian production, the combine concentrated on filling its theatres with imported films, and Australian production companies began to fade within months.

In 1911, more than 10 production companies had made 50-odd fiction films, but by the end of 1912 only five or six companies were in existence, and only 30 features had been produced that year. In 1913, less than 20 films had appeared, and the number declined even further in the following years. Filmmaking had become an early victim of competition between Australian businessmen for control of the marketplace. Local production thereafter depended entirely on shifts in the policies or sympathies of the men who ruled the distribution and exhibition trade.

By 1920, American companies broke the monopoly of Australasian Films and Union Theatres, but they rarely expressed interest in local production. Filmmaking after 1912 remained fragmented and defensive, and companies rose and fell as producers sought ways around the commercial barrier.

There were, of course, some exceptions to the apathy of the distribution and exhibition trade towards local production. Between 1925 and 1940, Australasian Films and Union Theatres were engaged in production, first in their Master Pictures series until 1929, and, after 1932, in their wholly-owned subsidiary, Cinesound Productions. Their motives for supporting production at these times are obscure. In the late 1920s it was partly fear of government intervention in an industry which allowed no room for Australian films, and in both cases it was partly to cope with a recurring shortage of films for the company's theatres.

Much of the initiative for this production at Cinesound (which shall be dealt with later) was also due to Stuart Doyle, managing director during the late 1920s and early 1930s. Doyle

Stuart Doyle, managing director of Union Theatres and Australasian Films during the late 1920s and early 1930s.

realized the potential commercial value of Australian cinema, and was lured by the romantic image that Hollywood had created around film production. His resignation in 1937 marked the end of the organization's interest in feature production, and the advent of World War 2 gave the new managing director, Norman Rydge, a convenient excuse to withdraw from the risks that Doyle had taken in production.

The Australian branches of American distribution companies also showed occasional interest in Australian production, most notably in the work of Hercules McIntyre, head of the Australian branch of Universal Pictures. From the early 1920s until the late 1950s, McIntyre provided a generous distribution service for Australian features. He also invested heavily in productions by Charles Chauvel — including **Forty Thousand Horsemen** (1940) and **Sons of Matthew** (1949) — but the personal commitment of McIntyre and Doyle to production was rare among the men in power. Others generally complained that they were hindered by their head offices in the U.S. or Britain, and that their primary responsibility was to safeguard the financial interests of their company, not to gamble with capital for the sake of any patriotic principle.

Government Assistance

Pressure on governments to protect film producers began as early as 1912 when filmmakers pleaded for a tariff barrier against imported films to protect them from excessive foreign competition; but the governments found it difficult to help. In 1926, the Victorian government legislated for a compulsory quota of British Empire or Australian films to be shown in every cinema in the state, but the quota was low enough to be filled by the regular showing of local newsreels or travelogues; it did nothing to boost the production of feature films.

A Royal Commission into the industry in 1927 recommended a more forceful quota, but the government failed to act because of doubts about its constitutional powers in this area, and the results were minor and ineffectual. In 1936, the New South Wales government imposed a quota for Australian films, but, despite successive amendments, its legislation was unproductive.

All these attempts to help feature film production emphasized exhibition and distribution, with the assumption that production

Opposite: Franklyn Barrett's **The Girl of the Bush**.

Miss Vera James
"A Girl of the Bush"

Scenes from Norman Dawn's 1927 adaptation of Marcus Clarke's classic novel, *For the Term of His Natural Life.*

would become viable if one could guarantee that Australian films would be shown under favorable conditions in Australian theatres. But as the post-1930 era of talkies progressed, production became increasingly the preserve of large companies. Production costs increased sharply with the requirements of sound, and the industry became more and more capital intensive. The cry for government assistance began to change its tune: no longer was adequate exhibition seen as the only major prerequisite, but the need for low-cost studio facilities and, above all, the availability of finance began to be stressed.

Governments may have shown some willingness to legislate to help Australian films to reach the screen, but they were less eager to spend money. A minor attempt by the New South Wales government in 1939 to guarantee the bank overdrafts of approved producers helped to subsidize four productions, but nothing of lasting value was achieved at state or federal level until the end of the 1960s.

Local and Overseas Markets

In the absence of government finance or legislative support, Australian filmmakers were forced to rely on their initiative to circumvent the problems that faced them. In most cases, the single goal of producers was to attract Australian audiences. Very few filmmakers took overseas markets into consideration when planning their work, and few even pursued overseas sales. If a sale did take place, it was regarded as a lucky break, and it did not alter the basic concentration on the home market as the mainstay of a financially-viable industry.

Occasionally, producers imported American or British casts and crews to work on Australian films, but the results seldom justified the expense. These producers found that the only Americans who were cheap enough were no longer in demand in Hollywood, and their presence in Australian films did nothing for their failing careers or for the Australian industry. In 1919, for example, E. J. and Dan Carroll imported several Americans, including actor-director Wilfred Lucas, and three westerns were made; they starred the Australian athlete, Snowy Baker. The Carroll brothers soon learnt that the American presence guaranteed neither outstanding efficiency in production nor rewarding sales on the American market, and the venture ended abruptly.

In 1927, Australasian Films also tried to make its productions attractive to the world market by hiring Americans to make them, but again the costs, especially with **For the Term of His Natural Life** (1927), were grossly out of proportion with the small return from overseas sales. In the 1930s, various producers, including Ken G. Hall and Charles Chauvel, made use of second-rate Hollywood or British figures; but Hall and Chauvel soon reverted to all-Australian casts and crews when it became evident that the main advantage of imported talent was to win prestige for their companies with local audiences, rather than additional sales overseas.

A series of co-productions with France in the 1950s, by the Australian team of Lee Robinson and Chips Rafferty, also failed to return worthwhile dividends. They found themselves being drawn into productions that

George Fisher as Rufus Dawes (left), and Gabbett (Arthur McLaglen) surrounded by his captors. **For the Term of His Natural Life**.

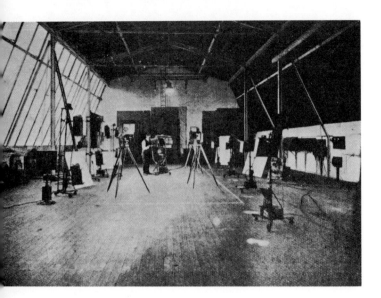

Inside the Spencer's studio at Rushcutter's Bay, Sydney.

were too expensive, and this finally caused the closure of their company, Southern International. Throughout, the moral was clear: overseas sales were always elusive, and even with American, British or French involvement in production the risks were not reduced. It was safer to make sure of the home market and not hope for too much from countries that already produced their own films.

The Studios

Production before the doldrums of the 1960s was primarily studio-based. Unlike the present industry, where individual films tend to be 'packaged' by companies that are formed for one production only, entrepreneurs in the past frequently tried to package a long-term studio operation to produce a series of unspecified films on a continuous basis. The concern was less with the nature of individual productions than with the mode of producing them. Not many companies achieved financial stability for more than two or three productions, but the establishment of a studio for continuous production remained an ideal from the earliest days of the industry until the Rafferty-Robinson venture of Southern International in the 1950s. The model of Hollywood, too, especially in the 1920s, led Australian filmmakers towards the goal of continuity within a studio system.

The early development of the fiction film in Australia was closely related to live theatre. After a few isolated ventures, like **The Story of the Kelly Gang** (1906) and **For the Term of**

His Natural Life (1908), production began to flourish at the end of 1910 and throughout 1911. In this early boom period, when a multiplicity of exhibition companies made it easy for producers to arrange screenings, many theatrical troupes made film versions of the most popular items in their repertoire. Cinema enabled them to reach markets they had not been able to afford before, in small country towns and the suburbs of large cities.

During 1911, some stage companies began to concentrate on film rather than the stage, while other groups specialized in film work. Perhaps the first major specialized film unit was the Australian Photo-Play Company, set up in June 1911 under the management of Stanley Crick. Before its collapse in mid-1912 (allegedly because of the unavailability of adequate exhibition outlets after the formation of the combine), the company produced about 20 'features': fiction films directed by Alfred Rolfe, made by a regular crew of technicians and with a stock company of performers. The films were 'quickies', with readily exploitable subjects, relying heavily on local appeal and novel publicity gimmicks.

The first production, **Moora Neya, or The Message of the Spear** (1911), about the exploits of a wicked overseer on an outback station, claimed to be the first dramatic film to feature 'real' Aboriginals, some of whom, according to the publicity, were wild, and were sufficiently carried away by their performances to assault the director during a fight scene. Another production, **The Cup Winner** (1911), ingeniously exploited public interest in the 1911 Melbourne Cup by inserting footage of the race into a ready-made melodrama about race-track intrigue; the film was released in Melbourne on the evening of Cup day, and in Sydney a day later.

One of the persistent ironies of the early industry was that the best production resources lay in the hands of Australasian Films and Union Theatres, who usually showed no interest in producing films themselves. This came about after the combine acquired the large production facilities of Cozens Spencer when Spencer's Pictures merged with the organization in 1912. Spencer was primarily an exhibitor, and his theatre interests were valuable to the combine. But his enthusiasm for production was barely tolerated and was discontinued in 1914 when he resigned from the board of his company. In 1912, Spencer had built a studio at Rushcutter's Bay in Sydney, and had set up a film unit there under the direction of Raymond Longford.

During 1912 and 1913, Spencer's company had also produced a series of expensive and ambitious films, including a 'costume' drama of European courtly intrigue, **The Midnight Wedding** (1912), and an 'epic' about the invasion of Australia by Asians, **Australia Calls** (1913). As with the Australian Photo-Play Company, the films starred a regular group of performers, including the young Lottie Lyell, who later became Longford's creative collaborator, and were handled by the same studio technicians led by the gifted cinematographer, Arthur Higgins. Longford's productions for Spencer were popular with Australian audiences, and Spencer became a vocal advocate of Australian production. His fall from power within Australasian Films seems to have been directly caused by conflict over his ambitions for production. The combine could not be pushed in directions it did not want to go, and it remained almost completely inactive in feature production for

the following decade, content only to lease Spencer's studio to other producers.

Despite their early reluctance to be involved in production, and their bad reputation among filmmakers, Australasian Films and Union Theatres became the sponsors of one of Australia's most successful production ventures in the 1930s with the development of the large studio operation of Cinesound Productions. Based at two Sydney studios (one at Bondi and the other at the old Spencer studio at Rushcutter's Bay), and one in Melbourne at St Kilda, Cinesound produced a series of 17 features between 1932 and 1940, achieving a record of continuous production and commercial success that stands alone in Australian film history.

Although the initiatives to form Cinesound were made by the managing director of the Union Theatre organization, Stuart Doyle, the operation was left almost entirely in the hands of Doyle's young personal assistant, Ken G. Hall, and the success of the company was largely due to him. Hall approached production with a strong sense of responsibility — to his

Raymond Longford, who headed the film unit at the Rushcutter's Bay studio.

Lottie Lyell, actress and long-time creative collaborator with Longford.

17

staff, whom he tried to keep employed during the Depression, and to the paying audience. Hall's philosophy of showmanship, which was shared by many of his contemporaries, has often been falsely characterized as anti-art and primarily concerned with the 'conning' of money from the public. Rather, Hall was concerned to ensure that his audiences were never cheated, and he gave them what he thought would please the Saturday night crowd at the local cinema. His films were made specifically for that audience, and, regardless of what some critics may think of his work today, he succeeded in winning the support of the Australian public in film after film.

In constructing a film production program for his audience, Hall devoted much attention to developing an 'image' for the Cinesound studio, based on the model of the great Hollywood studios of the time. He generated large volumes of publicity about the studio, its company of actors and actresses, and its production staff. Through its constant presence in the press and on radio, and its weekly newsreel in theatres, the studio became a familiar name to most Australians. The films made by Hall also encouraged the public to think of Cinesound as a Hollywood-style studio: stories were often modelled on successful American films and they usually played down overt 'Australianisms' to aim for results that would look like Hollywood products, sometimes even with Americans in the leading roles, such as Helen Twelvetrees in **Thoroughbred** (1936). Hall also tried to develop a local star system, and launched a lavish campaign to groom the Australian actress, Shirley Ann Richards, for stardom in a series of light comedies.

Other major studios were developed in the 1930s: one in Melbourne by Efftee Productions, and one in Sydney by National Studios. Efftee, under the personal control of Frank Thring sen., produced seven features after 1931. None of the films were outstandingly successful commercially, and the studio ceased operation with Thring's death in 1936. Unlike Hall, with his emphasis on Hollywood models, Thring tied his films more closely to the theatre, often with the cinema screen serving as a proscenium arch for static performances of stage routines. Thring's films were often awkwardly constructed around long vaudeville routines, and generally showed little sign of attempts to modulate theatrical gesturing or speech articulation for the different demands

Director Ken G. Hall and actress Shirley Ann Richards at a Cinesound premiere.

of cinema. At the same time, Thring did capture some outstanding comic sequences, albeit stage-bound, especially in two of his films with the local vaudeville star, George Wallace: **His Royal Highness** (1932), a musical comedy set in the mythical European kingdom of Betonia, and **A Ticket in Tatts** (1934), a race-track comedy with a stilted upper-class romance to balance the 'low-life' clowning of Wallace and the other stable hands.

The commercial success of Cinesound and its local fame provided incentives for other producers to attempt similar enterprises. In 1936, a large film studio was built at Pagewood in Sydney, with a powerful group of business and civic leaders on the board of the company, National Studios. Much publicity surrounded the production and release of its first feature, the erratic melodrama, **The Flying Doctor** (1936), but it failed to attract a profitable audience, as did the second production, the western, **Rangle River** (1936). As a result, the Pagewood studio fell into disuse. The failure showed that capital and publicity alone were insufficient to ensure public acceptance of a film.

Themes

In their concentration on the local audience, the most commercially successful of Australian filmmakers often relied heavily on the use of stereotype characters who were consciously distinct from the heroes and

Opposite: Frank Thring sen.'s **His Royal Highness**.

heroines of British or American cinema. The use of local stereotypes to establish immediate rapport with audiences was similar in the present industry to the way in which the Barry McKenzie comedies or **Newsfront** (1978) were structured around a 'private' Australian experience, and developed a sense of knowing complicity between the audience and the film-maker.

In the first great wave of Australian cinema from 1910-1911, films with bush settings were among the most popular, especially stories about bushrangers. The bushranging films followed similar patterns of action, whether based on fact or fiction, and they competed with each other in their stuntwork to achieve distinction. Raymond Longford, who began his film career as an actor in bushranging films, later described their method of production:

> "All they needed was [sic] horses hired from stables in Redfern, some uniforms, guns, a stagecoach, and enough men to play troopers and rangers. They would take their gear down to the bush at Brookvale, outside Manly, camp out for a week, and — without any script — make a film. Their action was usually a stagecoach hold-up, a lot of galloping, and a shooting match."[2]

Bushrangers had been the popular heroes of the larrikin class in the cities in the late 19th Century, and the New South Wales police (who were responsible for film censorship) thought fit to ban bushranging adventures from the screen because of a fear of a resurgence of larrikinism and ridicule to which the police were subjected in most of the films. From 1912, bushranging films were rare in Australian production because of the ban in New South Wales, a state that was essential for commercial success. Their early popularity, however, was an unmistakable, if brief, flowering of a distinctive local genre.

Despite the demise of bushrangers in the cinema, other bush themes remained popular throughout the 1910s and 1920s, with stories of wealthy squatter life as well as tales of the hardships endured by pioneers and selectors. In the local cinema, the big stations seemed to 'breed' women who were able to break free of social conventions and become the equals of men in many aspects of their daily life. The image of the squatter's daughter was particularly common, from films like **The Squatter's Daughter** in 1910 to **The Girl of the**

20

Poster for Ken G. Hall's 1933 version of **The Squatter's Daughter**.

Bush in 1921 and Ken Hall's re-make of **The Squatter's Daughter** in 1933. The figure even appeared in vestigial form in the 1940s and 1950s in **The Overlanders** (1946), **Sons of Matthew** (1949) and other outback dramas.

These capable young women were often in a position of managing the family estate in the absence of suitable men, and their ability to supervise the station hands and work with them in mustering, branding and other skilled station work was unquestioned and unself-conscious. In **Silks and Saddles** (1921), the girl even plays two-up with the station hands, without any visible qualms on their part. The difference between this attitude and the objections of the shearers in **Sunday Too Far Away** (1975) to having the squatter's daughter in the shearing shed is striking. However, women of poorer rural families, without hired domestic help, were less free to compete with men, and their role as mother and housekeeper was usually strictly observed. Older married women with children were rarely seen in stories of life on the big stations, but films of the pioneers and selectors often waxed senti-mental over Mum, the figure who provided spiritual strength for the family, as well as the security of a comfortable and homely dwelling.

Comedies about the rural poor began to appear in 1917 with a series by Beaumont Smith about the Hayseeds family. Smith often put more energy and imagination into pub-licizing his films than making them: the roughest production methods would do, so long as local appeal was strong and there were plenty of gimmicks for advertising. **The Hayseeds Come To Sydney** (1917) was promoted

as a film about the family's encounter with typical Sydney life, with, for example, would-be suicides queueing up at the Gap. But for the film's Melbourne release, extra scenes were shot to replace the Sydney references with Melbourne equivalents, and it was released as **The Hayseeds Come To Town**. Smith made four Hayseeds films in 1917, two more in 1923, and a talkie reprise in 1933. Only the last in the series is extant today, and it shows the careless haste of Smith's production methods, and his exploitation of crude sentimentality about Australia and the hardy pioneer stock repre-sented by Mum and Dad Hayseeds.

The inspiration for Smith's Hayseeds family were Dad and Dave, the father and son of the Rudd family, who had first appeared in the stories of Steele Rudd published in *The Bulletin* in the 1890s. Dad and Dave did not reach the cinema until Raymond Longford made **On Our Selection** (1920) and **Rudd's New Selection** (1921). The first of these survives today as one of the major works of early Australian cinema. It is a conscious attempt to make a naturalistic account of life on a selection where the family has to fight to gain a foothold, using its own physical strength and ingenuity, rather than the capital and mechanical equipment of the wealthy. The disappointments and joys of family life on the selection are the subject of Longford's film, and his approach is radically different from the farce and situation comedy of the Hayseeds series.

Dad and Dave re-appeared in the 1930s in a series of four features by Ken Hall at Cine-sound, beginning with a film version of the popular stage play of *On Our Selection* (filmed

The Hayseeds family.

Frame enlargement from Raymond Longford's 1920 version of **On Our Selection**.

Pat Hanna, who played the "Digger" in Australian films.

in 1932) and ending with an original screen-play, **Dad Rudd, M.P.** (1940). In the course of the series, the Rudd family was transformed from crude rustics into relatively sophisticated and affluent citizens of an idyllic countryside.

In Hall's hands, Dad and Dave were flexible characters, equally at home in slapstick farce, in expressions of nationalistic sentiment (**On Our Selection**), as participants in a satire of bourgeois pretensions (**Dad and Dave Come**

to Town — 1938) and as moralists in a simple allegory of European politics played out in the context of an Australian electoral competition (**Dad Rudd, M.P.**). There seemed to be no limit to the range of Dad and Dave, but Hall's manipulation of the characters was abruptly discontinued by the closure of feature production at Cinesound in 1940.

Unlike the variety of bush themes, urban subjects were generally nondescript and imitative of British models until the arrival of Longford's **The Sentimental Bloke** in 1919. In telling the story of a larrikin's transformation into a responsible and loving family man, Longford demonstrated a remarkable ability to underplay the comedy and drama of the tale to create characters who were far more credible in their simplicity and restraint than the original creations of C. J. Dennis' verse narrative, on which the film was based.

The leading actors, Arthur Tauchert and Lottie Lyell (who also collaborated in the production), immersed themselves with Longford in the life of Woolloomooloo and the Woolloomoolese vernacular; the result was a degree of easy naturalism in the performances that was rare at that time in Australia and overseas. The film was immensely popular, and Tauchert became inseparable from the character of the "bloke" for the rest of his career, playing similar roles in other films and on stage.

The bloke's ideals of mateship, his off-hand expression of his deepest feelings, his disrespect for authority, and his ironic sense of humour re-emerged in the early 1930s in the character played by Pat Hanna in three feature

John Faulkner, Robert Mackinnon and Brownie Vernon in John Wells' **Silks and Saddles**.

The closing dissolve of Ken G. Hall's **Dad Rudd, M.P.**

23

Lottie Lyell as Doreen in Raymond Longford's **The Sentimental Bloke**.

films: **Diggers** (1931), **Diggers in Blighty** (1933) and **Waltzing Matilda** (1933). In each feature, Hanna played the same character, Chic Williams, a "digger" in the Australian Army in France and Britain during World War 1.

The first two films depicted Chic's exploits in the army: trying to evade active service by malingering in the base hospital, attempting to steal rum from the army stores, and going on leave in England and encountering the social pretensions of the aristocracy. The third film, however, is set contemporaneously in the Depression, and, almost in self-pity, depicts the hardships and loneliness of ex-diggers out of work in the cities, drifting into the country in search of laboring jobs, and growing too old to succeed in romance with younger women.

The happiness which the sentimental bloke found in marriage and a stable home life eludes Hanna's digger, but the two characters remain closely linked. They are working class in origin, and both have dreams of a happy life in the bush which the bloke manages to make a reality but which the digger never finds. The bloke is a reflection of the ideal that the digger would like to be, and the original verse of *The Sentimental Bloke* found enormous popularity among such men in the trenches in the war in Europe after its publication in 1915.

Hanna in turn provided inspiration for the character played in numerous films by Chips Rafferty. Rafferty's first major screen role, in Charles Chauvel's **Forty Thousand Horsemen**, echoed not only the physical lankiness of Hanna but also his *persona* of a fun-loving digger. Chauvel's calculated myth-making saga of Anzac heroism cleaned up the digger image by matching the irreverence and mischievousness with loyalty to both mates and the national cause, and with a ferocious efficiency in battle. If Hanna's digger had achieved anything constructive in the war it was accidental, and his films were not really interested in exploring such matters. But

Chauvel made his film with the purpose of not only entertaining Australian audiences, but of contributing to national morale. Rafferty served a dual purpose of providing comic relief, and of showing the resilience and fighting spirit of an essentially lower-class Australian in the company of his more educated and better-bred mates in the army.

In Chauvel's second morale-boosting war film, **The Rats of Tobruk** (1944), the comic function of Rafferty was more subdued, and a grim realization of the horrors of war dominated the film. Consolidation of Rafferty's character was delayed until after the war in **The Overlanders**, in which Rafferty achieved the clearest expression of the *persona* that he continued to play for the rest of his career: the self-reliant and determined man of action, whether a drover (**The Overlanders**), a pearling contractor (**King of the Coral Sea** — 1954), a patrol officer in New Guinea (**Walk into Paradise** — 1956), or a constable in a rough mining town (**Wake in Fright** — 1971).

Thematic continuity between the past industry and the present is not strikingly evident. Nationalism, which in the past may

Charles Chauvel (left), Elsa Chauvel and Ron Taylor.

have been embedded throughout a film, is now more apparent in euphoric publicity for the industry than in the films themselves. Some links are apparent in the work of producer Anthony Buckley and writer-producer Joan Long, both of whom have made thorough studies of the past industry. During the making of **Caddie** (1976), produced by Buckley and written by Long, films of urban Sydney life, such as **The Sentimental Bloke** and **Sunshine Sally** (1922), were used to help strengthen the film's recreation of the 1920s and the early Depression years. Long also developed the screenplay of **The Picture Show Man** (1977) from her knowledge of Australian film history.

More subtle and less conscious links between past and present might also be traced from the 'ocker' of the Barry McKenzie comedies and Tim Burstall's films back to the urban heroes of **The Sentimental Bloke**, or the Hanna or Rafferty films. But, in general, the present industry seems divorced from the one that existed in earlier decades. In some ways, the 1970s industry is without a past, and that may well be one of its main problems.

Chips Rafferty (left) in Charles Chauvel's **Forty Thousand Horsemen**.

25

2 SOCIAL REALISM

Keith Connolly

Human kind, according to T. S. Eliot, cannot stand too much reality; Australian filmmakers seem to agree. Of the 150 or so feature films produced in this country in the past decade, fewer than 50 were realist in tone, while only a handful taxed audiences in the way Eliot meant. These few belong to a category which may be described as social realist — a convenient, if less than precise, label.

British critic and author John Willett describes social realism as a work of art that is "socially concerned, yet objectively presented",[1] and this is a serviceable definition. The term should not be confused with "socialist realism", a now somewhat modified and discredited theory, which seeks to apply the Marxist dialectic to social realism for didactic and ideological purposes. As well, the social realism of the kind ventured into by Australian filmmakers has little in common with the Italian neo-realist movement, a view of poverty, injustice and alienation in post-World War 2 Italy that proved more than many filmgoers, and even some filmmakers, could take.

Australian films of social realism to be discussed here are those which, in various ways, depict our society, and the individuals and groups within it. The films vary in scope, setting and approach, ranging from mannered elaborations of television series to a few which achieve genuine insights into the Australia one knows. Of course, in assessing any fiction film of realist stamp, one should always bear in mind that its realism is, actually, spurious. What the audience sees is simulation, and what filmgoers recognize as reality is what they have been persuaded (or previously conditioned) to accept.

In 1973, Australian director Bert Deling challenged the very nature of films which seek truth through pretence in his electrifying, but ultimately disastrous, **Dalmas**. But this venture was an aberration, and other filmmakers stayed within defined and accepted narrative patterns. In any case, most of them were more exercised by questions of content, though in a rather negative way.

Like the rest of the Western world, Australia entered the 1970s in a troubled mood. Challenges to established social, moral and political values had been quickened by Australian intervention in the war in Vietnam. It was a time of change, of political and social experiment. The first federal Labor government for 23 years was elected late in 1972; a Liberal administration had acknowledged changing community attitudes by relaxing cinema censorship; there was passionate public debate about human rights, sexual equality, morals, drugs, and ecology; and much else. Not a great deal of this was reflected in Australian films. Apart from a couple of small-scale productions — a segment of the Film Australia compendium feature **Three to Go** (1970), and Warwick Freeman's **Demonstrator** (1971), both of which dealt in less than direct fashion with radical ferment among the young — filmmakers shied away from politics.

But, for the most part, even those dedicated to depicting Australian realities were disinclined to grasp polemical nettles. And, as proliferating government bodies and expanding private investment gradually advanced the size of production budgets (still small by overseas standards), box-office considerations loomed ever larger. Not that contentious themes were ever very popular. Producer Phillip Adams, in his usual trenchant fashion, said in 1976:

> "The trouble is that Australia is such a bland, easy-going nation, whereas the significant film industries develop in countries with social problems, where there are class wars and political despotism ... To make significant feature films you need *content*."[2]

There were, however, significant, if qualified, exceptions. Two accomplished Australian films which discussed relevant political and social issues did so in terms of the recent past, but raised questions highly relevant in the present. The first of these was Michael Thornhill's **Between Wars** (1974), reticent as a social document, but important in the history of Australian cinema. Its reluctance to become

Dr Trenbow (Corin Redgrave) has his 'radical' broadcast cut short by an ABC announcer (John Chance). **Between Wars**.

involved in the issues it raises is a characteristic of the film's protagonist, Dr Edward Trenbow, played by British actor Corin Redgrave.

Set during the years 1918 to 1941, it convincingly depicts life in Sydney and New South Wales country towns, and alludes to major issues and movements of the time. But though the narrative (by leading author Frank Moorhouse) records stirring events, the film keeps its distance. Dr Trenbow is embroiled in controversial matters — democratic rights, the incipient fascism of the New Guard, the advocacy of and resistance to new social and medical ideas — in spite of himself. Thornhill ironically counterposes two periods in the doctor's life when, without really belonging to either, he is branded as being at opposite political extremes. Despite its rather affected detachment, the film is a worthwhile chronicle of the currents within Australian society. It is also notable for imaginative and technically-confident depiction of places and period.

Four years after **Between Wars**, and on a considerably higher level, came Phillip Noyce's **Newsfront** (1978), arguably the best film of any kind made in Australia, and certainly the outstanding example of social realism. It, too, is set in the past, but closer still to the present — 1948 to 1956. **Newsfront** is of major importance for reasons of content as well as technique, and is, so far, the only Australian feature film to discuss contentious political

questions (the mere recording of them is rare enough) from an identifiable viewpoint.

Newsfront ingeniously uses clips from Australia's two defunct theatrical newsreels, Movietone and Cinesound, to provide the film's central narrative thread and validate the representation of actual events. The screenplay, by Noyce and Bob Ellis, is peopled by fictitious characters who are seen shooting the newsreel footage, a clever and convincing marriage of illusion and reality. The choice of newsreel material accurately and tellingly reflects the outlook of the period (although Noyce, Ellis and producer David Elfick were only children at the time). Along with footage of the staple of such newsreels — sport, the doings of stage and radio personalities, bushfires, floods, the rabbit menace — it includes coverage of the great 1949 coal strike, the defeat of the Chifley Labor Government, the failure of the Menzies Liberal Government's attempts to ban the Communist Party (which gave rise to an intense struggle for civil liberties).

The film closely relates the personal problems of the newsreel staffs to the events they are seen recording, raising matters of sharp

In recreated footage, Chris Hewitt (Chris Haywood) battles against the floods of Maitland in 1954. Phillip Noyce's **Newsfront**.

religious, as well as political, identification, something no other Australian film has dared do. Although it delves less than exhaustively into these questions, and sidesteps others, **Newsfront** is an accurate portrayal of the Australian ethos, demolishing in the process the crude caricatures that have emerged from all too much of our filmmaking, from Dad and Dave to Barry McKenzie.

It is instructive, and not a little disconcerting, to contemplate how Australian filmmakers have pictured our society, in its urban concentration as well as rural dispersal. As might be expected, the country receives far less attention, with attitudes ranging from fact to fable. The list of full-length films about country life is not long. It begins in 1971 with the shallow glibness of Peter Maxwell's **Country Town**, a spin-off from the television series **Bellbird**, a simplistic soap opera which ran for more than a decade on the ABC. The film features the cast of television stereotypes in cliched dramatic situations evolving from a Victorian rural area in the grip of drought. It is about as close to reality as **Mrs Miniver** is to circumstances of the British people during the Battle of Britain.

Two scenes from newsreel footage of the time which is intercut with new footage, such as at left. **Newsfront**.

Rural workers on the job. Arthur (Peter Cummins) and Foley (Jack Thompson). Ken Hannam's **Sunday Too Far Away**.

At the other end of the credibility scale is a splendid picture of rural life: Ken Hannam's **Sunday Too Far Away** (1975). Principally concerned with the circumscribed existence of shearers in the outback, the film also illustrates the various tyrannies the harsh, distant environment imposes on everyone in remote areas. **Sunday** is also the only valid portrayal of any group of Australian workers on the job, and that alone lends it a seminal importance. The script, by John Dingwall, ripples with illuminative dialogue which, though laconic in tone, startlingly reveals the psychological and emotional pressures these men are under in the social microcosm of the shearing shed. Hannam's skilful introduction into the work sequences of a machismo-impelled rivalry between the "gun" shearers is the very essence of social-realist cinema. Elsewhere, the film is less felicitous, and the shortcomings aren't helped by evident post-production cutting. The significance of some incidents has been trimmed beyond intelligibility, and the confrontation during a major strike, which should provide the dramatic climax, is little better than a postscript.

These failings impair, but do not expunge, the film's great value, which lies in its unsentimental, though sympathetic, portrayal of a group of Australian workers whose calling makes great demands on them and their families. An old shearer ruefully calculates that he has spent only three out of 25 years at

29

The rivalry between shearers is symbolized by the tally board, which is scrutinized by Booker (Jerry Thomas), Jim (Graeme Smith), Ugly (John Ewart) and Beresford (Sean Scully). **Sunday Too Far Away**.

home, a statistic summed up by the title ballad, the lament of a shearer's wife: "Friday too tired, Saturday too drunk, Sunday too far away."

Sunday has been criticised for the undoubted sexism of the shearers' outlook, but it gives a fairly accurate account of male attitudes in the 1950s (views still widespread today).

The following year Hannam directed another, and very different, picture of rural life, one cosily established in the nostalgic cycle. Set in a Victorian country town in the 1920s, **Break of Day** (1976) convincingly represents some elements of life in such a community, then loses itself in glossy memorabilia.

A much more honest approach is that of Brian Hannant in **Judy**, his segment of Film Australia's **Three to Go**. This half-hour episode succinctly sifts urban-rural conflicts as it examines the pressures on a girl secretary who, hesitant about accepting the wife-and-mother role expected of her, heads for the city.

One other treatment of our wide brown land demands attention: Nicolas Roeg's **Walkabout** (1971). Because director-cinematographer Roeg, scriptwriter Edward Bond and star Jenny Agutter are British, it is arguable

whether this is, strictly speaking, an Australian film. Few would argue, however, that Roeg displays considerable perception of the harsh realities of the Australian landscape. Roeg and Bond turn James Vance Marshall's novel (about abandoned white children saved by a tribal Aboriginal) into a haunting metaphysical parable on the interaction between man and his environment. Roeg's poetic camera savagely points up the destructive disparity between the technological age's greedy insensitivity and the stone-age black's instinctive partnership with nature. Both cultures are shown to be vulnerable: the Aboriginal (Gulpilil) dies when his love-dance is uncomprehendingly rebuffed; the children return to the devouring rancour of the modern rat-race.

In choice of locales, Australian filmmakers of the 1970s have reflected the national preference, in that the vast majority opted for the cities. Hardly surprising, therefore, that aspects of city life also provided the meatier themes for films of a social realist bent. As, for reasons already canvassed, filmmakers were most comfortable dealing with effects rather than causes, the best results were obtained when they examined, without much attempt at elucidation, social phenomena like alienation. This subject has been seen from many ideological standpoints in modern times, but a most apposite definition comes from American Marxist author-critic Sidney Finkelstein:

"Alienation is the individual's estrangement from himself and his seeing the rest of nature and humanity in the despairing picture he finds when he regards himself."[3]

The Australian film renaissance virtually began with an oblique evocation of this theme in **2000 Weeks** (1969) — though one doubts whether director Tim Burstall would acknowledge it as such. Burstall's pioneering feature, a critical and box-office failure, has artistic as well as historic importance. Its melodramatically-expressed story about a young middle-class intellectual questioning in literate terms the values, relationships and goals of his life is an important step in Australian feature filmmaking.

It was soon followed by a film whose characters were on the farthest side of the tracks: Denis Cahill's **You Can't See Round Corners** (1969), another television spin-off. Given that the advent of television in 1956 had opened new avenues to Australian filmmakers, it was only to be expected that some features would acquire the technical gloss and thematic superficiality of television drama. Based on a Jon Cleary novel, **Corners** is a salient example of that tendency. In updating — from World War 2 to Vietnam — Cleary's novel about an army deserter, the film ignores the vast changes popular attitudes had undergone in the intervening years, and is equally cavalier about its back-street milieu, which also belongs in the past.

The following year saw the completion of **Jack and Jill: A Postscript** (1970), a marathon labor of love by Phillip Adams and Brian Robinson. Five years in the making (at odd intervals and with the slenderest of means), it rather charmingly blends amateur enthusiasm and professional capability to achieve something similar to the aggressive fiction-documentary style of maverick British director Peter Watkins. The brusque editing and Adams' laconic voice-over commentary are in the Peter Watkins' manner, although the narrative, about the doomed affaire of a bikie and a girl from a "respectable" working-class family, is emotionally, rather than ideologically, involving. Grainily shot in black and white, and using a minimum of lip-synch

sound, the film makes telling points about alienation and hypocrisy in our urban society.

Also a product of this age of relative innocence was Nigel Buesst's **Bonjour Balwyn** (1971), another, sterner, look at alienation from the middle-class viewpoint. A confused attack on bourgeois values, as well as anti-bourgeois role-playing, it criticises modern materialism, while indicating the pitfalls of reaching for hazily-perceived "alternative" lifestyles. The film's structure is rickety and the script, on which leading playwright John Romeril collaborated, is irritatingly vague in places. The witty, downbeat conclusion, although the most engaging part of the film, begs so many questions that the theme remains enigmatic.

A popular sub-genre of films dealing with alienation are those about youthful working-class bike and car freaks, as introduced in **Jack and Jill** and later celebrated in Sandy Harbutt's **Stone** (1974) and Michael Thornhill's **The FJ Holden** (1977). **Stone** is a bikie film, but besides depicting the leather machos of Sydney's bike gangs with apparent fidelity and (given the ribald vulgarity of their milieu) a certain amount of restraint, Harbutt also introduces such issues as the ecology, human rights and political repression. The story, a pastiche of the plausible and the improbable, links fascist-inclined big business with drug-dealing gangsters who eliminate unwitting

Leather machos *en masse* for the funeral of one of their gang. Sandy Harbutt's **Stone**.

The New Australian Cinema

bikie witnesses of a political assassination. Much of this is told with cloak-and-dagger chiaroscuro, although Harbutt manages to retain the film's basic verisimilitude — a not inconsiderable feat.

The FJ Holden is far more socially relevant in its depiction of working-class suburbia. In spite of the nostalgic connotations of its title (the FJ is the 1953 model of the first all-Australian car and is now something of a cult among car fanciers), the film is set firmly in the 1970s. A lyrically-photographed study of suburban teenagers, it is largely plotless, but generates interest and concern in its detached study of the unmotivated characters. Thornhill shows their uneasy, self-conscious relationships with each other and the gulf separating them from their resigned parents. The environment is plastic-kitsch, the lifestyle vapidly hedonist. If these kids are alienated, their response is largely passive. The only uplift life offers the boys is tinkering with cars, and Thornhill uses the FJ Holden as a symbol.

Under the loving hands of the film's anti-heroes the car blossoms from rust-bucket to hot-rod showpiece, but once the transformation is complete they lapse into apathetic vacuity. A confrontation with the law ends the film on a questioning note reminiscent of **Bicycle Thieves**. (Thornhill has professed his admiration of Vittorio de Sica's great neo-realist film.) With the help of some artfully

Serge (Sergio Frazetto) chats with Carrie (Kim Krejus) and Jeannie (Sonia Peat). John Duigan's **Mouth to Mouth**.

suggestive photography by David Gribble, Thornhill mounts an acutely-observed tableau of the new suburbia of the lower-income groups: manicured lawns, ticky-tacky boxed homes, bustling, gimcrack shopping centre, the fretful maintenance of established order. Gribble's camera also has its reflective, poetic moments, as when distant lights at dusk fleetingly ennoble the tawdry surroundings.

The film is a fine piece of observation, tolerant rather than empathic. It is a pity Thornhill thought it necessary to include several scenes which seem to be aimed largely at seekers of vicarious thrills, as in several gratuitous sex and car-chase scenes.

Easily the best film about Australian youth is John Duigan's **Mouth to Mouth** (1978). Duigan, who played the disaffected young man in **Bonjour Balwyn**, gets a good deal closer than Thornhill to expressing the feelings of his teenagers. Duigan's characters are of the same age group, but belong to a more recent phenomena in Australian society — the under-privileged, unemployed young. Duigan doesn't assume to present the whole picture, or even a particularly representative one, and unemployment isn't the film's basic theme; he is more concerned with depicting those children of the lucky country who have missed out on more than jobs.

The film's principals, two boys and two girls, are on the 'outer' of contemporary Australian society and Duigan denotes the extent of their deprivation with restrained sympathy. Fleetingly, they experience a degree of emotional security in their mutually-sustaining fellowship. The girls are on the run from an institution (one drifts into prostitution, the other goes back "inside"), the boys hopelessly search for work. They vent their frustrations on the consumer society — shoplifting, sky-larking, and disrupting the plastic palaces that exclude them. Duigan ends on a note of cautious optimism. One is left with the impression that, like resilient weeds, the four will survive, perhaps even thrive. The film, made on a very small, but commercially viable budget, is a milestone achievement.

The idea that any part of our young people could be regarded as deprived is a relatively novel one for Australian society. Until the economic downturn of the mid-1970s, the most common view saw them, at the very least, as well provided for. There were, however, others about whom society harbored a

Opposite: **Newsfront**.

less-than-easy conscience, notably migrants and Aboriginals.

Considering that so much of Australia's population is of recent migrant origin (Federal Community Relations commissioner A. J. Grassby estimates that 2.5 million have links with the Mediterranean countries alone), surprisingly few filmmakers show an interest in the lives of the newcomers. Only Oliver Howe's **Toula** (yet another useful section of **Three to Go**), Tom Cowan's **Promised Woman** (1975), both about Greeks, and Ayten Kuyululu's **The Golden Cage** (1975), on Turks, attempted serious, realistic portrayals. All three are set in Sydney and make the same error: in striving for audience communication, they depict migrants — some very recent arrivals — speaking broken English to each other in private. The incongruity of these passages, and the consequent lowering of verisimilitude, devalues otherwise admirable qualities in all three.

Promised Woman is the best of them. The second of three features directed in four years by Cowan, who is also one of Australia's most capable cinematographers, **Promised Woman** is about a proxy bride rejected upon arrival because she is older than the groom thought. To the surprise of other migrants, she elects to stay in Australia and Cowan achieves considerable insight into the problems faced by many migrants in his tracing of this lone woman's difficult adjustment. Similar tribulations are experienced by Greeks in **Toula**. Through the protagonist, a girl in her early

teens, Howes succinctly dramatizes the culture shock suffered by migrants, and the divisions between the two cultures are epitomized in traumatic confrontations between parents and children.

The **Golden Cage** is less successful in enunciating the even-deeper conflicts felt by Turkish migrants. The film centres on single males: their loneliness, sense of alienation, the pull of family ties and the effects of a vastly-different social ethos. Convincing when it deals with the men's inner turmoil, the film lapses into novelettish contrivance as the narrative progresses.

In 1979, two features went some of the way towards redressing the balance of films about migrants. Paul Cox's **Kostas** deals with a Greek taxi-driver in present-day Melbourne. The film is technically accomplished and, mercifully, Cox's Greeks all address each other in their own tongue. He somewhat artfully describes (from a screenplay by Linda Aronson) the romantic attachment of the Greek (Takis Emmanuel) and a middle-class Australian divorcee (Wendy Hughes).

What Cox fails to do — and it is symptomatic of Australian cinema's approach to social questions — is examine the very issues this relationship raises. Migrants of Mediterranean origin are, to say the least, still regarded with some reserve by the predominantly WASP milieu the divorcee inhabits. A couple like this is relatively rare, even in the city said to have the world's third greatest Greek population. The pair are parted by ethnic differences, contemporary as well as historical, in which questions of class and culture also arise. To this extent, Cox's rather facile romance is a worthwhile social document, even though the more important matters it touches upon are largely unexplored.

Donald Crombie's **Cathy's Child** (1979) may also be classed as a film about migrants, because it focuses on the enormous barriers which sometimes confront newcomers who seek to obtain, or even understand, their rights. A factual account of a *cause célèbre* — that of Cathy Baikas, a young Maltese woman who, with the aid of a Sydney newspaper, regained the infant daughter abducted by her Greek husband — it surpasses **Kostas** in the incisiveness of its glimpses of Australian city life and cultural divisions.

Crombie, scriptwriter Ken Quinnell (whose screenplay is based on a book by the prin-

A brief, romantic moment between Kostas (Takis Emmanuel) and Carol (Wendy Hughes). Paul Cox's **Kostas**.

Cathy Baikas (Michele Fawdon), with child, is escorted through a pack of waiting reporters by Paul Nicholson (Bryan Brown). Donald Crombie's **Cathy's Child**.

cipal journalist involved, Dick Wordley) and Michele Fawdon, in the title role, affectingly convey the plight of the young mother.

At first cut off by unfamiliarity, custom and conditioning from the people and institutions best able to help her, Cathy plugs doggedly ahead. Crombie neatly equates Cathy's growing worldliness and self-confidence with the progress of her quest. At the end, she sounds a note of faintly irrational, and insensitive, optimism — something else she appears to have acquired in the lucky country.

If some Australians were uneasy about the treatment of migrants, many more had a thundering bad conscience about Aboriginals. Yet not until 1976 did any fiction film deal with our oldest inhabitants. Phillip Noyce served notice of his powers with **Backroads** (1977), a short feature made on a small budget. An inconclusive road drama, **Backroads** follows a carload of social rejects driving across New South Wales. Two of them are Aboriginals and the film contains salutary insights into the way many black people live as the pair visit relatives en route.

Noyce's film, set in the present day, was an instructive prelude to one of Australia's biggest productions: Fred Schepisi's **The Chant of Jimmie Blacksmith** (1978). This poetic film, based on Thomas Keneally's novel, is set at the turn of the century, but the questions it raises about Aboriginals come uncomfortably close to our own time — too close, one suspects, for many urban whites who criticized the film's violence, but were in fact much more disturbed by its implications. Keneally's novel, a factually-based story about a Europeanized half-caste who runs amok and

turns outlaw, is indeed bloodily violent — but the violence is neither excessive nor gratuitous.

The simulated squalor of a blacks' camp on the outskirts of a country town in 1900 is little different from the reality of 1976 (as it was photographed by Russell Boyd in **Backroads**). Jimmie (Tommy Lewis), a quiet, mission-educated half-caste, does everything expected of him in pursuit of the anticipated happiness of admission to white society. But he is exploited, derided and rejected. This lyrical, passionate film falters only at the vital point where the young man torn between two cultures finally snaps. Because the effects of the psychological and emotional pressures he suffers aren't properly defined, his sudden passing from abject complaisance to raging rancour seems altogether too abrupt and capricious. In sum, however, **Jimmie Blacksmith** must be regarded as a considerable achievement, if only for its apposite contrasting of the timeless land's beauties and latter-day ugliness.

When it comes to assessing the cinema's treatment of underprivileged groups, one can't overlook the largest deprived class in our society: women. Much debate and campaigning about feminine status stirred Australian society during the past decade, and undoubtedly affected filmmakers, male and female. No film was devoted exclusively to a feminist topic, but a large number did, in one way or another, take into account changing attitudes towards and among women. Most significant, however,

Jimmie (Tommy Lewis) with the missionary, Rev. Neville (Jack Thompson), and wife (Julie Dawson). Fred Schepisi's **The Chant of Jimmie Blacksmith**.

Above: Husband (Byron Williams) and wife (Elke Neikhardt) in John B. Murray's **The Husband**, an episode of **Libido**.
Below: Low-income suburbia and an image of defiance, the restored FJ. Michael Thornhill's **The FJ Holden**.

3 COMEDY

Geoff Mayer

". . . humour is always considered a healthy thing until someone steps on our own toes or prejudices, or kicks our own crutches out from under our armpits or throws up all over our new Persian rug. Then the humour is in bad taste. It all depends upon the point of view."

Andrew Sarris[1]

When interviewed about his part in **The Odd Angry Shot** (1979), actor John Hargreaves said it was

"a film that couldn't have been made in America or England because it depends on a peculiarly Australian sense of humour. We can joke about some awful situation."[2]

Hargreaves is incorrect, in that there are a number of British (e.g., **The Virgin Soldiers**) and American precedents (**M*A*S*H**) for the film, although he does draw attention to the "peculiarly Australian sense of humour" in the film. Even here the mainstream of Australian humour is not quite as unique as is sometimes claimed. Parallels between the dominant form of Australian comedy and the broad 'roughhouse' populist strain found in many pre-World War 2 American comedies (and which surfaced recently in Clint Eastwood's **Every Which Way But Loose**) can be established. This is not all that surprising, given that the roots of this form of comedy go back to the frontier tradition which was, in some respects,[3] common to both countries.

In attempting to isolate some of the distinctive characteristics of mainstream Australian humour, T. Inglis Moore's comprehensive study of the social patterns in Australian literature is a useful starting point. In it he says that Australian society, through a blend of specific qualities, developed its own type of humour:

"On the one hand, the humour tends to have a robust crudity, to be simple, direct, and obvious in its humour of action as shown in tall stories, tales of tricksters and farce. On the other hand, the humour holds as its keynote an irony which demands a sophisticated detachment and an intellectual assessment of conflicting factors calling for a degree of subtlety."[4]

Inglis Moore's explanation for the development of this particular pattern derives from his notion of an 'ecological unity' where society is seen as being shaped by the interaction between the People and the Place. For example, he argues that the ironic quality is largely a result of the unpredictable variability of the seasons.

Another factor which helped shape the character of Australian life (including, of course, its humour) is revealed in Geoffrey Blainey's revisionist history, *The Tyranny of Distance*. Blainey says that many

"of the characteristics of Australia's population and life were shaped by the simple fact that Australia was so far from Europe."[5]

One of the most important consequences of this was the scarcity of women. Of the convicts who were sent to New South Wales, men outnumbered women by more than five to one. This imbalance persisted throughout the 19th Century, although the gap was gradually narrowed and by 1900 Australia had only 11 males for every 10 females.

The social consequences of this sexual imbalance persisted for so long that, according to Blainey, it must have "flavoured society in countless ways". He lists the use of alcohol and the heavy incidence of drunkenness; the tradition of mateship ("the collectivist idea that men should be loyal to the men with whom they lived and worked"); the relative neglect education suffered in the 19th Century; the heavy emphasis placed on sport; and even

"that curious custom, so common at dances or social evenings in many parts of Australia, whereby women gather at the opposite end of the room, seems to have had its origin in the era when women were scarce."[6]

Blainey's view that geographical considerations were significant in forming the archetypical patterns of Australian culture goes a long way towards explaining the masculine character of Australian humour, particularly its irreverence, broadness and crudity (which are not used here in a pejorative sense). These formative years were important in determining the shape and direction of Australian comedy.

This view is in accord with the thesis presented by Russel Ward, in *The Australian Legend*. Ward, inspired by the "frontier theory" of American historian Frederick Jackson, attempts to trace and explain the development of the "national mystique", the source of which he argued is found in the Australian bush.[7] Ward's book is invaluable in articulating the Australian ethos, the national self-image consisting of a range of attitudes, assumptions and beliefs about the unique quality of Australian life.

From this, the characteristics of the national stereotype are established; he is assumed to be rough and ready, pragmatic, an improviser, a hard drinker, sceptical about religion, culture and intellectual pursuits, egalitarian, loyal to his mates and deeply interested in sport.[8]

This national stereotype, Ward argues, was absurdly romanticized and exaggerated, and was taken to be characteristic of the semi-nomadic drovers, shepherds, bullock drivers, stockmen and other pastoral workers. The national mystique derived from the interaction between these People and the Place (i.e., the material conditions of outback life).

Ward acknowledges that this mystique emanated from a group of people who had disproportionate influence to their numerical and economic strength, and that it represented characteristics that were admired, but not necessarily practised. However, from the late 19th Century, through the growth of the trade union movement, periodicals such as *The Bulletin*, *Lone Hand* and *The Queensland Worker*, and writers such as Furphy, Henry Lawson and Banjo Paterson, Australians became actively conscious of a distinctive 'bush' ethos, and its value as an expression and symbol of Australian nationalism.

This ethos, according to Ward, was a distinctive way of looking at life. Its 'truth' or otherwise was irrelevant, and like most 'myths' (in the anthropological sense) it provided a conceptual framework which was taken as given. Inherent in this framework was the characterization and outlook of the 'typical'/ideal Australian. It is this framework which has formed the basis of Australian screen comedy. For example, films such as **Sunday Too Far Away** (1975), **The Picture Show Man** (1977) and **High Rolling** (1977) draw on, and manipulate, this ethos to celebrate aspects of Australian life. Similarly, David Williamson (**Don's Party** — 1976) and Barry Humphries (**The Adventures of Barry McKenzie** — 1972) tap the same source in their attack on the urban legacy of this ethos.

Earlier exponents of mainstream comedy, such as Roy Rene "Mo" and George Wallace ("the drongo from the Congo"), reached the public through the Tivoli, and other vaudeville outlets in the pre-war years. Slapstick and the double entendre, together with a strong vein of sardonic humour, which characterized these performers, were consistent with Australian screen comedy of the 1930s. For example, **Dad and Dave Come To Town** (1938) is a fine example of this tradition, and the nature of the comedy is established in the opening sequence with a shot of Dad's (Bert Bailey) foot caught in Dave's (Fred McDonald) fox trap. This is followed by Dave's attempt to extract a tooth by tying it to a cartridge fired out of a rifle. After the tooth is removed, the punchline reveals that Dave tied the string to the wrong tooth.

The broad, visual humour of the film (such as Dave's patented car running out of control and setting fire to a haystack) is accompanied by the double-entendre dialogue. For example, when Bill Ryan (Peter Finch) calls on Dad to

Arnold (John Clayton), a "poofter", grapples with Alby (Grigor Taylor) in Igor Auzin's **High Rolling**.

Early Australian comedy: Ken G. Hall's **Dad and Dave Come to Town**.

ask his permission to marry Sally (Valerie Scalon), Dad mistakenly believes that the purpose of the visit is to buy his dog, called Sal. Thus Dad extols the virtues and defects of his dog to a bewildered Bill:

Dad: If she likes your piece of meat she's liable to take it out and hide it under a stump.

and

Dad: She's liable to hop into anybody's bed if you don't watch her ... She's the best little bitch in the district.

For most of the film, the humour comes from Dad and Dave, and the rest of the family, moving to Sydney; the film follows the usual populist dichotomy of rough and ready rural folk adapting to the deceit and decadence of big city life. This is particularly evident in the blatantly effeminate depiction of Entwhistle (Alec Kellaway), the designer in the frock shop that

the Rudds inherit. (Dad describes him as a "natural born milker".)

Rarely in the context of the Australian film industry is it possible to evoke the auteur principle, but in the production of **The Adventures of Barry McKenzie** and its successor, **Barry McKenzie Holds His Own** (1974), the nihilistic, cynical outlook of Barry Humphries dominates. Humphries created the characters in the British magazine *Private Eye*, co-wrote the screenplay with director Bruce Beresford, and played three characters (Edna Everage, Dr Meyer de Lamphrey, and a member of the musical group, "The Disciples"). Humphries is aware of the legacy of the bush ethos, as well as the idiosyncrasies of life in the outer suburbs. As a result, his central character, Barry McKenzie (Barry Crocker), is a pathetic Anzac who comes from a brick veneer house in Moonee Ponds, Melbourne, and is addicted to beer and lamingtons.

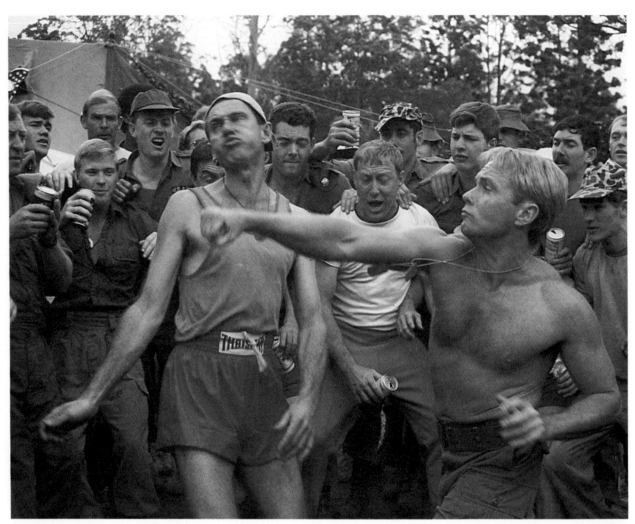

The fight resulting from Bung's (John Hargreaves) having stomped on a Marine's scorpion. Tom Jeffrey's **The Odd Angry Shot**.

Alvin (Graeme Blundell) accidentally steps on a shovel, but finds consolation from his schoolteacher's wife (Jill Forster). Tim Burstall's **Alvin Purple**.

A superb scene in **Barry McKenzie Holds His Own** captures the spirit of these two films. Barry, locked in gaol for being an illegal immigrant, is reduced to a pathetic, vindictive state in his abuse of the British:

"Our fighting men came over here when you Poms were ready to throw in the towel. Musso and their slimy element would have flattened this dump if it weren't for my uncles and their superlative fighting spirit. ... And if it hadn't been for Australians, Musso and them slanty-eyed pricks would have strung up every white kiddy and gone choc-a-block with all the nurses and bus conductresses."

The Adventures of Barry McKenzie is generally considered, like Vegemite, to be crude, juvenile and uniquely Australian. However, the comic structure of the film is in the universal mode,[9] based on the individual (McKenzie) who is out of step with society (British). The film is consistent with this mode, in that the protagonist is naive and infantile, and much of the comedy derives from his inability to cope with a hostile society.[10] Also consistent is the picaresque journey he undertakes which, in turn, gives the film an episodic narrative structure.

Humphries' film is very much a product of the cynical 1970s. It attacks many of the stereotype characteristics attributed to Australia (and Britain) in general, and the Australian male in particular: his inability to relate with women or match sexual boasting with actual deeds; castration complexes; etc. British decadence also comes in for a serve (Ronald Gort's den and Whippington Grammar obsessions), as well as the treatment of naive colonists (the British taxi driver who takes Edna and Barry from the airport to the city via Stonehenge and Scotland), together with the generally unhealthy state of the Mother Country (e.g., the newspaper heading, "Leprosy Panic Sweeps Birmingham", followed by a news-reader who claims there is no need to panic as the leprosy cases can be counted on the finger of two hands).

The Adventures of Barry McKenzie is a very uneven film. The opening and closing sequences add little, while some of the comedy sequences lack imagination and fall flat. This is particularly evident in the fight between McKenzie and Morrie Miller's men, and the repetitive sequence of the detective (Dick Bentley) being crushed behind a door. Other episodes are extremely funny, such as Barry's attempt to update his sexual technique based on the premise that British girls don't like it "clean and simple" like Australian women. Following the advice of the sex book, *The Perfumed Fanny*, Barry visits an Asian store for exotic spices. Later, as Caroline Thighs (Maria O'Brien) waits for him in bed, Barry excuses himself to pour a tin of curry down the inside front of his boxer shorts.

However, the film's greatest strength (or weakness, depending on your taste) is Humphries' dialogue. For example, Barry tells an obnoxious British snob that, "I hope all your chooks turn to emus and kick your dunny door down". Also, Barry confides to mate Curly (Paul Bertram) that, "If it was raining virgins, I'd be washed down the gutter with a poofter." There are also the seemingly endless euphemisms for urinating ("splash the boots", "shake hands with the wife's best friend", "strain the peas", etc.).

Barry McKenzie Holds His Own is a stronger film in most respects. The slapstick sequences work better, particularly the scene where Barry is accidentally locked in the toilet of a plane in flight ("Frogair") with Dr Meyer de Lamphrey. Barry tells De Lamphrey that he has this "small problem" and, as the plane suddenly lurches, De Lamphrey slips over until his face is in Barry's open fly, and he remarks, "It is a *little* problem."

Edna's sexual innuendoes are cleverer

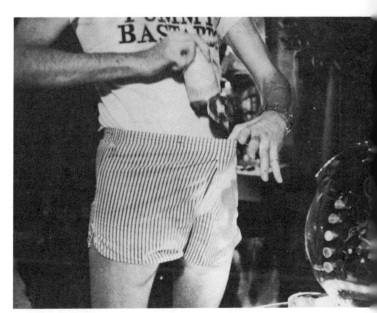

Barry McKenzie (Barry Crocker) spices up his sexual technique. Bruce Beresford's **The Adventures of Barry McKenzie**.

Aunt Edna (Barry Humphries) with Barry in a London taxi. **The Adventures of Barry McKenzie.**

("Lesbianism has always left a nasty taste in my mouth") and the social satire is sharper — particularly Edna's home movie designed to promote Australian beaches, which also shows the raw sewage outlet sign and the on-the-spot amputations when the sea wasps attack the surfers. Also effective is the Australia Culture Test, which is applied to all prospective British emigrants to Australia and where one applicant (John le Mesurier) is subjected to a rather vicious quiz game.

The second half of the film jettisons the loose episodic narrative which characterizes the first half (and the first Barry McKenzie film), and embarks on a parody of many of the conventions of war and horror genres. The excuse for this is provided by Count Plasma's (Donald Pleasence) abduction of Edna, when he mistakes her for the Queen. Barry and fellow Australians in London begin "Opera-tion Gladioli" to rescue Edna from the vampire's castle, and they interrupt the Count's blood-tasting ("full-bodied", "pleasant-tasting", etc.).

David Williamson, in an interview with Leonard Radic of *The Age*, said that satire could be an agent for social change, and he cited the example of Barry Humphries:

"Thanks to him, Australian sophistication has taken a great leap forward. No middle-class person, at home or overseas, wants to be identified with any of Humphries' monsters. He's often accused — wrongly, I think — of celebrating the Ocker image. But I'm sure it works the other way as well. I'm sure a lot of Australians distance themselves as rapidly as possible from the boozy philistinism of a Bazza McKenzie. In my own case I'd like to think that if you do a hatchet job in *Don's Party*, the Cooleys in the

A cynical view of Australian males *en masse*: Mack (Graham Kennedy), Don (John Hargreaves) and Mal (Ray Barrett). **Don's Party**.

audience won't, in the long term, dare to be as chauvinistic as they were in '69."[11]

Don's Party, scripted by David Williamson and directed by Bruce Beresford, is similar in many ways to the Barry McKenzie films. Its humour is broad, direct, irreverent and vulgar (the expatriate Australians who put out a studio fire by urinating on it in the first Barry McKenzie film are paralleled by the men in **Don's Party** who urinate on the bushes in the backyard).

The subtlety of the humour, or lack of it, is demonstrated by Mack's (Graham Kennedy) duck-hunter-with-a-toilet-role story, along with the four-letter endearments exchanged among the male guests. The visual humour is on the same level. For example, during the abortive love-making sequence between Don (John Hargreaves) and Susan (Claire Binney) in the backyard near the barbecue, the film

The irreverent, vulgar humour of Mal in **Don's Party**.

cuts to the not-too-subtle phallic image of sausages cooking on the barbecue plate.

John Clark, in his introduction to the published text of *Don's Party*, writes:

"Williamson is the most objective of dramatists. He never makes a moral judgement and he refrains from comment. His characters are drawn with cool detachment ... Williamson invites his audience to understand first and then judge if they wish."[12]

David Williamson displays many qualities in his screenplay for **Don's Party**, particularly the ability to orchestrate effective confrontations and devise cutting dialogue; but a cool detachment is not one of them. The film, set on the North Shore in Sydney (Lower Plenty on the outskirts of Melbourne in the play), is an undisguised attack on the trendy superficiality, materialism and selfishness which are presented as the dominant characteristics of the university-educated 'upward mobiles' who populate the film. These aspects are established in the film's opening scenes with Don and Kath (Jeanie Drynan) preparing for the party; while Kath is running around putting their young boy to bed, Don, beer in hand, fiddles with the television and resents Kath's request to put out the peanuts and chips. When Kath ridicules the purpose of the party to celebrate the ALP's election to power,[13] Don, watching the ABC election telecast, cites friend Cooley (Harold Hopkins) as being one guest with a sincere interest in the election result. However, the film undermines Don's defence by cutting to Cooley in a motel with his latest girlfriend, Susan, watching a television channel not covering the election.

The rest of the film is consistently cynical, and towards the end the only relationship to survive the party, the mateship between Don and Mal (Ray Barrett), is ridiculed. For example, as Don and Mal are slumped on the floor agreeing with each other, Kath remarks to Mal's wife, Jenny (Pat Bishop):

Kath: You won't stop them now. They're into the mutual admiration stage.
Jenny: Twelve glasses?

Earlier, Cooley tells Mal what a failure he has been, and cites his inability to attract the other women at the party ("You've been swinging your dick at anything available and missing by years"). However, the ultimate example of the cynical nature of the humour, which producer Phillip Adams describes as

being in the mainstream of Australian comedy, is Cooley's prolonged description of the diarrhoea he contracted on a visit to the South Australian wineries. Sequences such as this are not particularly humorous and their forced nature, lacking any semblance of inventiveness, make Barry McKenzie's chundering exploits seem like a masterpiece in subtle social comment.

However, it is consistent with Williamson's view of himself as a satirist of what he terms "bourgeois pseudo-problems": status, materialism and self-esteem.[13] Affluence, according to this former resident of a 4 ha bush retreat north of Diamond Creek, Victoria, encourages narcissism and self-worship:

"Problems that would seem minor in any other historical context are inflated to major ones because the people concerned have both affluence and leisure ... A person of 30 who has health, money and intelligence plus the capacity to change their [sic] life, would be better employed thanking their [sic] lucky stars that they're in such a position at this time in world history instead of sitting around, moaning about their [sic] lot, or going off to primal scream therapy."[14]

All narrative films are social documents, in that they incorporate values and a particular world view, although certain films much more overtly highlight their 'significance' and foreground their particular social concerns. Tom Jeffrey's **The Odd Angry Shot**, like **Don's Party**, is such an example. Set in a rain-sodden hell-hole in Vietnam at the height of the war, the film concentrates on the activities of the

Mal and Don in their "mutual admiration" stage. **Don's Party**.

Special Air Force Service, a group of professional soldiers led by Harry (Graham Kennedy), an embittered and cynical professional soldier. Similar in many ways to **Catch 22** and **M*A*S*H** (film and television series), the film attempts to evoke humour in the most appalling conditions. The humour is a lot broader (unsophisticated?), but equally irreverent, and throughout the film remains pretty much on the level of Harry's threat to urinate in the cook's scrambled eggs, or a close-up of Bung (John Hargreaves) squashing a scorpion after he had lost a bet with the Americans over a fight between his spider and their scorpion.

Consistent with this type of genre, **The Odd Angry Shot** attempts to express, through irony, the futility of war, although the Australian film is particularly heavy-handed in this regard: e.g., Harry punctuates the film with a number of speeches about the lack of interest back home in the welfare of Australian soldiers in Vietnam. Similarly, after the death of Bung near the end of the film, the audience is reminded (in case they have forgotten) that the communists will take over the area no matter what the Australians do. Finally, at the end of the film Harry and Bill (John Jarratt) enter a bar in Sydney and the barman asks Harry if he is back from Vietnam. Harry answers, "No!" The film then ladles on the irony with Normie Rowe's theme song, *Who Cares Anyway*, over the end titles.

The Odd Angry Shot deliberately eschews any overt acts of heroism, but nevertheless remains faithful to the Anzac mystique which, of course, is part of the ethos described earlier — particularly its anti-authoritarian tendencies combined with the image of the digger as being pragmatic with an intense sense of loyalty to his mates. In fact, **The Odd Angry Shot** is an interesting Australian example of the pattern American sociologist Will Wright discerns in his study of the American western.[15] Jeffrey's film approximates the narrative structure of the professional western (e.g., **The Professionals**, **Butch Cassidy and the Sundance Kid**, **The Wild Bunch**), where the hero's loyalty is to the group, not to society. In fact, the group is an elite unit which is seen as apart

Harry (Graham Kennedy) talks with Rogers (Bryan Brown) and Bung. **The Odd Angry Shot**.

from a society which is not presented in a favorable light. Wright argues that this form of narrative structure is a result of a corporate capitalistic form of economic organization which projects an ideology of technocracy.[16] Wright's thesis opens up the possibility of some parallel developments between Australia and the U.S. with regard to the narrative structure and the conceptual framework which shapes that structure.

A film which combines a critical examination of the Australian bush ethos, along with an understanding of it, is **Sunday Too Far Away**, arguably the finest Australian film produced since the revival of the early 1970s. Like the great majority of Australian films, it has an episodic narrative which studies a small group of men contracted to Timberoo, an outback sheep station, over a number of months in 1955. Like many other recent Australian films, it centres on the activities of a loser — Foley (Jack Thompson).

Foley, a former gun shearer,[17] returns to shearing with the intention of saving his money and leaving for good. Throughout the film, the parallels between Old Garth (Reg Lyle), a former gun shearer who is now a pathetic alcoholic, and Foley are emphasized. As well, his status as a loser is established in the opening scene when he crashes his car while driving back to the small outback town. Despite this, John Dingwall's script and Jack

Foley:	Where's the proper vehicle?
Undertaker:	In use. Old Mrs Taylor's got the use of it today.
Foley:	Couldn't you have hired one?
Undertaker:	Yes, from Smithfield. I have an arrangement there. Cost fifty quid all this way.
Foley:	So why didn't you?
Undertaker:	For Old Garth?
Foley:	If it had been the fucking cocky, you'd have hired it.
Undertaker:	Too right. But then I'd know I'd get paid for it.

(*Foley grabs the undertaker and slams him against the side of the van. He releases him, walks around to the back, lifts Garth's body and puts him inside the van in the passenger seat.*)

Foley:	If I hear, during the ride to town, Old Garth found his way to the back again . . . I'll come looking for you.

Near the end of the film, Foley and the other shearers strike when they learn that their prosperity bonus is to be withdrawn. As Foley and the other strikers fight the scabs in the hotel bar, words are superimposed on the screen informing the audience that, although the strike lasted nine months, the shearers won. The film cuts to a bloodied Foley, and as the scabs close in on him he brings back his fist to throw another punch. Over the frozen image the following words are superimposed:

"But it wasn't the money, it was the bloody insult."

The humour in the film, as in the other Australian films, is crude, direct, and irreverent. For example, Foley warns Tim King (Max Cullen), the contractor, to keep Dawson (Philip Ross), the station owner, out of the shed:

Foley:	He's driving us all mad. If he carries on running up and down like a headless chook, the place'll be ankle deep in pedigree balls.

Earlier, the shearers watch the approach of a car.

Tim:	This'll be the cook.
Foley:	Oh yeah. Who is the poisoner?
Tim:	Bloke called Quinn.
Foley:	Who?
Foley:	Tim. We pay the cook, we've got a right to a good one.
Tim:	I know. I know. This is a good one.

Shearing contractor Tim King (Max Cullen) takes his team to Timberoo. Foley (Jack Thompson) and Old Garth (Reg Lyle) doze on the back seat. Ken Hannam's **Sunday Too Far Away**.

Thompson's moving performance invest Foley with a dignity missing in the other films mentioned so far.

British critic David Robinson has perceptively summarized the quality which lifts this film above the others when he says that **Sunday Too Far Away** has the Fordian ability to perceive grandeur in people of limited horizons. This emerges in a number of sequences. When Old Garth dies, for example, Foley objects to the undertaker arriving in a utility van instead of a hearse:

Ugly (John Ewart) and Foley confront each other in the shearing shed. **Sunday Too Far Away**.

Foley: (*to the other shearers*): Anybody hear of a poisoner called Quinn?

(Nobody speaks out.)

Foley: Do you hear all that silence Tim?

As the car gets closer, one of the shearers, Ugly (John Ewart), tells the men a story of a cook with one arm that he and Foley had to get rid of when they worked on a property in 1952. This cook specialized in rissoles.

Ugly: Lovely rissoles. Best I ever tasted, till we caught him and had to get rid of him. Remember the day the machines broke down, Foley, and we got to the cookhouse early? We saw how the bastard made his rissoles.

Basher: How did he?

Ugly: He had all the stuff there (*Ugly gestures with his hand*), meat and onion and whatever other secret ingredient he used, 'cause they were bloody beautiful and he'd just pick a lump of it and . . .

(*Ugly throws an imaginary lump of meat into his armpit, and by flapping his wing produces a rissole which he throws down; he grabs another lump, manufactures a rissole; etc.*)

Ugly: Knocked them out one every two seconds. (*The rest of the shearers are groaning at the thought of it.*) We kept on finding hairs in those bloody rissoles, but we thought they were from his head!

Quinn, a huge man, is an alcoholic ("a lemon essence man") and a woeful cook. It is Foley's job, as union representative, to get rid of Quinn, and he is forced to make a deal with the station owner's daughter (Lisa Peers). She lets him take a number of bottles of lemon essence, so that Quinn can get drunk and Foley will have a better chance of beating him, in return for permission to watch the men shearing. However, when she enters the shed, one of the men calls out "ducks on the pond", and they stop shearing. Foley intervenes and they agree to let her watch one run. As she leaves, the girl thanks the shearers, but they virtually ignore her.

The position of women is reinforced in another sequence when, one evening, the shearers invite Beresford (Sean Scully), a young shearer, to inspect the next day's sheep with them:

Foley: You coming?

Beresford: I'll just carry on with my letter.

Foley: What's wrong with you Berry?

Beresford: What do you mean what's wrong with me, nothing wrong with me.

Foley: I mean, are you queer or something?

Beresford: I'm not queer.

Ugly: All he ever does is write letters. Who do you write letters to?

Beresford: My wife.

Basher: God bugger me!

Foley: (*shouting at Beresford*): What in the bloody hell's wrong with you?

At the end of **Sunday Too Far Away**, a series of shots of the empty shearing shed establishes an elegiac, nostalgic feeling of something having been lost. **The Picture Show Man** shares this mood.[18] Its episodic narrative centres on the activities of Maurice "Pop" Pymm (John Meillon) who travels around small outback towns with his son Larry (Harold Hopkins), and their combination moving picture show and song-and-dance routine.

The humour complements the rather gentle mood of the film and revolves around Miss Lockhart (Judy Morris) dancing in the Isadora Duncan fashion, together with Freddy Graves' (John Ewart) liaison with Mrs Duncan (Jeanie Drynan), a lonely widow, and the ensuing double entendre. For example, as Graves tunes Mrs Duncan's piano:

Graves: A very beautiful instrument. I see it hasn't been tuned for some time.

Duncan: Not since my husband died . . . he used to attend to things like that.

Consistent with the leisurely elegiac quality, virtually every incident in the film is underdeveloped. This includes son Larry's periodic attempts to establish his independence from Pop; the bush race meeting where Pop's horse takes off in the wrong direction; and Pop's attempt to form a romantic attachment to the wife of an alcoholic magician.

A film which shares much the same topic, but is expressed in an entirely different comic mode, is **That's Showbiz** (1973), a 20-minute feature written and directed by Phil Noyce. The similarity is in its concentration on an ageing, second-rate vaudeville act, The Saddler Troupe, as it travels the small-town circuit. However, the sentimentality of this situation, which characterizes **The Picture Show Man**, and the first section of this film, is ruthlessly discarded with the return of the youngest son and his successful attempt to bolster falling attendances by importing the outrageous Madam Lash and her strip/whip act. Business booms until the oldest member of the act, Percy (George Till), runs off with Madam Lash. In an effective punchline, his elderly wife, Marjorie (Sarah Willis), decides the show must go on, and substitutes for Madam Lash — whip, leather, wrinkles and all.[19]

With **The Picture Show Man** and **That's Showbiz** one returns to the same pattern mentioned earlier. The former film generally celebrates the national mystique, while the latter draws on the ethos to present a much more cynical view. The same could be said of Richard Franklin's **The True Story of Eskimo Nell** (1975), which examines this mystique amid jokes about faeces and flatulence, and Igor Auzin's **High Rolling**, although this includes an extroverted American, Tex (Joseph Bottoms), who tends to dominate at the expense of the main Australian character,

Freddy Graves (John Ewart) accompanies a silent comedy which is being shown in an outback town. John Power's **The Picture Show Man**.

Pop (John Meillon) leads his horse and cart through the mud of inland New South Wales. **The Picture Show Man**.

Tex (Joseph Bottoms) glares at a passenger during the hold-up of the sightseeing coach. **High Rolling**.

Alby (Grigor Taylor). The obvious quality of much of the humour (e.g., Alby in bed with two girls asking what to do next; Tex setting fire to a dollar note to impress the girls), and the episodic quality of the script, which is often rather aimless (particularly the attempt to rob a sightseeing coach), negate a lot of the film's energy.

The same could be said of Tim Burstall's **Petersen** (1974), although it is structured around the interesting premise of a man caught between two irreconcilable lifestyles. Linda Gross, reviewing the film, which was released in the U.S. as **Jock Petersen**, wrote in *The Los Angeles Times*:

"**Jock Petersen** is a wry and poignant Australian comedy about a man who lives in an age where virility is valued more than integrity, intellect or courage ... It lacks polish, suffers from glib conclusions, but still exudes charm."

The humour in the rather durable formula of the Australian sexploitation film — e.g., **The Naked Bunyip** (1970), **Fantasm** (1976) and **Fantasm Comes Again** (1977) — along with such television spin-offs as **Number 96** (1974) and **The Box** (1975), does nothing to alter this

pattern. Neither does **Alvin Purple** (1973), one of Australia's most financially successful films. Shot on a budget of $202,000, the film has grossed almost $4 million. From the credits, which are superimposed over alternative shots of bouncing bed springs and four feet protruding from the end of the bed, to the double entendre dialogue delivered by Alvin's father to his son at his 21st birthday party ("There are openings everywhere for the right man ... In this world no one can afford to be

Broad, farcical humour during a milk-bar conversation. John Duigan's **Dimboola**.

58

slack"), the film is firmly rooted in the vaudeville tradition of Roy "Mo" Rene and George Wallace.

From the opening strains of *Going Back To Yarrawonga*, the film version of Jack Hibberd's participatory play, *Dimboola*, invokes the use of farce and the broad humour of the "Dad and Dave" films of the 1930s — complete with Chad Morgan as an updated facsimile of Dave. However, the difference between **Dimboola** (1979) and **Dad and Dave Come To Town** is in the confused viewpoint of the former film. Whereas **Dad and Dave** is essentially an affectionate celebration of the bush ethos, **Dimboola** is much more ambiguous. On occasions there appears to be a sincere attempt (albeit self-consciously) to recapture elements of this feeling through performance of songs like *Riding To The Never Never* at the Star Theatre, coupled with Tom Cowan's photography of the bush and the town, and the characterization of British visitor, Vivien Worcestershire-Jones (Max Gillies), where the formality and culture of the stereotyped Englishman is juxtaposed against the easygoing, uncouth residents of Dimboola. However, on other occasions, the film adopts the **Don's Party/Barry McKenzie** point of view, with its attack on such middle-class rituals as the kitchen tea party, the buck's turn and the boozy wedding, with the usual stereotypes. Nevertheless, it is all part of the same world discussed in the opening section of this chapter.

A. G. Stephens once selected Steele Rudd as the representative Australian humourist on the grounds that his work stands not for sophisticated wit or satire, but because of its sheer fun, its obviousness and its rough and hearty qualities. These qualities, along with an irreverence and a strong ironic vein, dominate Australian screen humour — for example, the scene in **Sunday Too Far Away** where Dawson, the property owner, tells the shearers

The clash between British values, represented by Vivien Worcestershire-Jones (Max Gillies), and an uncouth youth. **Dimboola**.

that Timberoo is a stud property, and that

"one of those rams in there won first prize at the Royal Show last year, and we paid 10,000 guineas for him. Most of my others would bring half of that and more at auction. You all know how easily a money-hungry shearer can incapacitate a ram, consequently instead of the usual double rate I have decided to pay double plus half."

Tim King then steps forward to interpret Dawson's speech to the shearers, who aren't particularly overwhelmed by the offer:

"What the cocky ... uh ... what Mr Dawson is saying, these rams are worth a quid, careful of their pizzles, careful of their knackers."

As in A. D. Hope's poem *Australia* ("The learned doubt, the chatter of cultured apes which is called civilization over there"), Tim King's reply to the station owner captures the ability of Australian humour to prick pomposity and perpetuate the egalitarian basis of the bush ethos.

4 HORROR AND SUSPENSE

Brian McFarlane

Horror and suspense have not been major elements in the Australian film renaissance of the 1970s. Many of the most popular films — **Caddie** (1976), **Storm Boy** (1976), **The Devil's Playground** (1976) and **The Getting of Wisdom** (1977), for instance — have been characterized by a pervasive nostalgia for Australia's past, a dwelling on pictorial beauties and gentle evocations of youth. Even while admiring these films, one has often longed for something gutsier or tougher-minded. It is not a matter of wanting **Frankenstein Down Under** or **Murder on the Southern Aurora**; rather, that our emerging filmmakers respond to the threat of the Australian landscape, instead of lyricizing it, or to the potential excitement of its cities, instead of ignoring it.

Equally, it is not a matter of urging filmmakers to work in the Hollywood-established genres of the horror film or the suspense drama, both of which reached their peak in the studio output of the 1940s. These genres certainly produced some honorable achievements, but at their most impressive — e.g., the dozen remarkable horror films Val Lewton produced for RKO, or Robert Siodmak's suspense-thrillers for Universal — they had a way of transcending the expectations of the genre. Thus, a film like Jacques Tourneur's **I Walked with a Zombie** (produced by Lewton) subsumes its elements of horror in a haunting and poetic study of conflicting ideologies, while Siodmak's **Phantom Lady** and **Uncle Harry** generate suspense out of an exploration of the dark possibilities in human nature. Australian directors have only just begun to excite audiences in these ways.

If one is to feel a sense of horror at work in films, one will be looking to directors and writers whose vision of life is sufficiently inclusive for them to be aware of the extraordinary lying beneath, or lurking at the edges of, the ordinary. Such filmmakers will understand the kinds of fears to which everyone is prey: fear of the unknown, the supernatural, sudden death, of destructive passions within us and dangerous forces around us.

Suspense may often accompany a growing sense of horror, but it need not do so. In Sophocles' *Oedipus Rex*, for example, the audience's horror at the fate it knows has overtaken Oedipus intensifies the suspense over when Oedipus will understand things for himself. Uncertainty about the outcome of a relationship (even in a work like Jane Austen's *Pride and Prejudice*, where the emphasis is generally comic) can also create suspense as effectively as a police chase.

Suspense depends initially on the screenplay. If a film as a whole is to generate suspense, it will need a script that knows how to build to climaxes, pace and vary the tone of its episodes, and realize how much an audience needs to know to secure its interest, while holding back enough to retain it. This is not, of course, to suggest that an incompetent or unimaginative director cannot defuse a promising screenplay.

The over-riding weaknesses in Australian films of the 1970s can be attributed to inadequate screenplays. Too many films have suffered from unduly episodic treatment in which the episodes fail to add to a coherent whole. **The Mango Tree** (1977) is an obvious example; **The Picture Show Man** (1977) another. **The Picture Show Man**'s faults are almost wholly derived from a screenplay that moves at a snail's pace, as if pace or energy were vulgar. This kind of excruciating slowness also made **Storm Boy** an endurance test for many, including children.

Another major fault of local screenplays (curiously, it is endemic in Australian novels, too) is a relentless determination to spell out themes, as though — and sometimes with good reason — they don't trust their narrative structures to make the points for them. Fred Schepisi, a fine director but a less confident scriptwriter, is guilty of this undue explicitness in **The Chant of Jimmie Blacksmith** (1978).

Opposite: Peter Weir's **The Last Wave**.

Arthur Waldo (Terry Camilleri) with the Mayor of Paris (John Meillon). Peter Weir's **The Cars That Ate Paris**.

Though the film's moments of horror and mayhem are done with imagination and a responsible sense of what the horror derives from, the screenplay cannot resist hammering home its message in statements about the destruction of a way of life.

No amount of blood-spattered violence, with its calculated visceral effect, however, is a replacement for the subtle and potentially cathartic working on the fears that lie, if suppressed, in all of us. Peter Weir's trio — **The Cars That Ate Paris** (1974), **Picnic at Hanging Rock** (1975), and **The Last Wave** (1977) — perhaps come nearest to achieving this result. As one watches the reluctant growth of fear in Arthur Waldo's response to the vicious opportunism of Paris in **Cars**, in the superficially demure schoolgirls and increasingly distraught headmistress in **Picnic**, or in David Burton's uneasy acceptance of forces beyond

his educated comprehension in **The Last Wave**, one becomes aware of a more sophisticated perception of horror. The audience responds to it as an inward pressure on that precarious state of psychological balance which is described crudely as normality.

Picnic enjoyed the greatest popular and critical success of the three, but it is not a film which grows richer in recollection: occasionally it seems to find visual style an end in itself, and its central enigma (What *did* happen at Hanging Rock on St Valentine's Day 1900?) has to fight for attention with the film's pervasive sense of a smothered sexuality. The parallel suggested between the surface of giggling excited schoolgirls, with its suggestions of real but repressed desire, and the surface beauty of the Australian scene, with its lurking horror, could well have been developed further by Cliff Green in his otherwise capable screenplay.

The Last Wave very intelligently explores a rational man's mounting fear when confronted by the irrational, but after a brilliant opening it loses some of the narrative tautness with which it establishes its dualities, and which it needs to pursue them. Like **Picnic**, it tends to become too much a matter of atmosphere, with ideas tantalizingly dangled — and each film *has* ideas — rather than pursued in dramatic terms. Both films show seemingly stable societies — the English-style, upper-class girls' school, incongruously set in the Australian bush; the suburban comforts of a professional, middle-class home in Sydney — which are about to disintegrate under the threat of unknown fears hovering at their edges.

Cars is a less complex work, but in some ways more exciting and satisfying. This is not just to express a preference for a trimness and coherence that grew out of an enterprise that was easier to organize, but also for Weir's integration of the elements of narrative swiftness, sharp observation of faces and places, and the awareness that apparent ordinariness barely masks violence and terror. It makes us privy to the horror which is at the heart of Weir's vision.

After crashing his car outside the little town of Paris, and killing his brother, Arthur Waldo (Terry Camilleri) is welcomed into town by the Mayor (John Meillon). He is taken to the Mayor's home where, in a nicely cryptic scene at dinner, earlier suggestions that all is not what it seems in Paris are intensified. And, as Arthur becomes aware that Paris lives off road accidents, Weir cuts to a brilliantly-handled

sequence where an accident victim is stripped of his belongings; a drill is applied to his brain; and his car is first dismantled then set on fire, while faces, including the Mayor's, watch from the window.

In the next sequence, Arthur decides to leave town, watched again by curious eyes. While waiting at the run-down bus station, he is asked to step down to the Council Chambers for a few words with the Mayor, who tells him, "You're basically normal . . . but you may not stay that way", and draws his attention to the "veggies" in the Bellevue Ward of the hospital — accident victims who don't even know their own names. Arthur's confidence is convincingly undermined by the knowledge of "two lives on his conscience" (his brother's and an old man he struck down a year earlier), by his inability to persuade anyone that he was dazzled by lights on the night of the accident, and by the sense of the whole town's being terrifyingly caught up in the accident trade. In one unobtrusive shot, an old lady trades a shining hub cap for clothes; in church, the clergyman (Ted Mulray) speaks of his two hobbies: the past, "manifest in lovely old towns like Paris", and the future, which is with the young and the forthcoming car gymkhana.

When the Mayor pursues Arthur into the countryside on a sunny Sunday afternoon, one gets a quintessential Weir image: a deceptively sleepy town nestling in the hills, but which increasingly, one realizes, is an inescapable death-trap for anyone trying to get in or out. Part of the film's horror is in its claustrophobia: one longs to be reassured that there is whole-

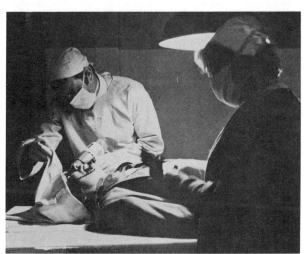

A road-accident victim is transformed into a 'veggie' by Doctor Midland (Kevin Miles). **The Cars That Ate Paris**.

A Paris local puts the torch to the stripped-down car of a crash victim. **The Cars That Ate Paris**.

some life out there, but Weir, true to his belief that horrifying things exist from which there may be no easy escape, doesn't allow such comfort.

The film moves in a series of fluent sequences which show a flair for narrative rhythm and tonal variety that Weir has not surpassed in his later, more ambitious films. What is so exhilarating, however, is the way the film spikes its mounting horror with black comedy. (So, incidentally, does Richard Franklin's **Patrick** — 1978.) The wit is there in the odd line, like the clergyman's words at the funeral, "Gosh, Lord, sometimes you work in ways that are incomprehensible", or the callous talk of the "midnight chorus" of the hospital "veggies". But, more importantly, it is worked into the texture of crucial sequences, like the morning service at church when beat-up cars circle the car wreck which acts as a monument in the town's centre. Also, the crash and bang of these cars nicely competes with "Immortal, invisible, God only one" in the church. The clergyman's position is teasingly enigmatic; one does not know where *he* stands until his corpse is brought in.

In the film's final sequence — the mayoral fancy dress ball and the attack of the spiked monster-cars — comedy and horror jostle for audience response, the one heightening the other. The authentic sound of the country town dance band floats outside to be drowned by the arrival of the cars, bent on reprisal for the burning of the car of one of the gang. The spikes on the leading car climb into the frame from the bottom right corner, then fill the

screen. The orgy of destruction which follows is directed with a fine eye for clarity and horror: the Mayor attacks the cars with a pole; someone else is caught on the spikes of a car while trying to spear it; and Arthur, forced to become part of the mayhem, regains his confidence as a driver by squashing a car and killing its "yobbo" driver. Arthur drives out, as traps are laid to stop him leaving the ruined town; smiling triumphantly, he heads for ... what?

Suspicious, potentially dangerous intruders in a watchful community are also an element of Ken Hannam's **Summerfield** (1977). Like other similar films (**Patrick** and **Long Weekend** — 1978), **Summerfield** understands the dramatic value of the contrast between the superficially ordinary and the horrors that may or may not erupt. At their best, these films recall the Ivy Compton-Burnett character who said, in *A Family and a Fortune*, "I am appalled by the threat and danger of life." Where **Summerfield** goes wrong, however, is with Cliff Green's screenplay. The disappearance of a young schoolteacher, Michael Flynn, from Banning's Beach, and the strange, elliptically-presented goings-on at the Abbotts' place are linked by some fairly obvious clues. The audience is led to expect that discovery of the "secret" of Summerfield will somehow be linked to Flynn's disappearance. The attitude of the town to Flynn (hostile, suspicious on the one hand; "We all liked Mr Flynn very much" on the other), and to the Abbotts (curious but detached) is sharply sketched. But in the end neither "strand" of the film's plot is adequately developed.

The more orthodox suspense of whatever-became-of-Flynn is developed by the new schoolteacher, Simon Robinson (Nick Tate), discovering Flynn's discarded car (which he identifies by a missing hub-cap found on a rocky beach) and by the policeman's refusal to interest himself in the discovery. Simon also locates Flynn's photographic equipment, and photos of the Abbotts and island wildlife in a drawer in the guest-house room he has inherited. However, Flynn's anti-climactic appearance in the last sequence renders all this narrative clue-dropping pointless and his connection with the Abbotts remains resolutely obscure.

As for the Abbotts, the audience is asked to be excited about incest between Jenny (Elizabeth Alexander) and her brother David

Schoolteacher Simon Robinson (Nick Tate) with the incestuous Abbotts: David (John Waters) and Jenny (Elizabeth Alexander). Ken Hannam's **Summerfield**.

For a survivor of a car crash, the horror is about to begin. **The Cars That Ate Paris**.

Michael Fitzhubert (Dominic Guard) struggles to climb the rock. Peter Weir's **Picnic at Hanging Rock**.

The security of a middle-class home is destroyed by the malevolent weather. Richard Chamberlain as David Burton in **The Last Wave**.

65

(John Waters).[1] Jenny's daughter, Sally (Michelle Jarman), is also revealed as the result of this relationship, and this revelation is signalled by some rather heavy-handed references. David has, for instance, killed some new kittens because "the cats on this place are a pretty poor lot; they're all inbred." Elsewhere there is a shot of David and Jenny looking much more than siblings as they stand at Sally's window. Jenny, we are also told, went away 10 years ago and came back with the child.

The film then erupts in a horrifying but uninvolving bloodbath, yet from the moment Simon peers at David and Jenny's love-making (takes his time about it, too) nothing is convincing. It is as though Green has no way of reconciling the interests of mystery-thriller and psychological drama, and one feels cheated by the hints of connection the film has so liberally strewn.

Hannam is not yet a director who can weld together a slack-minded script. What he does well, if finally to little purpose, is to create a suspicious, uncommunicative township, vaguely hostile to the intruding new teacher; to contrast the shadowy graces of Summerfield life with the immutably dreary procedures of an Australian guest-house; and to manage his actors with a sensitive regard for their personal qualities. He is particularly successful in playing off Nick Tate's athletic and relaxed Simon against John Waters' tensely withdrawn David. Their scenes together, and those with Elizabeth Alexander's properly-strained Jenny, are

good examples of a director's use of the attributes three excellent actors can bring to a film.

Whereas Weir and Hannam locate their visions of horror in deceptively ordinary little towns, Richard Franklin places his in the recognizable cinematic framework of 1940s Hollywood.[2] **Patrick** belongs to the honorable tradition of films about plucky heroines, obtuse heroes, and eerie institutions run by mad doctors and sinister matrons. In combining elements of Gothic horror, easy sensuality and sharp wit, it emerges as a fitting stablemate for such notable *films noirs* as Curtis Bernhardt's **Conflict**, Peter Godfrey's **Cry Wolf**, and Siodmak's **The Dark Mirror**.

The screenplay is by Everett de Roche, the most sophisticated and coherent scriptwriter at work in Australian features, and it clearly understands the demands of the genre: a promising central premise (psychokinetic patient with a yen for his pretty nurse and alarming ways of showing it) which gives rise to a variety

A terrified Dr Wright (Bruce Barry) is comforted by nurse Kathy Jacquard (Susan Penhaligon) after he nearly drowns in his swimming pool. **Patrick**.

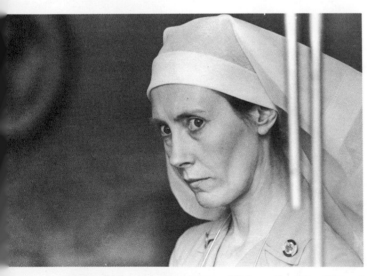

Julie Blake as the sinister Matron Cassidy. Richard Franklin's **Patrick**.

Kathy is attacked by an "intruder". **Patrick**.

Dr Wright assures Kathy that the comatose Patrick is quite incapable of psychokinetic terrorism. **Patrick**.

Kathy and Dr Roget (Robert Helpmann) in the hospital cellar where they find Matron Cassidy murdered. **Patrick**.

of lively action; characters whose individual quirks are sufficiently sketched without being allowed to clog the film's movement; some excellent throwaway dialogue; and a series of well-paced shocks. Franklin knows how to build on this framework, how to direct his cameraman, Don McAlpine, to get the maximum suspense from an episode, and how to use objects and locations to create a sinister atmosphere.

In one scene, as nurse Kathy Jacquard (Susan Penhaligon) dangles her legs in the swimming pool of a doctor boyfriend (Bruce Barry), the rippling light of the water assumes an unsettling quality, intensified as the camera takes the audience underwater. The doctor seems to be having trouble reaching the surface, and before he finally stumbles out, a victim of Patrick's malevolent playfulness, Franklin chillingly plays on that fear each of us

has experienced in nightmares of not being able to move from under a terrifying weight.

Elsewhere, Kathy is seen getting her new flat into order, and there is a very satisfying shock when an intruder leaps out as she arrives home. (This is none too logical in the context, but is not too worrying at the time.) Later still, there is another good shock when Kathy returns home to find the place wrecked. (That Patrick! And all the time he's flat on his back in a hospital bed.)

Franklin's use of staircases, street lamps, billowing curtains, an electric radiator, and a flickering "Emergency" sign recalls the great days of Val Lewton at RKO, in films like **Cat People** and **I Walked with a Zombie**. In these, the horror works largely by suggestion, and by imbuing objects with an iconographic significance. So too with the actors: Susan Penhaligon's nurse is blood sister to Ella Raines' secretary in **Phantom Lady** and Frances Dee's nurse in **Zombie**; Julia Blake's sinister matron is Katherine Emery or Gale Sondergaard to the life; and, in the rather lumpish heroes (played by Bruce Barry and Rod Mullinar), Tom Conway and James Ellison live again. They understand exactly the nature of their involvement in the film.

But **Patrick** is more than just a happy hunting ground for 1940s Hollywood buffs. Technically, it is a very accomplished film — certainly one of the most stylish of the recent boom — and its technique is at the service of a coherent point of view that comprehends easily such dichotomies as normal/abnormal, innocent/corrupt, wholesome/ugly. This point of

Above: At first fearful of rape, Kathy soon realizes that the assailant is her husband Ed (Rod Mullinar). **Patrick**. Below: Kathy returns to her flat with Dr Wright and finds it ransacked. **Patrick**.

view expresses itself in its images (e.g., excrement and flowers) and its teasing use of faces to create an enjoyable ambiguity, and skilfully orchestrates the contributions of a sophisticated screenplay, a cameraman who is receptive to what his director wants, and brilliantly-inventive special effects.

It has been argued that **Patrick** is not a profound film, and that it does not push a social message, or, indeed, a message of any kind. That is true, but what makes Franklin a director to watch is the trust he shows in his medium, the confident relish with which he uses the conventions of the genre, and the way he creates his meanings in images.

Everett de Roche also wrote the screenplay for Colin Eggleston's "ecological" thriller, **Long Weekend**, and, as in **Patrick**, there is an impressive coherence that owes much to the screenplay. The film opens superbly as the camera pulls back from a close-up of a crab on a rock to reveal a vast and lovely stretch of coast; it then cuts to a city street where there is a flutter of birds as a car starts. Fern fronds edge into the screen; there are ferns in the bath of a trendy suburban house; there is a news report that white cockatoos are attacking houses; and Marcia (an excellent, edgy performance from Briony Behets) closes the curtains, as if to shut out the threat of nature, and takes a frozen chicken from the refrigerator. Peter (John Hargreaves in another intelligent, complex performance) arrives home, trains his rifle on her, and a tense relationship is set up — between two people, and between suburban man and the natural world.

The screenplay does not spell out this latter suggestion in pretentious abstractions, but in skilful juxtaposition of images. The sophistication of the young couple proves inadequate to the threat of the landscape as they set up their camp on a remote beach: she brimming with resentment (affaire, abortion and breakdown in sexual communication are deftly sketched by De Roche's screenplay); he determined to prove himself equal to the demands of this isolated weekend.

Screenplay and direction work smoothly together to establish the threat of the coastal retreat. Once or twice the film over-signals its thematic intentions: e.g., "I ran over a kangaroo tonight", Peter remarks while his wife tartly disapproves, and there is an eerie response in the night bush, like a baby crying. Such explicit moments, however, are com-

pensated by the steady, imagistic build-up: Peter mindlessly hacks at a tree; a dark shape appears in the water while he swims; ants crawl menacingly over the food; Peter throws an empty beer bottle into the sea and shoots at it; Marcia finds an eagle's egg and later breaks it against a tree; and, after another "shark" scare, Peter shoots what proves to be a dugong, and the gulls hover as its blood darkens the water.

As the images multiply, so does the friction in the young couple's relationship: Marcia refuses to make love; she is bored and he is randy; and, as he goes off to surf, she masturbates. And, against the conflicts adumbrated in the film's opening, their campsite, a small pool of light, begins to look threatened by the foliage: an eagle attacks Peter, and a possum eats the food; and the beauty of the sunset mocks the increasing ugliness of their relationship and the danger of their situation.

The film is intelligent about suburban man's maladaptation to the natural world, and is critical of Marcia's refusal to accommodate herself to its challenges and Peter's romanticized view of reality. It loses some of its momentum towards the end, but Eggleston

Peter (John Hargreaves), alone against an encroaching nature. Colin Eggleston's **Long Weekend**.

Peter, his nerve broken, screams hysterically in the forest. **Long Weekend**.

A cockatoo attacks a semi-trailer driver, who, in swerving across the road, strikes and kills Peter. **Long Weekend**.

sustains an eerie sense of his humans being observed by silent, menacing forces. Sometimes these are embodied in an animal; sometimes there is threat in the way boughs or vines frame and cross the screen. The flight and death of Marcia, the breaking of Peter's nerve, and his being run down by a truck driver, whose attention is distracted by a bird, bring the film to a violent but poetically apt conclusion. It is a film of vivid images — as are many recent Australian films — but it welds these together to create a coherent and frightening vision.

A film as self-consciously Grand Guignol as Terry Bourke's **Inn of the Damned** (1975), with all its Gothic paraphernalia, doesn't begin to create the *frissons* of the Weir films, or De Roche's screenplays. It offers no recognizable reference point, no sense of a "normality" to be violated, no character with whose connection with a real world one can identify. In the absence of such prerequisites, **Inn of the Damned** becomes no more than a series of melodramatic gestures. And Judith Anderson's Caroline is so resolutely strange and sinister that it is hard to feel for her supposedly-tormented mind the sympathy that might have given the film — and the audience — a point of view.

The film's best asset is cameraman Brian Probyn's splendid evocation, mainly through skilful use of overhead shots, of a wayside house nestling suggestively in a green valley among forested mountains. Generally, however, the film fails to build the eerie house atmosphere of such minor classics as Andre de Toth's **Swamp Water**, with poor Merle Oberon driven out of her wits in a mossy, crumbling Southern mansion, or Charles Vidor's **Ladies in Retirement**, where Isobel Elsom is strangled in a Romney Marshes cottage. Even if it did succeed on this physical level, **Inn of the Damned** would still fail for the psychological reasons suggested above.

Equally unsuccessful is Tim Burstall's **End Play** (1975), an absurd mystery-thriller (to use the term loosely) adapted by Burstall from a Russell Braddon novel. The film opens with the murder (third in a series) of a hitch-hiker on the highway near Kyneton, Victoria. The pre-credits sequence is neatly handled: the opening shots fasten on the girl's legs with cars racing past; then her face is framed in the windscreen of the car that stops. The audience does not see the face of the driver whose gloved hand cups her face, then moves over her body, before reaching into the glove box of the car. Then come the credits, with Peter Best's appalling theme song, and Mark Gifford (John Waters) arriving at a country house to be greeted by his paraplegic brother Robbie (played without style or subtlety by George Mallaby). Some interesting tension is established between the two brothers, as conversation gives way to Robbie's archery practice during which he misses Mark by inches. Then, while Robbie is away at a local paraplegic centre, Mark brings in the body of the hitch-hiker, props her up on a couch, puts her hat on and sits down to observe her.

Soon after this, the film falls apart. Why on earth should Mark go to so much trouble to dispose of the body? Disguised in a long blonde wig, hat and sunglasses, he takes her in Robbie's old wheel-chair to the Rex Cinema, Kyneton (it is a surprise to find Kyneton has daytime screenings), bundles her into a seat and then leaves in the wheel-chair. None of the film's ramifications, including the nature of the feeling between Margaret (Belinda Giblin) and each of the brothers, or the black-and-white flashback intended to explain Robbie's bitterness, is convincing.

The final physical clash between Robbie and Mark, with javelins, axes and arrows, has some exciting moments, but these founder on the improbability of Mark's not being able to escape his crippled brother — and on our indifference to the outcome. The exposing of

the murderer, and the explanation of how the murders were carried out, is in the manner of Agatha Christie's denouements, but without the style and logic to make us forget the earlier improbabilities. There is only one camera set-up which effectively heightens the tension and that is of the bottle of pills which Mark puts in his brother's drink: this merely calls attention to how visually uninteresting most of the film is, and how the camera is almost never used to create suspense.

Another mystery-thriller is Terry Ohlsson's **Scobie Malone** (1975). Adapted from *Helga's Web*, a Jon Cleary *policier*, it adopts a steadfastly simple-minded approach to its hearty mixture of violence and sex, corruption in high places and thuggery in low. It comes as a shock to see the distinguished name of Casey Robinson on the credits as producer and co-writer,[3] because there is little sign of the old mastercraftsman in this story which centres on the murder of an avaricious and notably unsubtle call-girl, Helga Brand (Judy Morris). Could Robinson really have provided a script which involves: (a) a detective who can't remember which air hostess' bed he is sharing (a running joke derived from a 1960s farce called **Boeing Boeing**); (b) puerile smut like "Mummy's got a position to make you forget your position in the community", as Helga goes to work on the Minister for Cultural Development; (c) witless camaraderie between Malone and his

The climactic clash between the brothers: Robbie (George Mallaby) and Mark (John Waters). Tim Burstall's **End Play**.

rookie offsider; or (d) a morality as jejune and specious as that expressed in Malone's righteous cry of "Is there one law for them [i.e., the rich and mighty] and one for the Helga Brands?"

In the matter of its moral sententiousness, the film seems to be modelling itself on another urban thriller, **The Maltese Falcon**. That classic of the genre, however, wore its moral concerns with organic laconicism; they were as much a part of its dark view of the way things are as the sleazy streets and sleazier people. In **Scobie Malone** they are merely imposed on a ramshackle narrative structure, mouthed piously by a thuggish, smart alec cop (played with neither charm nor conviction by Jack Thompson), whose treatment of women — of *people* — is so mindlessly amoral that one can't believe in his moments of sudden righteousness. The audience could only be properly horrified by the girl's death, in the Sydney Opera House, if it could feel that somewhere, among all the avarice and squalor, Malone stood credibly for a respect for human life. But life at every level of society in this film is too venal for the audience to have a steady viewpoint about anyone involved in it.

As it is, nothing is convincing. The film fails to make good use of its city exteriors; it has a hideous theme song; its sense of humour is relentlessly smutty, tied to an unusually repellent approach in all its sexual encounters;

its characterization is almost uniformly crude; and its idea of high society (James Condon and Jacqueline Kott stiffly theatrical as the Minister and his enamelled wife) is naive in the extreme. Even though Judy Morris, a very good actress, tries hard, it is not possible to care about Helga, or anyone. And the film, despite its bursts of violence and blood-letting, is never riveting enough on a simple narrative level to make one indifferent to its absurdities.

In terms of use of city locations, Brian Trenchard Smith, in **Deathcheaters** (1976) and **The Man From Hong Kong** (1975), is far more inventive, though neither he nor Ohlsson is able to imbue the urban scene with any real sense of menace.

One doesn't have to adduce master-works like **The Maltese Falcon** and **The Third Man**, or even lesser examples of the big-city thriller like John Farrow's **The Big Clock**, Peter Yates' **Bullitt** and Jules Dassin's **The Naked City**, which so effectively created a sense of the dangerousness of a huge city sweltering in the heat, to point up the failure of Australian filmmakers to exploit the thriller potential of city streets, their criminal underworlds, the visual threat of their burgeoning high-rise aspirations, and the sort of horror that innocent-looking suburbia can sometimes suggest. There are gestures in the direction of urban menace in **In Search of Anna** (1979), but they are apt to get lost in the overall artiness.

The abandoned corpse (Delvene Delaney) in the Kyneton cinema. **End Play**.

Urban, industrialized menace: Tony (Richard Moir) and the naked Gerry (Chris Haywood). Esben Storm's **In Search of Anna**.

Opposite: Fred Schepisi's **The Chant of Jimmie Blacksmith**.

Jim Sharman's **The Night The Prowler** (1978) opens well with its deceptively "normal" shots of affluent suburbia, but does not capitalize on this promise. Following the dictates of Patrick White's over-emphatic screenplay, the film is too concerned with insisting on the repulsive underbelly of the scene to do anything as straightforward as exciting the audience. It spends so much time disgusting one with glimpses of upper-class poops and concentrating on the grotesque elements of its view of Sydney night-life that the viewer loses his sense of the city as a real and frightening place.

The one really successful use of the city landscape is in Peter Weir's **The Last Wave**. As David Burton (Richard Chamberlain) drives through the city's rain-washed streets, its buildings obscured by the downpour, a fine tension is evoked. There is a suggestion that the kind of society these buildings represent is in heedless opposition to, and threatened by, natural and supernatural forces, a point which critic Jack Clancy has perceptively developed in his review of the film:

"Much of the film's sense of menace, of imminent, apocalyptic doom, comes from the very strong feeling of disjunction, of white civilization as no more than a historical pimple on the vast, timeless body of the ancient continent."[4]

Clancy also writes of the "balance Weir manages to hold between ... the busy, dirty civilization of the city against the constant threat of overpowering natural forces". Weir's direction makes clear that the balance is precariously held and creates a potent sense of horror through that very precariousness. Neither the seeming solidity of those city blocks nor the pleasant suburban home of the lawyer in the end offer a substantial bulwark against these unknown forces. And this point, made in the film's *mise en scene*, provides a physical analogue for its decent, rationalist hero's growing attraction to, and fear of, the mysterious and the irrational.

Generally, though, the menace of place in Australian films has been better caught in rural settings. One thinks especially of **Picnic**, with its oppressively Victorian school and its in-

John Waters as "Rabbit", the gentle man badgered into joining the posse by a socially-conscious wife. Tom Jeffrey's **Weekend of Shadows**.

scrutable, ancient monolithic outcrop; of the raw, lonely, exposed mountains and forests of **Jimmie Blacksmith**, and its inadequate, isolated huts; of the encroachment of violated flora and fauna on the solitary camp of **Long Weekend**; of some of the shots establishing small-town suspicions in **Summerfield, Cars**, and Tom Jeffrey's **Weekend of Shadows** (1978).

Jeffrey's film suffers from some heavy-handed scripting, but Richard Wallace's camera deals remarkably well with the bigoted little town and the alarming emptiness of the surrounding countryside. The film is short on real suspense — we can never believe that the hunted Pole is truly a murderer — but John Waters' thoughtful performance as "Rabbit" does generate a more interesting tension. This grows from the exploration of how far a simple, but not stupid, and inarticulately good man can be pushed before his mind snaps and his life breaks apart. Waters, perhaps the subtlest actor in Australian films, deserves a full-length role to do justice to his watchful intensity.

The idea of horror's being used to moral ends is one that has scarcely been touched by Australian filmmakers. Apart from Weir's use of it in **Cars** to confront the audience with the hideously venal possibilities dormant in ordinary lives, it is only Schepisi in **Jimmie Blacksmith** who warrants a mention. Schepisi's account of his treatment of the violence in the film is an accurate reflection of how it appears on the screen: "... though I have tried to stylize it and do something different, in the end you have to front it head on."[5]

The murder of the Newby women *is* horrific and that is how it appears. It has been prepared for in the film's imagistic insistence on cutting edges: the sharp stone used in Jimmie's tribal initiation, the axe used in cutting the chicken's head, the deft use of the blades in the shearing shed, kitchen knives and butcher's knives hacking their way through meat, and the axe Jimmie has in hand when he hears of the birth of his child. When the climactic horror comes, the audience responds to its orgasic quality and recognizes its place in the context of casual brutality which has persisted throughout the film.

There is also an element of stylization, almost a balletic sense of movement, but this does not blunt the horror the episode inspires, and which is intensified by observant touches

Felicity (Kerry Walker) is comforted by her mother (Ruth Cracknell) after the alleged attack. Jim Sharman's **The Night The Prowler**.

of ordinary life, like the brief glimpse of home preserves the camera catches during the massacre. This is not mindless violence: it carries the emotional charge appropriate to the film's climax and offers the most intense epitomization of the complex situation of rage, frustration and paternalism that is at the heart of the film's experience. The audience can't merely respond appalled to this scene without being forced to consider why it is so.

There are a few moments in Sharman's **The Night The Prowler**, in which Kerry Walker, as the unraped heroine, is on her nocturnal prowl through Sydney's streets and parks when it looks as if we may get some insight into the horrifying potential in human nature. A repressed, ordinary, lumpish girl is "liberated" by an assault that didn't happen. In seeking revenge on the society that has tried to force her into an ill-fitting mould, she comes face to face with violent possibilities within herself (and others) and gives vent to these in unusual ways. However, this potentially interesting situation founders on the pretentious and obsessive qualities of Patrick White's screenplay and on Sharman's flashy direction, both of which are more concerned with making points than understanding people.

Sharman's earlier effort, the ludicrous **Summer of Secrets** (1976), has some of the same trademarks. It offers a highly schematized account of two sets of memories, with

Beverly (Arthur Dignam) engaged in his nightly multi-media ritual. Jim Sharman's **Summer of Secrets**.

two sets of characters united by their attempts to recapture the past. The young boy, Steve (Andrew Sharp), holidaying on a lonely beach with his girlfriend, Kym (Nell Campbell), is pursuing childhood memories in the wooden shack among the tea-tree. In a large house nearby, Dr Beverly Adams (Arthur Dignam in an improbable blond wig) and Bob (Rufus Collins), his black companion, engage nightly in a weird multi-media ritual in which Adams recalls the great love of his life, Rachel (Kate Fitzpatrick), while Bob projects exotic filmed backgrounds of Rio or Paris and appropriate music to aid the processes of memory.

In a tedious manner, Steve and his girl are caught up in this nonsense, Rachel is brought back to life, and Steve finds a "purpose" by the end of the film to replace his earlier apathy about passing his examinations. Unfortunately, the film is so inept that it can't even play its trump card — the resuscitation of Rachel — for any kind of excitement.

Pretension and artiness are certainly death to the creation of suspense, and Esben Storm's **In Search of Anna**, full of sensitive suffering and fouled-up narrative habits, is another example. Storm's screenplay records the

search of Tony (Richard Moir), after five years in gaol, for his first love Anna; his involvement with Sammy (Judy Morris), a liberated young woman; his recalled snippets from his past; his coming to terms with his relationship with Sammy; and the revenge he has sought against his treacherous former accomplice, Gerry (Chris Haywood).

This brief account makes it sound much more coherent than is in fact the case. Not that I am suggesting direct linear development is a prerequisite for the creation of tension or, indeed, for the telling of a story. The trouble with **Anna** is that it is so concerned with drawing attention to its flashy technique, and so pretentious in its thematic interests, that it is hard to care about its characters and their situation.

The climax to the revenge story, when Tony has Gerry at his mercy high up on a tower, does work well, chiefly because of Chris Haywood's excellent acting; but even here suspense is vitiated by irrelevant anxiety about whether Storm will play the scene for all it is worth, or insist on cutting to something else — he settles for the latter, of course. Storm seems fascinated by the inter-relation of past, present

Geraldine Fitzgerald as Grandma Carr. Kevin Dobson's **The Mango Tree**.

and future; he also seems interested in creating suspense. His screenplay, however, does not offer a firm enough structure to support these aspirations.

In the Australian films of the past decade, the most persuasive manifestations of horror have been felt in those in which horror was seen as a potentially disturbing element in the comprehensive vision that informed the films. As I have suggested, Weir and Franklin are the two directors who have understood this notion most clearly, and whose work has provided chief evidence for it. Elsewhere, horrific elements have too often been grafted on to, rather than growing organically out of, the director's and/or scriptwriter's concept. When this has been the case, there have been bursts of unassimilated violence, unilluminating indulgence in grotesquerie, and stiff-legged narrative procedures all too obviously lacking the coherence of a unifying vision.

I do not believe Australian filmmakers will achieve the kind of suspense that belongs, not merely in a Trenchard Smith thriller but in any tightly-told story, until they insist on better screenplays. Without a script that knows exactly where it is going, that can build convincingly within and between episodes, and is literate without being literary, a director will not normally be able to make a film in which the story matters. Too many screenplays have been thin in characterization, and actors have often been left building bricks with straw. A performance as richly detailed as Geraldine Fitzgerald's in **The Mango Tree**, or Bill Hunter's in **Newsfront**, is a rarity in Australian films of the 1970s. Suspense may be created by a camera's stealthy stalking of empty passages, or horror by some outrage against human dignity. These will be incidental effects though if they do not grow out of, and add to, an understanding of what it means to be human.

5 ACTION AND ADVENTURE

Susan Dermody

Somewhere in the background of a shot in **Oz** (1976), as small-town Dorothy reaches the city in search of the Wizard, is a striking sign that is masked to read "MITH UNLIMITED". Whether it is there by chance or by design, the sign appears as an almost magical clue to a thematic reading of the action-adventure film. For while there is considerable surface variety of themes in the 30-odd Australian films in this category in the past decade, the apparent profusion of myths and meanings is powerfully limited and organized by a set of conventions arising from an underlying story form common to all.

This ancient form has been called the "quest-romance", and it informs the organization of meaning in stories as diverse as Homer's *Ulysses*, the biblical story of Moses, nearly every fairytale, Shakespearean romances, such as *The Winter's Tale*, and the action-adventure film in all its manifestations. It comes most clearly to the surface in the children's films of the group; in the adult action-adventure, the elements of the quest-romance may be displaced, transformed, or even inverted, to the point where, at first, they may be hard to recognize. What is shared by both kinds of film is an articulation of ideals through plots based on adventure into difficult or unknown terrain, with action sequences as the crux of the adventure, putting to test the ideals and the hero.

In a sense, every film with a traditional narrative structure embodies a quest, in that a problem or question is posed at the start that is answered to close the narrative. What places the action-adventure film in the romance mode is that the quest is fulfilled through a series of physical challenges in unfamiliar territory, and the governing motivation of the hero is idealist rather than comic, tragic, or satiric and pessimistic. The quest-romance can also have comic elements, as in **Oz**; tragic ones, as in **The Chant of Jimmie Blacksmith** (1978); but only in inverted form can it accommodate a deeply pessimistic and ironic outlook,

as in **Long Weekend** (1978) or **The Money Movers** (1979).

The romance-based quest of the action-adventure film can be compared with fantasy, in that it projects a search or struggle to fulfil a desire in ideal terms, but against a background of real anxieties. Hence, there is a tension between verisimilitude and realistic detail on the one hand, and a highly conventionalized plot on the other, which may pull so strongly toward a set of ideals that reality becomes distorted.

The other important pattern to be observed is the strong influence of landscape on the unfolding of adventure and the staging of action. The *look* of the specifically Australian landscape is important in recent films because of the long-preceding drought, in which one never got to see the Australian landscape as part of an imaginary world.

In the quest-romance, the natural (as opposed to the man-made) landscape is an important repository of traditional, even conservative, values, while the city is seen as a sterile wasteland in which those values wither. This ties in strongly with the dichotomy, crucial throughout Australia's cultural history, between city and country; the city-based action-adventures (like **The Money Movers**) or those imbued with city consciousness (like **Backroads** — 1977) are dangerously, if not fatally, infected with pessimism, and a predetermined failure of the quest. And even in the most beautiful landscapes, there is frequently a sense of guilt and nostalgia stemming from Australia's collective memory of the colonialist and industrialist ransack of that landscape, and dispossession of its Aboriginal inhabitants.

This is important, thematically, in the action-adventure films because the quest-romance uses the natural domain as a ground against which the moral figure of the story emerges. Characterization is the key to this process.

Since the action-adventure conflict is cast in

idealist terms, most of the characters are either heroes or villains. But there is another morally ambiguous, or even amoral, group of characters, strongly associated with the natural domain. These characters are largely peripheral to civilization (which is the context that makes sense of the hero's idealist quest); they are children or spirits of nature, often helpful, usually benign, but essentially of another order of being, inscrutable to the hero.

The character-function can be filled by an animal — think of Barney's unfortunate wombat, Storm Boy's pelican — or even by a tree, in **Let the Balloon Go** (1976), or the entire wilderness in **Journey Among Women** (1977). Frequently it is filled by an Aboriginal (**Storm Boy** — 1976, **Walkabout** — 1971, **Mad Dog Morgan** — 1976), in which case the role of helper may shift into victim, which is the structural principle of **Jimmie Blacksmith**. (A comparable situation is the use made of Indians in westerns.) Sometimes, one has to look hard for the link with the natural world: for example, in the post-post-industrial wasteland of **Mad Max** (1979), the association with nature seeps into the name — and song and behaviour — of Jim Goose, Max's faithful offsider. Only in the radically-inverted romance of a film like **Long Weekend** does nature become a moral force, a flood of malevolence instead of a vast reservoir of regenerative forces and magical creatures.

One final general point: the 'hero' of the action-adventure is usually literally that, and not a heroine. Australia's culture historically assigns men to action, women to *being* (wives, mothers, objects of sexual desire), and I have already noted the conservatism of the action-adventure film. The adventure of film heroines is generally confined to the enclosed world of the domestic melodrama, and the struggle is to adjust, with feats of self-limitation and self-sacrifice. While men and boys risk their lives in open physical adventure, the greatest risk for women is not so much physical as psychic: will the self-sacrifice protest itself, in madness?

The action-adventure films of the past decade fall into groups of variations on the general body of themes I have discussed. The first, and perhaps simplest, ties in loosely with a highly-recurrent motif of Australian culture, that of 'lost in the bush'.

Peter Dodds' 60-minute film, **Lost in the Bush** (1973), treats the theme as folk-history

retold for children, developing an account of an 1864 incident of three children lost for eight days in the Wimmera district of Victoria. Dodds uses amateur actors, ad-libbed dialogue, handheld camera, and a pleasantly rough-edged use of Wimmera locations and locals. Many of the shortcuts forced by the small budget actually help achieve the folkloric feel of the film: for example, locals with their shirt collars turned under for authenticity, re-enacting a memory of their district.

The adventure of this group of films springs from the displacement of the characters into the bush, the difficult terrain of the uncivilized wilderness, with episodic crises in the struggle to survive. Each small success tends to prove some attribute of civilization, against the orderless, indifferent wilderness. And the quest is for home, parents, the ordered relations of society.

Barney (1976) is another example of trial by separation, as heavily over-determined as a film for children as any Disney product. There is also a sense in which colonial Australia is confused with 18th Century Britain — the bush is a kind of verdant parkland, a children's zoo of picturesque animals, and the adventures are picaresque encounters with roguery in the *Tom Jones* or *Joseph Andrews* comic mode, rather than simple survival. Barney (Brett Maxworthy) is cast into the sea during a shipwreck and washed ashore with a twinkle-eyed convict, Rafe (Sean Kramer), and captive wombat. The wombat's only function in the plot, apart from being cared for by Barney as Rafe should care for him, is to signify long-suffering cuteness.

Barney (Brett Maxworthy) and Rafe (Sean Kramer) meet a gypsy on their journey home. David Waddington's **Barney**.

Opposite: Tom Cowan's **Journey Among Women**.

A surreal contrast between school uniforms and outback Australia. Lucien John and Jenny Agutter in Nicolas Roeg's **Walkabout**.

The natural world has no central thematic function here, it is merely a pleasant backdrop to the moral education of Rafe. While Rafe sets out accompanying Barney to his home, with more of an eye to exploitation than protection, his moral bearings are constantly corrected by the vulnerability of Barney, and by their shared confrontations with the chicanery of others: that is, the adult world is a little confusing but ultimately benevolent. Besides, Barney's father is always only as far away as the last location, hot on the trail, so there is never any real anxiety that the quest for home might fail.

When British filmmaker Nicolas Roeg picked up the theme of children lost in the bush in **Walkabout** it was with didactic, adult purposes in mind. The theme of trying to relocate civilization and to survive in the meantime is present, but inverted with ironic effect. The children (Jenny Agutter and Lucien John), very British in private school uniforms and accents, wander through dry inland wilderness after their father attempts to ambush them into a family suicide.

This is a film by an outsider conscious of the outsider mentality of Australian culture.

The visual imposition of British-style school uniforms onto dry country landscapes of almost shocking beauty makes the point. So does the radio 'wallpaper' that emanates from the girl's transistor radio with mindless energy and irrelevance to the landscape; its invasion of the silent desert — whose perceptible changes have been measured in geological aeons — with busy clock time filled to the brim with opinions and information suddenly makes the desert seem fragile, a mirage that may collapse or crumble into minerals.

The tribal Aboriginal (Gulpilil) who guides them towards the macadam highway of the mining town is shown, by comparison, to be in such rapport with the land that he *is* the land. His inability to woo the girl in a way that will reach her, leads to his suicide, and this seems to be Roeg's deeply pessimistic view of the consequences of our alien insensibility towards this continent — one which sees it as a series of mining operations and sites for port cities for the rapid shipping out of the spoils.

The children begin to lose their cultural defences against the countryside. They gradually adjust and rearrange their clothing until it acquires a kind of exoticism that fits in with the landscape. But the road surface belongs to another cultural and historical dispensation; the feet that descend upon it are, once more, guarded in school shoes and socks; and it leads, imperviously, to the aluminium houses and sprinkler-assisted lawns of the nearest mining operation. The neurotic disease of being a people inappropriate to the landscape produces both suicides of the film (from different directions) and the final glimpse of the girl, married, some years later, and still unable to make usable sense of her enforced walkabout.

The guilt of the intruder, lost in the bush in the sense of seeing it with eyes of a hopelessly other time and world, is also present in Peter Weir's **The Cars That Ate Paris** (1974), **Picnic at Hanging Rock** (1975) and **The Last Wave** (1977), although none of these are strictly action-adventure films. (**Cars** is like a freakishly arrested road-film, with a captive adventurer, and almost totally repressed action. It becomes a Gothic horror story of the barely inhabited sparseness of our culture, the substitution of material fetishes for a lived culture.)

To some extent the same kind of guilt has thematic influence in Tim Burstall's **Eliza**

Captain Fraser (Noel Ferrier) and Mrs Fraser (Susannah York) with some tribal Aboriginals. Tim Burstall's **Eliza Fraser**.

Fraser (1976), but it jostles with so many mixed genre influences that the point is lost. The story of the real Eliza Fraser, shipwrecked on Fraser Island (while greatly pregnant), and living for months as an honorary or con-scripted member of an Aboriginal tribe, has rich possibilities in terms of the action-adven-ture sub-type. Burstall, however, seems to have been unable to take a woman and a tribe of Aboriginals seriously, or straight. Bedroom farce replaces serious characterization of Mrs

A convict woman adapts to the natural world of the bush. **Journey Among Women**.

Fraser; comedy of manners insulates and trivializes the encounter of two worlds; and the *grand-guignol* of the convicts' premature mutual cannibalism drowns any attempt by the audience to fine tune towards the meanings of this encounter.

The substitute themes, of class and social relations in a penal colony, are mainly com-ically exploited by a comic strategy with no serious purpose. The film becomes the saga of a lone woman, surreptitiously succeeding in her own, covert scheme, despite being prey to the lustful schemes of many men, including a tribeful of Aboriginals.

Journey Among Women, on the other hand, changes the 'lost in the bush' theme by making it 'found in the bush': women convicts are freed by a young upper-class woman in a moment of self-realization, and take refuge in the wilderness where they find themselves, and each other. There they form a new tribal civilization of women, free from sexual oppres-sion. As they shed clothes, they shed the signs that locate them in 19th Century history, and the images of their bodies in the bush are framed to suggest a re-discovered rapport with nature that is timeless.

The blend of myths in the middle of the film — a kind of poem about the natural spirit of women — is interesting: there are hints of

Fear begins to take hold: Marcia (Briony Behets) and Peter (John Hargreaves). Colin Eggleston's **Long Weekend**.

Dionysiac creative disorder, bacchic madness and, when the red-coated soldiers ride stiffly into the green bush, the women fight with the militancy and invincibility of Amazons. There is another kind of *mythos* revealed by the shedding of period clothes as well — that of radical-feminist Australian women of the 1970s — since the women who acted in Tom Cowan's film participated because of their political convictions, and brought with them distinct (and undisguised) marks of that affiliation.

The problem is that the overriding myth of the film is the frequently reactionary one that sees women as mysterious creatures who are close to nature, bound to the biological functions of their bodies, more intuitive than logical and, therefore, not well fitted to the rational decision-making world dominated by men. So, the women escape sexual servitude on one level of the story, only to re-enter it on another.

Another confusion is between action-adventure narrative and a kind·of thinking in images that has no strict spatial or temporal logic. The film wavers between the two, opting mainly for the second, to the detriment of the first. The ill-effects of this indecision are especially noticeable in the action sequences of escape and battle. In a controlled action-adventure film, such sequences are not a vicarious spectacle but work to draw together the lines of force emerging from the narrative in a sudden,

intense acceleration of that development. Yet the choreography of the battle sequence fails, either at the level of direction·or editing: the action is spatially vague; its breaks in continuity have no clear motivation and are readable as failure of continuity; and it adds nothing to the meaning of the women's journey, except vague gestures of heroism.

Colin Eggleston's **Long Weekend** is worth mentioning in this thematic group since it is, in a sense, a pared-down allegory of the 'lost in the bush' theme of alienation from nature. A married couple leaves the city for a long weekend at a virtually deserted beach to camp wild; they take a landcruiser loaded with camping consumer goods, and gradually litter the campsite. Their malaise stems from their mindless material appetites, and it is these that provoke the natural world into the terrifying trial and judgment of the long weekend, which neither survive. Each is guilty of specific crimes against nature, like the Ancient Mariner: Marcia (Briony Behets) has aborted the child she conceived after carelessly sleeping around, while Peter (John Hargreaves) stupidly shoots a harmless dugong, and the creature climbs like Judgment slowly towards the camp.

This theme of wilderness edged with menace and certain of revenge for every mindlessly-sprayed ant and frozen chicken is the **Walkabout** theme of the guilty, alien despoiler taken one step further, from judgment to sentencing. By this stage, a complete inversion of the quest-romance value system has been effected, while retaining its form. Nature is turned into a severely moral force. The anti-heroes, Peter and Marcia, invade the natural domain in a futile and ritualized escape. The little-known terrain into which they venture is

Peter patrols the deserted beach. **Long Weekend**.

intended to give them relief, not the adventure of struggling for their lives in a doomed contest. Each dies in deeply ironic circumstances, and it is the absence of any motivating idealism that transforms the adventure into a trap, and the action into slaughter.

The other anti-quest films to be discussed later include **The Money Movers, The FJ Holden** (1977), **Pure S...** (1975), **Backroads**, and, to some extent, **The Odd Angry Shot** (1979). In terms of the idealist quest-romance whose form they borrow, all are fatally infected with pessimism and city consciousness.

The next rough group is of films which involve a search for experience that will prove the hero. This is predominantly a children's film preoccupation. The hero is born by moving out of the protection of childhood, and the action-adventure is a rite of passage. Frequently this involves conflict between parent and child — almost an oedipal conflict generated by the parent or authority figure's deep reluctance to admit the child to the adult world where the child shall begin to be an equal, instead of a dependant. "School" films like **The Getting of Wisdom** (1977) and **The Devil's Playground** (1976) share some of these themes, but instead of overt action of a structural kind they take the form of a sentimental education. And the hierarchy of school authority replaces the parent.

Storm Boy and **Blue Fin** (1978) should be examined together since they centre on these themes, and share Colin Thiele as their writer, Matt Carroll as producer, and Greg Rowe as the child protagonist. But while **Blue Fin** focuses its action-adventure construction on the characteristics of a specialized industry (tuna fishing), **Storm Boy** de-centres its action-adventure components in a kind of meditative response to the characteristics of a special place — the isolated coastal marshlands of the Coorong.

One of the strengths of the film is the way it manages to admit the Coorong as a presence, as idiosyncratically influential as any of the three main human characters: Storm Boy (Greg Rowe), his taciturn, reclusive father Tom (Peter Cummins), and his symbolic father, the Aboriginal, Fingerbone Bill (Gulpilil).

This is partly achieved through bridging passages of images of the landscape itself, but,

A storm at sea hits the tuna boat, and a man is washed overboard. Carl Schultz's **Blue Fin**.

more importantly, the Coorong infiltrates the characters: Fingerbone is its intelligence, Tom is its white recluse, Storm Boy is literally its child and Mr Percival, the wild pelican, is its semi-magical gift to Storm Boy. Mr Percival helps Storm Boy as he moves through the conflicts with his father, and releases him (by dying) for the move to the town neighboring the Coorong, where he will go to school, and where he and his father will be integrated into a community. Greg Rowe plays a much younger boy here than in **Blue Fin**, and, in fact, Storm Boy doesn't so much conflict with his father as register the conflicts in him as he faces the difficult move back to the town and the social life which has scarred him in the past.

The New Australian Cinema

In **Blue Fin** the people are in pragmatic, rather than spiritual, harmony with their watery landscape. Where the action erupts in storms, shipwrecks and invasions of dune-buggies of shooters in **Storm Boy**, in **Blue Fin** it is inherent in the nature of the activity of tuna-fishing, which is explored in extended sequences. For Snook (Greg Rowe), a normal fishing trip is adventure, but the patriarch of the family (and skipper of the tuna fleet) has other plans for him, particularly since Snook makes irritating mistakes on a trial run. But in his second chance, reluctantly conceded, extra-ordinary adventure overtakes him: a freak storm disables the boat and drowns all the crew, except for Snook and his badly-injured father (Hardy Kruger). The climacteric strug-gle of the hero is Snook's battle to find the endurance and ingenuity to keep the tiny world of the boat afloat, restart the engine, and make home port. It is a triumphant reversal of the growingly claustrophobic role of being depen-dent on the will of the father. The final freeze-frame of Snook, lifted to the shoulders of the men on the pier, is the appropriate "exaltation of the hero" phase to complete the strict romance form of this film.

Oliver Howes' **Let the Balloon Go** is the quest of a partly-disabled child (Robert Bettles) to cut the umbilicus and be permitted to risk experience: "A balloon is not a balloon until the string is cut." On the first free afternoon of life, when his mother relinquishes her terrible care and leaves him alone in the house, he climbs the tallest evergreen tree in the front

The partly-disabled boy (Robert Bettles), with his parents and the local doctor. Oliver Howes' **Let the Balloon Go**.

yard. The string of adventures to this point has been the misadventures of his attempts to express his misery — of being "at a difficult age", of being "different", like the town's crazy, once-glorious major who runs out roar-ing at the first sound of a child's stone rattling down his tin roof. But suddenly the boy is granted a chance in which to prove himself. In a nice reversal of the outward quest, this one is upward, rooted in the front yard of home, as green as the tree of life, and risking death.

It is a glorious quest, cheered on by the major from his topmost window, witnessed by all his schoolmates and townspeople, and the furore it causes accidentally triggers the release of the giant balloon, which soars. And, in hav-ing to come down, the boy learns as much as in having to climb. The strength of the film is this honest admission of some of the real nastiness of life — even in tiny details, like the girls' chanted skipping rhyme:

"On the way her britches busted,
How many people were disgusted?
One! two! three! ..."

The Irishman (1978) also admits death into its world-view, though more profoundly in the thumbnail sketches of the aged grand-

Michael (Simon Burke) meets his father, Paddy (Michael Craig), after a long search. Donald Crombie's **The Irishman**.

parents than in the elegiac death of the "Irishman", Paddy Doolan (Michael Craig). But its view of the world is in some ways more severely G-rated than **Let the Balloon Go**.

The Irishman is about a father-son relationship. The younger son, Michael (Simon Burke), is protected by order of birth from the violent oedipal struggle between his brother Will (Lou Brown) and his father which ends by driving Paddy, last of the draught-horse teamsters, into exile from the family.

Michael loves his father and the superseded glory of the work he did; he tracks him down, only in time to witness his death and bring back the pitiful mementoes of his life. But throughout the film, as though sensing the doom laid by stubbornness on his real father, he casts about for father-figures, wavering between a canny occasional horse-thief and a stern Scots station-owner, for whom he works and towards whom he finally turns, as if to home, but riding on the last of his father's great draught-horses.

The Mango Tree (1977) fits in here to

some extent, except that its lack of sustained action-adventure structure finally excludes it. The film is more similar to the sentimental education films like **The Getting of Wisdom**; the action-sequence of the manhunt for the crazed hell-fire preacher is only a passing, even gratuitous, concern of plot. (It is like a ritual exorcism of the town's combined prurience and prudery.) It is even difficult to decide who to regard as the hero: should one centre on the birth of the adolescent, or the death of the grandmother? A choice is necessary because, again, there is no structural relationship binding these two chief movements of the film.

The Irishman comes close to the same danger of using action and adventure in non-functional ways, but escapes through its use of symmetry. The action-adventure elements finally add up to Michael's quest for a paradoxical 'birth' as a hero through bearing witness to his father's death, and choosing rebirth to a less equivocal kind of father.

The FJ Holden could also be mentioned here, but its potential action-adventure form is arrested, and even negated, by the very confinement of suburban streets. To some extent it is an 'anti-quest' version of this group of films: the emergence of the central boy or girl as a hero is never a likelihood. Endless circling, even in heroicized FJ Holdens, fatally replaces any directed quest, with the circle literally closing in on the hero in the final frame.

However, it is possible to place **Jimmie**

Jamie (Christopher Pate), the adolescent who learns about life. Kevin Dobson's **The Mango Tree**.

Jimmie (Tommy Lewis) with his white wife, Gilda (Angela Punch). Fred Schepisi's **The Chant of Jimmie Blacksmith**.

Blacksmith here, at least in terms of some of its thematic concerns. And it is interesting to see how the themes so far discussed are transformed by the insertion of this strictly adult film into a group dominated by children's films.

Jimmie's (Tommy Lewis) quest is for adulthood in a white society, where adulthood, in the sense of psychological, sexual and social autonomy, is not granted to blacks in any completed way. When Jimmie and his brother run amok with an axe among undefended white women and children, they are striking out for that denied freedom in a way that is finally not paradoxical, but relentlessly logical. Jimmie was a good boy, an assimilated Aboriginal. He was even a cop, though confined to the most menial rung of power. But he makes mistakes; in marrying a white girl, Gilda (Angela Punch), whose child he may have fathered, he steps too far out from under the oedipal yoke of white colonization, which makes sexually mature non-white males eternal boys. In what they take to be obvious generosity, the white women of the station arrange to take Gilda and the child away from Jimmie's hut. But their terrible punishment comes down upon them more from meanings that are enacted through them, than by them.

Arguably, contradictions facing a black male in white culture can be seen to centre on white women, in that, since women in general are sexual subordinates in almost every present culture, the greater social power of white women presents black males with a deep sexual contradiction. So, in a sense, white women are a more powerful sign of oppression to black males than the white males who oppress both. This is the kind of complex of deferred meanings expressed by Jimmie's action when he finally snaps from social paralysis. His moment of birth as a hero is also instantly his moment of suicide as one. His death can only be stalled, by flight.

Jimmie Blacksmith could also be placed among the themes organized as quests for justice/revenge (yet to be discussed) but its comparison with the themes of this group points to the deep ironies of that quest, and indicates that the film has serious tragic intentions for its action-adventure sequences, not those of gratuitous spectacle.

The next group of films involves a quest in a literal way — the physical search — whether a journey, a road film, or a search (or flight) for justice or revenge. The reason that **Oz** is one of the clearest examples is that it is only several short removes from the fairytale material that Baum's *Wizard of Oz* consciously selected, condensed and modernized. And the fairytale is a very old pared-down (though not necessarily uncomplicated) oral prototype of the romance form from which the action-adventure derives. In this further modernization, Dorothy (Joy

Dunstan) becomes a small-town rock-band groupie; in an accident, she is thrown clear off the band's van into unconsciousness, through which she journeys to the city in search of a rock star called the Wizard. This is a sexually-ripe Dorothy, so the trio of misfits she collects along the way are a gentle surfie (Scarecrow), a lustful acned mechanic (Tin Man) and a chicken-hearted motor-cycle yob (Lion). And the malevolent truckie, bent on revengeful rape, is the figure of sub-conscious fears.

Against the odds, Dorothy makes it, even to the penthouse party and private bathroom of the Wizard, but when she sees the puny human being inside the charisma, she falls back into consciousness, in the countryside, with "Fame and fortune fuck you up" reverberating in her head. The film does not disguise the fact that it is projecting fantasy; by framing Dorothy's fantasy with reality, it even analyses the process of heightened desires and anxieties, and dream-like transformations of reality. And it is an interesting fantasy, charting that creative phase of a young girl's sexuality in which magical events, that will rapidly transform the girl and carry her to a high plane of union with a remote rock star, are always on the verge of happening — until, suddenly, the

Young males in search of a good time. Christopher Fraser's **Summer City**.

perspective shifts a fraction, and the idea is as distant as childhood.

The road film is an interesting sub-type for the way it partly inverts the idealist quest form. Perhaps it would be more accurate to describe the process as subverting the quest's idealism with existentialism, and so scattering its structured quest form by losing the object of the search. It involves people on the move from some place to some place else, an indeterminate journey, taking existential pleasure in being without bearing or conscious goal, lost on the road, perhaps. **Summer City** (1977) and **High Rolling** (1977) are typical versions: young males abroad on picaresque adventures in search of a good time and finding, for the audience if not for themselves, yawning gaps in the adequacy of their philosophy of existence.

In Search of Anna (1979), on the other hand, is hardly a road film, except that the two road sequences, from Pentridge gaol to Sydney, and from Sydney to somewhere in southern Queensland, are crucial in the meaning and organization of the story. It is a complex exercise in ordering the narrative out of time and space sequence and logic, so that the theme of mental disorganization and conflict is enacted on the level of narrative structure.

What holds the film together, and ultimately also its protagonist, Tony (Richard Moir), who is released from gaol into a world that has since disintegrated, are the two trips with Sam (Judy Morris), the woman he picks up. (Perhaps the best moment in the film is when Sam, driving in the night, examines the

The sexually-ripe Dorothy (Joy Dunstan) off on the road to see the Wizard. Chris Lofven's **Oz**.

contents of Tony's airline bag, while he is asleep; she finds a bottle and a gun; she looks at each with equal gravity, sliding the gun back, and, after a pause, raising the bottle to her lips for a considered swig. The later neurotic disintegration of Sam, in the context of her sick relationship, is not as bad as it would be without this earlier sequence.)

Each stage of movement north with Sam (she accompanies Tony in his search for Anna who, if found again, will mend his collapsed world) ends by being a stage towards reintegration. Finding Anna's house, at last, he realizes that it is Sam he is in search of, and they will go on together — once they get the car started again. It is also worth noting that Tony has a small, nondescript dog who stays close as a talisman, a small nature-spirit ensuring survival and sanity, and that the final mending of his consciousness is achievable only in the countryside, on a lost backroad, far from the city.

Pure S . . . and **Backroads** have the fatal infection by city consciousness that makes them romantic expressions of anti-romance. **Pure S . . .** is city-trapped, like **FJ Holden**; its inevitably circling quest is for "pure shit", in the sense of good-quality heroin. It is a one-night adventure conducted in confusingly-lit darkness, breaking abruptly into absurd bursts of half-comic action to try to grab some of the deadly grail. Finally, finding some offers relief, but nothing more climacteric than a long vacant period on a bed, followed by a bust. The girl whose FX Holden is the literal vehicle of the quest, is a heroin initiate; the final, almost accidental, achievement of her 'first hit' provides an ironic inversion of the birth of the hero, as she lines up like a beast being stunned at the slaughter yards.

In **Backroads**, a red-necked white and an Aboriginal aimlessly tour remote back-country roads in a stolen car, picking up and shrugging off a variety of people in a joyride that ends, just short of the city, in the passionless murder of a man ordering them out of his car as they prepare to steal it. Direction is finally pointed for the two men by a gun in the back of the neck of one of them, when the police suddenly emerge like agents of accelerated doom. The backroads in this film are not havens of country peace, but monotonous tracks through a world that is fallen, and will stay down.

Finally, there are action-adventure quests for justice or revenge, involving either pursuit or escape, depending on the situation of the protagonists. **Journey Among Women** and **Jimmie Blacksmith** find some of their actions and concerns here — pursuing a kind of wild justice while escaping capture and death.

More direct examples of films with parallel themes are **Ned Kelly** (1970) and **Mad Dog Morgan**, which work in the familiar Australian territory of sympathy for the underdog, and the rise and fall of a bushranger, which is not

Sam (Judy Morris) and Tony (Richard Moir) pause during their travels to Queensland. Esben Storm's **In Search of Anna**.

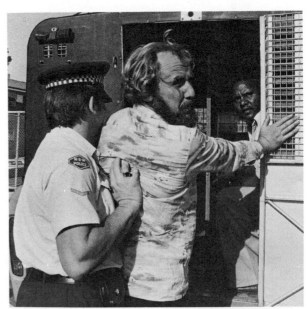

After murdering a car-owner, Jack (Bill Hunter) and Joe (Zac Martin) are arrested. Phillip Noyce's **Backroads**.

Two underdogs: Billy (Gulpilil) and Daniel Morgan (Dennis Hopper). Philippe Mora's **Mad Dog Morgan**.

American cinematic values in an Australian setting. Russell Hagg's **Raw Deal**.

so far removed in psychology from the rise and fall of **Little Caesar**. In both, the landscapes are ravishingly beautiful, as if the country is in nostalgic sympathy with the doomed Robin Hood figure of the bushranger. But where the Robin Hood romance — of the man in green in powerful harmony with the green world of nature — posits an invincible moral hero, the bushranger can carry the identifying approval of the audience only so far, before meeting annihilation by the organized forces of oppression.

The bushranger is a solitary figure, flanked by a few sympathizers, but representative of a whole oppressed class; the 'traps' are interchangeable, uniformed men in numbers, who die like foolish flies in the interests of the state, or survive like grim bull-terriers to become the unshakeable nemesis of the hero; and the ruling class are moral degenerates interested only in the fact, and not the purpose, of power.

A similar moral (and historical) framework is imitated in **Raw Deal** (1977), with the solitary hero expanded into a bunch of solitary heroes, recruited, western-style, as mercenaries to deal with not one Irish-born outlaw, but an army of them, planning an Irish-Catholic takeover of the government of New South Wales. But **Raw Deal** is a 'meatpie western'. It transposes themes developed in a culture quite different to the one that gave rise to the class-loyalty, myth of the underdog and blighted heroism of the bushranger film, indifferent to the resulting thematic confusion, and failing to recognize the deadly boredom of action that expresses nothing of thematic importance and coherence. When the two surviving heroes

light out at the end for Tombstone, capital of the Hollywood West, the film strikes its first true note.

Inn of the Damned (1975) shares similar problems; of pastiche at the level of genre and themes, and indigestion at the level of the film's action sequences. Where **Raw Deal** has mercenaries destroying 'revolutionaries' (and then being, themselves, eliminated by their recruiters), **Inn of the Damned** is a period setting of the theme of justice investigating and eradicating an enigmatic evil. Again the Gippsland location has no intrinsic relation to the themes of the film; it is just a conveniently open landscape permitting pursuit action sequences as a bonus to the enclosed suspense of the inn itself. And both films reflect a gestation period as ideas for television, rather than film.

It is probably true to say that the effect in both, of action-adventure values being imitated from without, as spectacle, rather than generated from within, as necessity, derives from television's habit of skimming the top off a given film genre, and having no time for the thematic complexity below.

A number of other films develop the same theme — of justice single-handedly solving a violent riddle — but in city landscapes, without a period picturesque. Sandy Harbutt's **Stone** (1974) is the quest of a clean-cut drug-squad undercover man, Stone (Ken Shorter), to infiltrate a bikie gang and find out why they are being systematically murdered. The juxtaposition of bikie milieu and political scandal, of two different social echelons and value-systems, of brotherly loyalty and cold-blooded

91

profit motive could all have been rich stuff for the action-adventure form to articulate. But the film is thematically impoverished: the bikies' milieu is fetishized for itself and its picturesque and spectacle values, and Stone is — for a character in a film with city consciousness — fatally lacking in ambivalence as its moral protagonist.

Mad Max, on the other hand, develops its bikie gang to a richer thematic level; the Nightrider's gang become horsemen of the apocalypse, a pestilence breeding from and preying upon the advanced rot, somewhere in the future, of Australian post-industrial society. The landscape of (present-day) Melbourne hinterland lends itself wonderfully to the film's theme of the victory of urban sterility over the wilderness, and roads are used as a gladiatorial maze for the struggle between the last zealots of a defunct justice and growing forces of darkness. This is far from the use of the open road as muse to the restlessness of the existential road-film hero. Max (Mel Gibson) gradually loses Jim Goose (Steve Bisley), his offsider, and then his Jessie (Joanne Samuel), and their child, in horrific sacrifice to the Nightrider's (Hugh Keays-Byrne) infinite appetite for torture and vengeance, until Max's madness is ignited into his own holocaust of revenge. **Mad Max** is to **Stone** as horror comics are to *The Boy's Own Annual*, in the hyperbole and suggestive power of its action sequences, and in their moral force, although the moral ground of both is very similar.

Deathcheaters (1976) and Brian Trenchard Smith's earlier Hong Kong co-production, **The Man from Hong Kong** (1975), also share this form, of a violent riddle solved through a series of encounters of growing intensity and shrinking odds for the slightly enigmatic force of justice. Where **Deathcheaters** engenders poorly-motivated spectacle in its anxiety to duplicate the successes of **The Man from Hong Kong**, the earlier film is a witty marriage of the Hong Kong kung-fu film and a Sydney locale. Fang Leng (Jimmy Wang Yu), a leading Hong Kong narcotics police officer, comes to Sydney to extradite a Chinese suspect and stays to clean up Dodge City, finally soaring like an avenging angel by hang-glider to invade the penthouse fastness of the enemy, who sits, Satan-like, stoking the flames of a roaring fire.

A comic-book fundamentalism is again in evidence, but this time the tongue is more in

Opposite: **Mad Max**.

Fang Sing Leng (Jimmy Wang.Yu) scales a Sydney building in Brian Trenchard Smith's **The Man From Hong Kong**.

cheek than rolling out in helpless horror. But Fang Leng, like Max, has to be goaded into full use of his faculties for destruction, and again, the ultimate goal, after a period of physical and spiritual recuperation in the bush, is the senseless destruction of the hero's true love. But one culture-specific difference is that, whereas **Mad Max**'s road accidents possibly have cumulative fascination, the kung-fu fights of **The Man from Hong Kong**, despite their intricate choreography, seem to be affected by a reduction principle similar to that of hardcore pornography: more is increasingly less.

An honest co-production, like **The Man from Hong Kong**, is more likely to produce coherent action-adventure themes and uses of convention than the **Raw Deal** model of "co-production", in which the dominant partner is absent, invests nothing, but effectively co-opts the entire project.

Lastly, there are two recent action-adventure films which fall into the anti-quest mode of pessimism, irony and satire; but there are no corresponding positive films to compare them with. **The Money Movers** is to some extent the inverse of the last four films — since it is a crime film, with the point-of-view of the doomed criminal — but it is repressed, and contained within the steel-riveted wall of armoured cars, the counting house depot, warehouse gates and the cramped lives, and is denied open physical expression in open landscape, like the other literal, physical quest films.

In the old morality tale, money is death, and in this film, out of a patchwork of ugly male urban faces, emerge three who work in the counting house, and have been 'infected'.

Below: Eric Jackson (Terry Donovan) is threatened with a loss of toes if he doesn't cut Jack Hendersen (Charles Tingwell, centre) into the action. Bruce Beresford's **The Money Movers**.

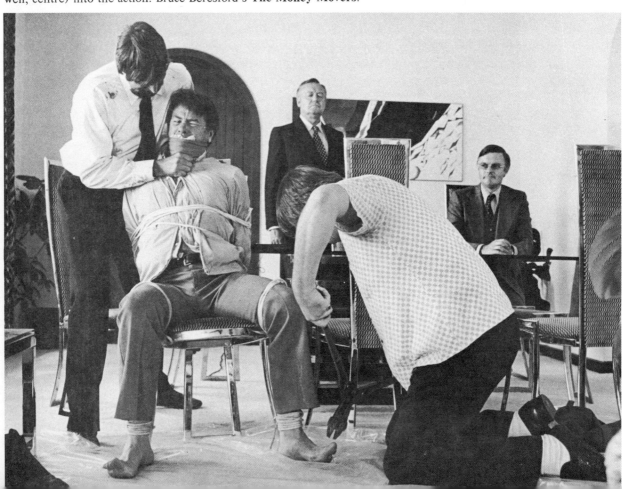

The puns of the actions are grim: for example, a seller of sly meat at the racecourse is caught in the crossfire of an armoured car hijack, and becomes meat. Women are brusquely dismissed from the action, except as momentary hitches or casualties to the mechanics of male greed. The countryside — a trip to the mountains is made by Jackson (Terry Donovan) and his wife (Jeanie Drynan) to establish an alibi for a brutal robbery — is no recuperative force, but a function of ugly city consciousness: in a clutter of roadsigns, "Hump" stands out grimly as they approach the tatty tourist cabins where this couple will come not even as close to each other as cynical sexuality might allow.

The masterplan, taken over by bigger fish, who plan merely to permit the inside men to carry it out, before eliminating them, collapses into a carnage, after an ex-cop security guard notices something odd about the numberplate of the armoured car in front. In a crowning irony of police corruption, the ex-cop is to be reinstated (after major surgery) on award wages, while the corrupt detective picks a clue off a corpse that would gaol the big crime syndicate, and sells it to them for his 20 pieces of gold.

Tom Jeffrey's **The Odd Angry Shot** is a kind of anti-quest of the straight war film's use of war as a proving ground for ideals of nationalism, self-sacrifice, etc. But there is a tradition, extending from *The Good Soldier Schweik*, *Catch 22*, **M*A*S*H**, and its television spin-off, that uses men at war as a metaphor for the black comedy of human society at large. It is from the end of this tradition that **The Odd Angry Shot** derives, with its loose organization of briefly-developed, episodic scenes, each structured towards a verbal or (rarely) visual gag, frequently centred on Harry (Graham Kennedy) and using Kennedy's television persona and its upstaging effects on the characters around him. The only theme to survive Jeffrey's apparent desire to generalize this war out of history and into human nature (Where is the thematic com-

War as a proving ground: Bill (John Jarratt), Bung (John Hargreaves), Roger (Bryan Brown) and Harry (Graham Kennedy). Tom Jeffrey's **The Odd Angry Shot**.

plexity of Australia's Vietnam adventure?) is stolid survival. Thus, Vietnam (or Korea) replaces a morally-admissible war like World War 2, episodic structure replaces the epic of the war film, irony replaces heroism, and only the stoic virtues remain, framed now to look absurd.

The Odd Angry Shot is an exception that seems to prove a fundamental rule of the action-adventure films. It is not the withholding of the epic coherence of a string of marvellous adventures developing towards a culminating struggle by the hero — **In Search of Anna**, and to some extent all the road films, survive this variation. It is not the inversion of heroic ideals — a number of the films do so, but they are proving a bitterly moral point, whereas **The Odd Angry Shot** proves only the bitterness, with none of the fierce moral energy of the original *Good Soldier Schweik*. The fragmented structure of this film has no analytical design, its comedy has no serious moral purpose, and it is this, finally, that points up the fundamental ground-rule of the action-adventure films: that its impulse is didactic, conservative, moral.

6 FANTASY

Adrian Martin

". . . some intellect may be found which will reduce my phantasm to the common-place . . . which will perceive, in the circumstances I detail with awe, nothing more than an ordinary succession of very natural causes and effects."

Edgar Allan Poe,
The Black Cat

Most conventional films attempt to create a world and lure the audience into it. If that world is the suburban milieu of **Mouth to Mouth** (1978), or a fiction blended with newsreel, as in **Newsfront** (1978), then that passage is accomplished without too much difficulty. Fantasy films take this process a step further. It is a dangerous and uncertain step, because the world evoked by the film mixes the familiar with the unfamiliar, the known with the unknown, the believably real with the purely possible. The success of a fantasy film depends largely on how meaningfully it can relate these different spheres of experience, and how completely it can set the audience on an adventure of seeking out — even creating — that meaning.

I am indebted in all that follows to the categories elaborated by Tzvetan Todorov in his book, *The Fantastic: A Structural Approach to a Literary Genre* (Cornell University Press, 1975). The framework he uses to discuss literary works is easily applicable to the cinema, because in both one is dealing with narrative: i.e., the construction of a fictional world with an internal logic that is bound by particular conventions and rules. In discussing fantasy, many of these conventions are uncovered, and it is possible to judge how well or badly they have been used by the Australian cinema.

The fantastic requires the audience to interpret the unusual events they see. This *hesitation* defines the fantasy genre proper. If they decide on a rational explanation (such as a dream or coincidence), then the film is part of the *uncanny* genre. If they accept a supernatural influence, then the film enters the realm of the *marvellous*.

True works of fantasy — perhaps among the richest of films — are open-ended, suspending themselves between possible explanations. Peter Weir's **Picnic at Hanging Rock** (1975), for example, ends as it began, in mystery. It is up to the audience to investigate the film and take up the clues by which they are most intrigued.

"It's been waiting a million years, just for us," remarks one of the girls as they ride towards Hanging Rock. The film suggests that the disappearance is predestined. Also, it is St Valentine's Day, and the year is 1900 — the beginning of a century. All this lends an aura of great historical moment to what happens. The rock stands, as it were, apart from the rest of the world that surrounds it. One of the girls aptly comments that, from where they are, the people below look like ants, "possibly serving some function unknown to themselves".

On the rock, all watches stop at noon. Miss McCraw (Vivean Gray) puts it down to magnetism. The supernatural interpretation is the literal one: time has stopped, and life on the rock exists in a different dimension. Time no longer follows a logical course of cause and effect. Rather, as Miranda (Anne Lambert) says, "Everything begins and ends at the right time" — perhaps at the same time, the frozen moment of noon.

The atmosphere of the rock is linked to a release of sexual constraints. The idea is conveyed by a visual comparison. At Appleyard College pigeons sit on the grass, silent and still. When the school party arrives at the rock, birds fly out in a great roar, an explosion of activity. Similarly, the girls discover a new freedom, while seeming not to realize it themselves. The film superimposes, in slow motion, images of the girls taking off their stockings upon the dance-like sway of their bodies, an intimation of sexual experience.

These evocations of sexuality open up two interpretations: a rational and a supernatural. The rational explanation is that the girls are abducted by someone lying in wait on the rock. Later, one of the townspeople comments: "It

Opposite: Peter Weir's **Picnic at Hanging Rock**.

The girls at their St Valentine's Day breakfast, before their journey to the rock. **Picnic at Hanging Rock**.

Right: Michael Fitzhubert (Dominic Guard), who finds Irma on the rock. **Picnic at Hanging Rock**.

must be someone from another town. No one around here would do such a thing!'' Yet when Irma (Jane Vallsi) is found alive by Michael (Dominic Guard) she is ''intact''; her head is bruised and hands scratched, but the rest of the body is unmarked.

Of all the girls who go on the expedition up the rock, it is Miranda who is presented as having a special awareness of the significance of what they are doing. It is even suggested that she has been gifted with a premonition of the disappearance. Early in the film she tells Sara (Margaret Nelson): "You must learn to love someone apart from me. I will not be with you for much longer.'' This might just mean she is going to another school, but the hint of the supernatural is strong. As well, the film's last shot returns to a gesture that is charged with great significance: her farewell wave to Mlle de Poitiers (Helen Morse), as if she is bidding goodbye to the world. The frame freezes as she turns her head, to stress that finality.

Twice in the film Michael thinks of Miranda, and Weir dissolves to a shot of a swan, so that the two figures appear for a moment in the image together. This carries the hint of a mythic explanation, for in Greek mythology Leda bore children to Zeus, who had intercourse with her while she was in the form of a swan. Miranda, too, has perhaps been borne away by a god in a recurrence of the legend. This is reinforced by Mlle de Poitiers describing her resembling a Botticelli

angel. But what of the others? Miss McCraw? Irma, left on the rock? And why does Michael appear to go through much the same experience as the girls? The audience is allowed to become as sceptical of the supernatural interpretation as of the rational one. Neither reading will guarantee a full, secure knowledge.

For the characters in the film, as well as for the audience, a crisis arises. How does one even begin to understand a mystery when it is not only the extraordinary events on the rock that prove elusive? — nature itself, in its most common manifestations, also contains elements of the *marvellous*. As Michael makes his way up the rock, Weir cuts to the animals around him — watching, knowing (as we might imagine). In the greenhouse at Appleyard College, when one man insists "There's gotta be a solution", his friend demonstrates the life in one of his plants: "Did you know they could move?" This theme is echoed in the tiniest details. The girls hold a seashell to their ears — and how does a small shell contain the sound of the entire sea?

The horror of never knowing, or understanding, is all pervasive. Mrs Appleyard (Rachel Roberts) remarks, after Irma is found, "It's worse that only one has been found." Having no memory of what occurred, Irma, in time, is hated by all. Michael, and then her school friends, batter her with the question, "What happened?", but they know it will

never be answered. Ironically, at one point, the girls sing the hymn *Rock of Ages*, but rather than praising the God whose wonders are known and loved, and whose church is everlasting, the song brings one of the girls to tears, reminding her of that other rock of ages which escapes the certainties of Christian religion. It is this horror that finally, as the closing narration tells us, sends Mrs Appleyard to her death; she falls while trying to climb the rock.

The film suggests meaningful connections, but only to frustrate the audience. What are they to make of Sara and Albert (John Jarratt), brother and sister orphans who, separated in life, are touched by the mystery of the rock? Sara pines for her brother while she is alone; Albert seems to have a vision in a dream (coincidence or telepathy?) as Sara, utterly desolate at the loss of Miranda and unable to remain at Appleyard College, kills herself.

Other relationships in the film are left ambiguous. As Mrs Appleyard becomes more and more distraught, she confesses to Mlle de Poitiers her total dependence on Miss McCraw. Implied is a sexual attachment, the repression of which was so complete that it now expresses itself in revulsion: "She let herself be raped on that rock!" Similarly, Miranda's goodbye wave to Mlle de Poitiers suggests an important link between the two women that is never clarified.

Such details are left in abeyance, and thus suspends the audience in what the French call *signifiance* — traces of meaning, fragments of sense, but never a coherent, fixed, final truth delivered easily to us by the film's end.

I have dealt with **Picnic** in some detail because I believe it to be the finest film of its kind produced in Australia. Its excellence is

Below: Miss McGraw (Vivean Gray) at the base of the rock. **Picnic at Hanging Rock**.

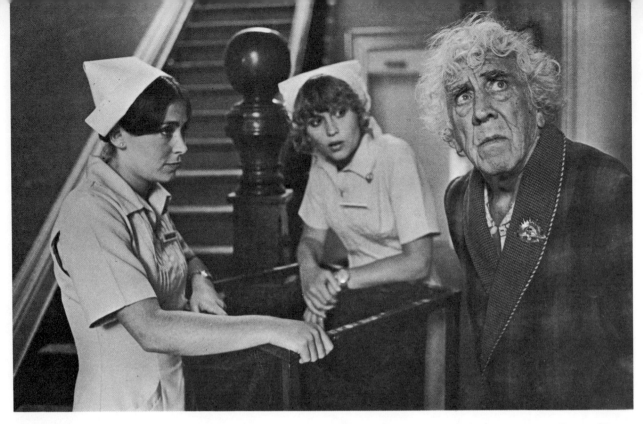

A disturbed Anzac (Walter Pym) is observed by Sister Williams (Helen Hemingway) and nurse Kathy (Susan Penhaligon). Richard Franklin's **Patrick**.

typical of the classics of the fantasy genre, such as Carl Dreyer's **Vampyr** and Jacques Tourneur's **I Walked With a Zombie** — films as much, if not more, about themselves and their shifting, disorientating relationship with the audience, as about a world full of mysterious events. **Picnic** also provides a model of the fantasy film, in which a *hesitation* is set up between two kinds of explanations: the rational and the supernatural. The film, and the audience, is put in a position of deciding whether something is, or isn't. Most fantasy films can be discussed in this way.

In Richard Franklin's **Patrick** (1978), the condition of the character of the film's title is, to begin with, one of a human vegetable — "limp meat hanging off a comatose brain", as Dr Roget (Robert Helpmann) remarks. Patrick (Robert Thompson) has the unusual power to effect the physical properties of objects — to move them, change their temperature, make machines function or malfunction. This is given a pseudo-scientific rationalization: Patrick has developed his remaining mental faculties to the point of psychokinesis.

The film reserves the *hesitation* characteristic of fantasy until the end. In an impressive shock effect, Patrick's supposedly dead body leaves its bed and crashes to the floor. Is this a final muscular reflex or, as is suggested, the moment when the soul leaves the body? The supernatural here takes on a Judaeo-Christian religious aspect, as it does in so many Hollywood fantasies of the 1940s. The final shot of the film, which shows Patrick opening his eyes, also makes one wonder whether he is alive or dead, his nature mortal or immortal.

A brilliant ambiguity of effect is also created in Colin Eggleston's **Long Weekend** (1978).

After the death of Marcia, Peter (John Hargreaves) faces the elements alone. Colin Eggleston's **Long Weekend**.

Preceding pages: **Picnic at Hanging Rock**.

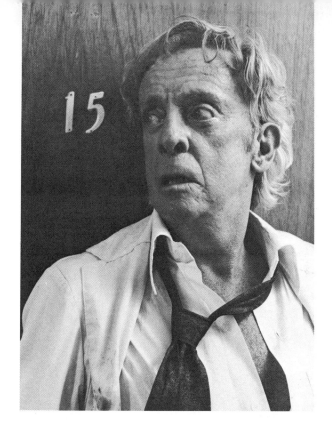

A tortured Dr Roget (Robert Helpmann) at Patrick's door. **Patrick**.

Threatening incidents occur when Peter (John Hargreaves) and Marcia (Briony Behets) are on a camping holiday by the beach: a spear-gun accidentally fires, barely missing Marcia; a possum bites Peter on the hand when he tries to touch it; and, at night, as Marcia tries to leave, birds fly "suicidally" into the windscreen, smashing the glass. Eventually, Peter and Marcia die: Marcia is shot accidentally by Peter when he mistakes her for an intruder; and Peter dies the next day, run over by a truck which he signals to stop — a bird flies at the driver's face, blurring his vision and causing the truck to go out of control.

Taken to this hideous point of death, one looks for another reading of the events. One is led to suspect, for example, that Peter and Marcia are being avenged for their irresponsible treatment of nature: Peter chopping a tree and aimlessly shooting at birds to amuse himself; Marcia, in a panic, destroying an eagle's egg left near their tent; the couple running over a kangaroo on the road, and crabs on the sand; and Peter shooting a large dugong, believing it to be a shark, the dying animal continually emitting an agonized cry, like that of a baby.

There are other clues which hint at a supernatural explanation. If nature is exacting revenge, it may not just be on this couple; it may be a preliminary step in a more inclusive plan. Farther down the beach, where Marcia and Peter find a car in the water, one can only speculate whether the mysterious situation is a mirror image of Peter and Marcia's; after all, they are not the only people guilty of offending nature. The film also alludes to this by commenting on oil mining at sea which has almost rendered some species of fish extinct.

Peter lies on the highway, killed by the truck he tried to flag down. **Long Weekend**.

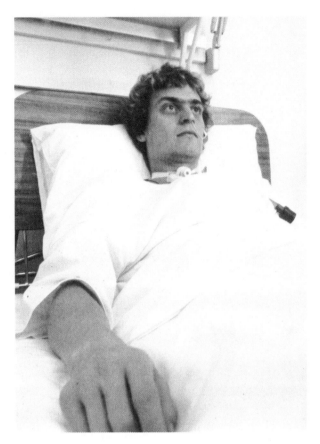

The hospitalized and comatized Patrick (Robert Thompson). **Patrick**.

Felicity's mother (Ruth Cracknell) by the hall mirror. Jim Sharman's **The Night The Prowler**.

Yet another version of the events is possible. The external world merely mirrors the relationship between Marcia and Peter, intervening to express the tensions between them, the violence they wish upon each other. Early in the film, and before they leave for the beach, Peter sights Marcia in the line of his gun — a grim private joke that turns into reality when he accidentally kills her. Again, after smashing the eagle's egg, Marcia is reminded by Peter of what the act so vividly resembles: the abortion of the foetus conceived during her affaire with another man. The mutual destructiveness, the murderous reciprocity of their marriage, deforms nature, and when their drama is played out on such a level, the only possible finale is death.

A different sort of *hesitation* is employed in Jim Sharman's **Shirley Thompson Versus The Aliens** (1971). Here it is a question of madness: is Shirley's (Jane Harders) story, told in flashback to two psychiatrists in the mental institution where she is kept, the outpourings of a hallucinating mind? Or was she given a mission by aliens who were stationed within

Luna Park? The film deliberately takes a ludicrous situation, never far from total self-parody, to turn the fantasy genre into an elegant game. Structurally, however, it is still a conventional fantasy film because it puts the filmgoer in the position of having to decide between two explanations.

For a time Shirley has followers — the members of the gang she knocks around with (this is the 1950s) — but there are no witnesses to her contact with the aliens. Consequently, no one can prove that what she describes actually happened. Similarly, the aliens speak through Prince Philip at a sporting event to warn earthlings of the danger of total annihilation if they pursue the path of war — but who listens to official speeches? So the aliens' radio broadcasts are thought by everybody to be another Orson Welles' *War of the Worlds*-type joke.

The psychiatrists rationally describe Shirley's condition in terms of "trauma leading to schizophrenia"; and her family life, represented in the form of the most grotesque caricatures, is enough to make us accept the

Peter under attack in **Long Weekend**.

diagnosis. In Shirley's words, suburbia has sent her "up shit creek". After the aliens leave earth, seeing nothing but the prospect of repeated failure in their attempts to communicate with the world, Shirley falls back into the cycle of a dull marriage to the nice boy her mother has picked for her. It is not a great distance from this into madness, a flight from an intolerable reality.

The final scene of the film condenses its treatment of the themes of the fantasy genre. Strapped to a bed and treated with injections, Shirley imagines herself spinning in a delirious ecstasy; this is echoed by Jeannie Lewis' song, *Fly Like a Bird*, on the soundtrack. Shirley is again experiencing the glimpse of the "power of pure thought" the aliens have. But the same image changes its tone, and is resignified as tension, entrapment and futility. The music builds to a screaming effect, as the camera watches her spinning from above. Perhaps she is just mad, or the uncomprehending world which refuses to see the truth of her story has finally succeeded in destroying her. The ambiguity and the response it elicits mark the

extraordinary, expressive power of the scene.

The stories of Edgar Allan Poe, like **Shirley Thompson**, play obsessively on the structural properties of the fantastic. Ignoring the thematic concerns with death, decay and anxiety that undoubtedly exist in his tales, they are pleasurable in other ways. Their construction of a rational-supernatural *hesitation* is all too evident; language outruns the illusory world offered by the narrative. Ralph Marsden's adaptation of **Sabbat of the Black Cat** (1973) provides all the details in Poe, expanding the story of a man who descends to the point of killing his wife and walling her up in the cellar. The cause, in his eyes, is the black cat, Pluto, who fills him with an irrational dread, having seemingly risen from death, and who finally reveals the murder to the police. But, as ever, it might all fit a pattern of coincidence. Marsden provides the narrative, but not the pleasure, of Poe's tale, which, to use Roland Barthes' phrase, "has been entrusted solely and totally to the power of the word" — i.e., it is unfilmable. One can only use Poe as an inspiration for something utterly different, as

Roger Corman did in his adaptations.

But even accepting **Sabbat** as a faithful transcription of Poe's fantasy world, the film illustrates the greatest pitfall of the genre: fantastic films must, paradoxically, be the most realistic. There must be a familiar, credible world established before any intrusion of the unusual can be effective. **Sabbat**, a historical film, is full of embarrassing anachronisms in dialogue, costume and acting style. Its failure to achieve the illusion of realism, and create a naturalistic flow in its narrative situations, puts the audience at a distance, thus preventing the film from dealing successfully with the fantastic.

I have so far dealt with films that belong with the fantasy genre, as it is defined, in which no clear explanation of strange events is chosen by the film — or the audience. Films that opt for a rational explanation are part of the *uncanny* genre. Chris Lofven's **Oz** (1976) is the only Australian production in this category. Since the main character is named Dorothy (Joy Dunstan), wears red magic shoes and is off to see the Wizard's (Graham Matters) final performance — he is a rock star — one may infer that this is a remake/reworking/modernization/parody (take your pick) of *The Wizard of Oz*. As in the original story by Frank L. Baum (of which there are several film versions), Dorothy is, after all, only dreaming.

Interpreting Lofven's film as a dream makes sense of the various fantasy elements encountered in it. The same actors appear in numerous roles, with a particular *idée fixe* on the Wizard, who is everything from a tram conductor and record dealer to an usher at the theatre. Dorothy's shoes guide her through the unfamiliar labyrinth of the city to the Wizard's concert, and eventually save her from the advances of a truckie rapist (i.e., she kicks him in the appropriate place).

Dorothy's dream exists to teach a moral lesson. It does not open the world of the *marvellous* to the dreamer, but rather serves to return her into waking reality, wiser than before. In the famous 1939 Judy Garland version of the story, the moral delivered by Dorothy at the end was befitting the idealism of romantic small-town America: "There's no place like home." In **Oz**, 37 years later, the modern Dorothy leaves home and the romantic aspiration relates to rock music, life out on the road and a search for self-discovery and fulfilment. The moral speaks out against the excesses of egomania and greed: "Fame and fortune fuck you up."

Oz is a difficult film with which to come to terms. If it takes itself and its moralizing seriously, then its presentation of sexuality is quite offensive. Dorothy, the innocent, is the prize to be won by whoever gets to her first (one of the Ross Wilson songs in the film is *Who's Gonna Love You Tonight?*; indeed, all the songs are of men speaking or men desiring, and never about Dorothy's point-of-view). Even worse is what the film does with Glenn (Robin Ramsey), who sets Dorothy on her mission to find the Wizard. He is the stereotype gay, down to the sparkling white suit and predictable effeminate gestures. As well, Glenn is revealed to be the evil purveyor of all this fame and fortune, the corrupting entrepreneur. The moral might as well read: "Homosexuals are ruining the world." If, alternatively, one takes the film as parody — of Hollywood, rock music culture, the pretentious philosophy of finding your 'real' self — then the stereotypes are, perhaps, jokes at the expense of those very stereotypes and the mentality from which they emerge. But the vagueness of such an interpretation places **Oz** a long way behind, say, **Shirley Thompson**, which is clearly parodic.

Peter Weir's **The Last Wave** (1977) deals almost exclusively with the *marvellous*, this time in the form of the Aboriginal mythology

Dorothy (Joy Dunstan) and the Good Fairy (Robin Ramsay). Chris Lofven's **Oz**.

of the dreamtime. Rational explanations of the unusual weather in the film — the position of the planets, air pollution, etc. — are peripheral, and carry little weight.

David Burton (Richard Chamberlain) is a lawyer, a member of that profession which epitomizes rationality. Step by step, he comes to realize that every event in the external world, and every message in the internal world of his psyche, announces a coming apocalypse in a universal cycle of destruction and rebirth, and his predestined part in it. Situations and experiences, at first random and unconnected, as they are usually taken to be in life, become charged with *pan-determinism*: everything has a specific meaning, and occurs in relation to a definite order and purpose. David, in retrieving and deciphering the dreams of his childhood (which include a premonition of his mother's death), learns that he is, and always has been, the medium through which the spirit, Mulkurul, speaks, bringing the news of the apocalypse and breaking the sacred rituals of dreamtime law to bring it about. When the tribal leader Charlie (Nandjiwarra Amagula) chants before him, "Who are you?", he knows he can no longer answer with his family name; that identity has been left behind. He tells his uncomprehending father, whose religion, like the white man's law, serves to pacify and explain away mystery: "I've lost the world I thought I had."

The main figure in this drama of the *marvellous* and supernatural is nature. With the elements no longer conforming to a predictable pattern, it becomes clear how awesome and beyond our control they are. The film has many images which ironically point out the ways in which people like to think they impose an order upon nature, and turn it to their service: the harnessing of water through drinking taps and sprinklers, etc. Equally, they believe they can keep nature away when it is an annoyance, with umbrellas and windscreen wipers. But nothing, finally, will hold back the last wave, which is utterly indifferent to the insignificant societies of men and women.

The film is constructed around a series of polar oppositions. In each case there is, on one side, the superficial and the reassuring; on the other, a richer level of experience which has been repressed. Most importantly, everyday waking life is set against the dreamtime. Our society has rationalized dreams, given them interpretations, attempted to master the self. But David learns that ultimately his self is insignificant. The things he will do, even down to beating Chris (Gulpilil) to death with the sacred stone, have already been mapped out, and telegraphed to him in his dreams.

Civilization can attempt to repress the *marvellous*, but it can never make it disappear; as David tells his father, "Our dreams come back, and we don't know what they mean."

White law and black defiance: David Burton (Richard Chamberlain) and Chris Lee (Gulpilil). Peter Weir's **The Last Wave**.

Chris and Charlie (Nandjiwarra Amagula) describe to David aspects of tribal law. **The Last Wave**.

The final sequence when David finds the secret cave, then crawls out along the sewers onto the beach where he awaits the wave. **The Last Wave**.

This is conveyed powerfully in another comparison, one of a physical, concrete order. Below the city streets, where one doesn't have to be reminded of their existence, run the sewers. It is here that the Aboriginals can hide their tribal identity and the sacred place whose walls foretell in drawings the cycle of the last wave. They can be sure that no white people would ever dirty themselves enough to stumble upon them. This is what gives so much power to the final scenes where David, having lost all traces of his civilized identity, tries to

crawl his way out of the sewer, but finds the steel door locked; he wades through the sewer again until he finds a passage onto the beach, where he sees the wave.

Two laws are contrasted: the Aboriginals' law against the civilized law. The Aboriginals' law is strictly bound by ritual and a secret set of rules which has been handed down unchanged from the forefathers. As Chris tells David, "It is more important than man." The civilized law is based on liberal ethics. David's colleague accuses him of "middle-class paternalism" towards the Aboriginals. Aspiring to knowledge, objectivity and truth, the proceedings in the courtroom never touch the reality

altogether absent (significantly, Marcia in **Long Weekend** has had an abortion). In **The Last Wave**, Weir grants children more importance. At the beginning, children in a schoolyard play joyfully in the rain, while their teacher tries to herd them inside; later, David's two children are delighted at the sight of water from an overflowing bathtub making its way down the stairs. Often during the film, David gazes at his daughter sleeping, as if she holds the key to the secret in which he is enmeshed. The suggestion is that children are closer to the *marvellous,* and have a potentially keener perception of it — that is, before the adult world socializes it out of them forever. This Weir demonstrates in the scene where David's daughter has a vivid dream; perhaps she too is connected with the supernatural. But the content of the dream is described by the child in Christian terms — which, we have seen, serve to explain away mystery — and ends with a pious, reassuring lesson: "I love Jesus, mummy." She has lost contact with the violence, the terror — and the beauty — of nature and its marvellous design.

Many films that are broadly termed fantasy fall outside the definitions which relate to a model of realism. Weir's **The Cars That Ate Paris** (1974), for instance, begins in an unreal world: beautiful people travelling through a countryside conjured for us by television advertising. The violence wrought on this couple when they reach the small town of Paris has no claim to credibility. Closer to allegory, the film demands to be analysed for the way it presents a microcosm of Australian society (the fetish of the motor car; the smouldering violence of delinquent youth), rather than evoking the world of the fantastic.

Dave Jones' **Yakkety Yak** (1974), a brilliant satire on the theory and practice of radical cinema, the animated **Marco Polo Junior Versus The Red Dragon** (1972), by Eric Porter, and Richard Franklin's **The True Story of Eskimo Nell** (1975) similarly obey few of the conventions of realism. They can correctly be titled poetic, but not fantastic.

Fantasy films can also belong to two other groups: themes of the *self* and of the *other.* Themes of the *self* investigate the individual and his/her perception of the world. Within fantasy, this can be a highly abstract perception. Mind and matter mingle; past, present and future lose their fixed chronology. The cinema is particularly suited to realize these themes through its deployment of a system of

of why the Aboriginals killed one of their own, preferring to acknowledge it as a drunken brawl. The two laws have no common ground, conveyed in the image of hands — one white, one black — on the Bible, as oaths are taken. The words, "so help me, God", that the Aboriginals are made to recite are, of course, irrelevant to them, reiterating the spiritual gap between the two cultures.

One final motif in **The Last Wave** should be noted: the contrast between adult and child. It is a theme not often dealt with in Australian cinema, where children are either on the brink of entering the adult world (**Libido** — 1973; **The Night The Prowler** — 1978), or are vision — the camera looks, characters within the fiction look, an audience looks at the film. Any or all of these can be made unstable. For example, in **Shirley Thompson** the audience is treated to the spectacle of objects and people, seen not as real, but as an essence — the "pure perception" Shirley claims to have received from the aliens. The film, in black and white at this point, uses the combination of a fast zoom, the sudden intrusion of color, and a flickering of the image to convey such a perception — but not very convincingly.

More subtly introduced are David's visions in **The Last Wave**: as he sits in his car, the rain teeming on the windscreen slowly blurs his field of vision. One image of the ordinary present (people crossing the street) can thus be replaced by another (bodies floating in the aftermath of the great wave). The film's dramatic, final shot signifies David's approaching death simply and effectively by showing him closing his eyes. In **Patrick**, the situation is different. Faced with Patrick's impassive, unblinking stare the audience is disconcerted and wonders whether he sees anything. Is his vision different, psychic or supernatural? That is why the film's final shot returns to the same eyes, open, but frustratingly telling us nothing certain.

Another Richard Franklin film, **The True Story of Eskimo Nell**, which has been unfairly underrated, presents a most poignant example of fantastic vision. Dead-Eye Dick (Max Gillies) has travelled the world to claim his Nell. When he reaches his destination, the audience and his companion, Mexico Pete (Serge Lazareff), see the brutal truth: Nell is merely a dream, a legendary name that a less-than-glamorous lady uses to bolster business. Dead-Eye sees nothing of the sort: through his eyes is conjured the Nell he has always desired, and whose photo he has kept lovingly under his hat. **Eskimo Nell** talks intelligently and interestingly about what it means to be a voyeur — to see only what one desires. And that, by extension, also reflects upon our situation as viewers of a film, for the cinema is, to quote Laura Mulvey, "an illusion cut to the measure of desire". In a cinema, we are all voyeurs.

In these cases, the *self* is enclosed and solitary. But a transition can occur whereby an individual enters society and establishes relations with others. It is when he catches his reflection in a mirror — i.e., for a moment he

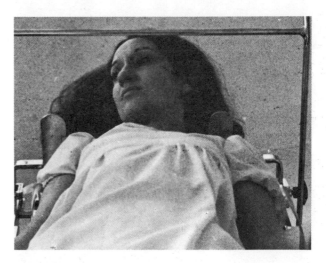

Jane Harders as Shirley Thompson in the asylum. Jim Sharman's **Shirley Thompson Versus The Aliens**.

can step outside and see himself as someone else. This pivotal moment occurs often in fantasy films. In **Oz**, for example, Dorothy smashes her reflection with the all-important red shoes when she realizes the moral of her story.

A more thoughtful and complex use of the image is in Jim Sharman's **The Night The Prowler**. Felicity (Kerry Walker) is confronted not only literally with a mirror image, but also symbolically — the dying man who has withdrawn from contact with others. In her aggressive rebellion against the norms of a middle-class family, Felicity sees that she too may be drying up emotionally. Thus, in the last line of the film when the police ask her about the old man — "Did you know him?" — she replies, "I knew him . . . as I know myself." Her mother (Ruth Cracknell), by contrast, is constantly looking in the mirror, but never seeing herself as she really is.

Themes of the *other* explore directly the relations between people. In Giorgio Mangiamele's **Beyond Reason** (1970), the doctors and patients of an asylum are locked together in an underground shelter while nuclear war rages above. The question is: how does one define madness? An individual can never be analysed separately from others, for it is with these others that he or she develops a particular configuration of need, demand and desire. There can be no distinctions between doctor and patient, asylum and the world at large. All people are caught in the image created for them by others.

The film choreographs its action carefully to emphasize choral-like arrangements of people

— not this or that individual. There are types rather than characters; symptoms rather than personality traits. Sexuality is presented in extremes — from frigidity to nymphomania; aggression runs on a scale from sadism to masochism. It is a very schematic but valiant attempt at describing social relations in the light of Freudian psychoanalysis.

The fundamental social unit is the family. **The Night The Prowler** is the most ambitious film involving family relationships yet produced in Australia. Felicity's sexuality has been denied and repressed by her parents, leading to the other extreme, an inverted neurosis. Fantasy turns, to use the language of psychoanalysis, into "phantasy". She longs to be raped by "a real man", a prowler in the night. Later, she becomes a prowler: the intrusion of the repressed into the homes of a middle-class neighborhood. The link between the family and Felicity's unleashed violence is made through repeated emphasis on certain objects: she cuts her 16th birthday cake with a knife; later, as a prowler, she slashes and defaces a family portrait.

But her violence is futile, for who is to blame? Each member of the family has, in a way, been forced into a role that conceals the free expression of desire. The film reverberates with many hinted-at sexual possibilities: Felicity desires her father, the mother imagines herself for a moment being raped. It is a pity that, towards the end, the film changes direction abruptly, so that Felicity's dilemma is presented as being purely individual ("I know myself") and no longer related to the family.

Finally, it remains to indicate some of the particular pleasures to be found in fantasy films. Being narratives, they are at liberty to play with such story-telling virtues as symmetry, economy and balance. This is a self-evident delight in Keith Salvat's **Private Collection** (1972), where the film sets up one collector (Peter Reynolds) employing a thief (Graham Bond) to steal an antique statue of an eagle from a teacher (Brian Blain); a piece that is the pair of his own eagle. Meanwhile, the teacher, who is also a collector, hires the same thief to steal an eagle from the first collector . . .

Marco Polo Junior Versus The Red Dragon has a narrative line as pure as the fairy tales it draws upon. Marco carries half the medal of Kublai Khan, and is helped in his travels by a magical guru and a seagull. In Xanadu, the Princess Shining Moon, who holds the other half, escapes from the evil villain, with the help of a friend and an elephant. When the pieces of the medal are joined, a love story begins, and order is restored in Xanadu. Every detail fits into a precise symmetrical pattern of narrative rhyme.

To discover how completely cinematic fantasy films can be, the audience should close its eyes and listen to the voluptuous, intricate soundtracks of **Picnic** and **Long Weekend**. In most conventional films the sound is neutral, redundant, secondary to the image; in these films, natural sounds are selected and worked over for optimum emotional charge. Conversely, the musical scores, rather than being the wallpaper they usually are, express very precise ideas, drawing significant connections between elements within the fantastic world.

In the fantasy genre, one receives an occasional glimpse of the delirious possibilities of the cinema; where everything expresses meaning and creates a world, while at the same time engaging the filmgoer in a direct relationship with the material of the film itself, and the building of each image and sound. But, however one may wish to interpret these films, one must first accept the challenge to, in some sense, create them ourselves. A phrase describing the nature of dreams from **The Last Wave** neatly captures the flavor of the finest fantasy films: a mixture of "seeing, hearing, talking", they can be ultimately "the way of knowing things".

7 HISTORICAL FILMS

Tom Ryan

*"History in cinema is nowhere other than in represen-
tation, representing exactly the historical present of
any film. Which is to say that the simple relation of
film and history-as-theme, as past to be shown today,
an obvious strategy for a cinema developed in the
perspective of a certain conception of nationhood, is
an idealist abstraction, an ideal of life and an ideal of
history."*

Stephen Heath[1]

To initiate a reading of Australian 'historical'
films, it is necessary to locate them within a
broader analytic method: to see them simply as
Australian is not enough. Certainly the characters who are constructed within their images
inhabit landscapes, towns and cities that are
identifiably Australian. Their voices usually
resound with an Australian accent, and a
number of them have come to assume the
status of archetypal figures — the Aboriginal,
the white settler, the bushranger, the shearer,
the farmer, the businessman. And though
these characters have come to occupy specific
positions within the Australian legend, much
still remains to be said about the films in which
they appear.

One might begin with a categorization of
these films in terms of generic sub-groups:

i. The outback/wilderness film (similar to
the American western), with its recurring characters (the wanderers, the law-
men, the stabilizing woman *et al.*) and
themes (the community of the township
versus the community of those who
brave the outback; the place of the outsider, who may be outlaw, black or
female): **Sunday Too Far Away** (1975),
Inn of the Damned (1975), **The True
Story of Eskimo Nell** (1975), **Mad Dog
Morgan** (1976), **Raw Deal** (1977),
Journey Among Women (1977), **The
Chant of Jimmie Blacksmith** (1978),
The Irishman (1978).

ii. The films of small-town Australian life,
with their narrative patterns setting old
against young, the traditional against the

new: **The Mango Tree** (1977), **Break of
Day** (1976), **The Picture Show Man**
(1977).

iii. The films of the city, introducing the
problem of anonymity of the individual
in a world in which he or she becomes
faceless amidst 'the crowd': **Caddie**
(1976), **Newsfront** (1978).

iv. The films about growing up, setting
innocence against experience, the individual against the repressive influences of
institutions (which are usually linked
with a British pomposity and a Victorian
morality), with only the wisdom of a
matriarchal presence to act as a guide:
The Child episode of **Libido** (1973),
The Devil's Playground (1976), **The
Mango Tree**, **The Getting of Wisdom**
(1977), **The Irishman**, **The Chant of
Jimmie Blacksmith**, **My Brilliant
Career** (1979).

v. The films about 'outsiders', dealing with
those characters who strive to come to
grips with their identities as Australians,
or to overcome their past in order to
enter the community, or to find their
place within the movement of Australian
history: **Between Wars** (1974), **Mad Dog
Morgan**, **Caddie**, **Break of Day**, **The
Chant of Jimmie Blacksmith**, **The Odd
Angry Shot** (1979), **Dawn!** (1979), **My
Brilliant Career**.

vi. The comedy films, in which a number of
characters from the other groups are
drawn more broadly, their accents and
manners stressed more heavily, while
the theme of sexuality is treated more
openly: **The True Story of Eskimo Nell**,
Eliza Fraser (1976), **Don's Party**
(1976), **Dimboola** (1979).

The list of possible sub-groups, of films
which might be included in them, and of recurring characters and thematic concerns is far
from complete. Such a process of classification

Shearers at work on an outback station. Fred Schepisi's **The Chant of Jimmie Blacksmith**.

inevitably creates an area of overlap, in which, for example, **Jimmie Blacksmith** could be appropriated to three of the six sub-groups I have arbitrarily selected. The result of this categorization is the construction of a framework in which various films can be examined in relation to each other, and the indication of several points from which a particular film's thematic patterns might be viewed.

From this freewheeling approach within the methodology of 'genre' criticism, much fruitful insight can be gained. Similarly, an examination of the works of particular directors (Peter Weir, Don Crombie, Tim Burstall), or scriptwriters (Cliff Green, David Williamson, Joan Long) can provide the critic with an additional body of knowledge (stylistic predispositions, thematic preoccupations), which is helpful in uncovering the layers of meaning present in any given film. The usefulness of 'genre' and 'auteur' criticism has already been established, and it is implicit within much of the film commentary which is available to date on Australian films.

However my concern here is to find an alternative critical route into those films which have, as their settings, recognizable periods of Australian history. If I give little attention to demands that these films should be "historically accurate", or to the view that they are "nostalgia trips", it is because neither approach takes us very close to the workings of individual films. Doubtless there are a number of occasions when both positions might be appropriate, but they are more often the result of a lack of critical imagination than the fruit of a probing analysis.

My view is that one is best rewarded by an examination of the relationship between the historical period or social world as it is represented by the images of particular films and the characters represented as inhabitants of that world, and whose drama is ostensibly the *raison d'être* for the film. To approach some understanding of this relationship, it is first necessary to identify, albeit in an abbreviated fashion, the machinery by which narratives and histories are produced, their similarities and differences.

Narrative Films as Histories

Narrative films are the constructions of histories. They have a beginning, a series of events and an ending; and they are all subject to a logical order. There are times when these events are presented out of chronological sequence, the implied role of the viewer being to sort them out, like pieces of a jigsaw puzzle, before the story is seen to be complete.

What needs to be emphasized is that the order of these events is a logical one — i.e., it is not the result of some natural accident, but the creation of a complex of machinery, which combines the history of film language and the individual filmmakers in the production of the logical order of a narrative film. The filmmakers are subordinate to the rules of narrative construction, to the methods by which one image is linked to another (cuts, wipes, dissolves), to a specific method of locating perspective (the use of the conventions of Renaissance space) and to the demand that sound and image should be synchronized, all of which go towards a definition of narrative realism.

The impulse of this narrative realism — according to Christian Metz, "its defining quality"[2] — is to conceal its status as a language, to obliterate the signs of its construction and to assert its order as a natural one. However, it is only if the process of watching becomes a self-conscious one, primarily concerned with the way in which meanings are constructed, rather than with the meanings themselves, that one becomes conscious of language. This might simply lead to an understanding of how particular visual or aural effects were achieved, a customary concern of much writing about film. But it might also result in an examination of the implications of the rules of narrative and visual construction, which attempt to present meanings as transparent rather than as the product of language.

Histories as Narratives

The writing of a history[3] is the imposition of an order upon a number of past events which are selected according to the author's discretion. Its usefulness is generally measured by how comprehensive and coherent the connections and explanations it constructs are deemed to be. Yet it also can, and should, be scrutinized as a discourse, as a construction of language, rather than as a window through which the past can be seen. Its order, more often than not, is subject to the same rules that apply in the building of narrative fictions. Given a recognition of these facts, any belief in the production of history (or of any other discourse) as "objective" or "impartial" needs to be treated with extreme suspicion.

A far-reaching approach to this question might concern itself with the route by which a particular history came into existence: as the product of an industry, of a collective of some kind, or of an individual. The scope of my concern is limited to the way in which a handful of Australian films which deal with "history-as-theme" share certain attitudes towards their different narrative subjects.

Perhaps the only fictional narrative which refuses to take its historical representations seriously, as history, is **Eliza Fraser**, directed by Tim Burstall and written by David Williamson. While its narrative can be seen to take as its starting-point a collection of characters and a sequence of events which have been documented by historians, its development shows little concern for an accurate reproduction of that documentation. Where the impulse of the historical research has been to create what Keith Connolly has properly observed as "a human drama of epic proportions",[4] the makers of the film subvert their characters' heroic status and adapt the material to a comic mode. The critical vituperation with which the result has been rewarded is based on a misunderstanding of the nature of historical record and its place in the preparation of narrative fiction, and on a refusal, or an inability, to see the way in which the film is working.

Below: Rory McBryde (John Castle), Captain Fraser (Noel Ferrier), Mrs Fraser (Susannah York) and Captain Fyans (Trevor Howard) at Moreton Bay. Tim Burstall's **Eliza Fraser**.

The film's full title, **A Faithful Narrative of the Capture, Sufferings and Miraculous Escape of Eliza Fraser**, immediately announces its adherence to the tradition of the picaresque and its parody of those films which seriously aspire to offer faithful renditions of "the way it really was"[5]. And if the point of the extended title is not immediately clear, the subsequent comic cavalcade serves to emphasize the obvious.

The film's comic mode and the neat structuring of its narrative proceed to invert the prevailing myth of the propriety of British mores and the primitive savagery of the native — in this case the Aboriginal. The sentiments expressed by the pompous Captain Fraser (Noel Ferrier), fearful of having to venture inland to Moreton Bay after his latest shipwreck, evoke a dominant view of the Aboriginals ("Savages! ... cannibals!") and are forcefully counterpointed by the patterns of savagery, deceit, betrayal, sexual jealousy, and cannibalism engaged upon by the white intruders into Australia. A nice irony has Captain Fraser later killed by an Aboriginal hunting spear thrown by a British soldier. Fraser's fears are directly contradicted when he and his wife (Susannah York) fall into the hands of the "savages" and find that the worst they have to face is the humiliation of being disrobed, the insult of having the dress that marks their class mocked by those as yet untarnished by British manners, and the threat of a proposal of marriage from a tribal elder.

The parody that lies beneath the film's surface rumbustiousness and the apparent disconnectedness of its picaresque narrative is one that intentionally confronts the literal-minded historians and critics. A determination to see the film as simply belonging to the tradition of **Stork** (1971) and **Alvin Purple** (1973) seems to have encouraged a superficial response to the place which the film's treatment of sexuality occupies within its broader thrust. The key passage in the film which illuminates this is the one which covers the night when the main characters come together at Moreton Bay after Fraser's brigantine has put in there to unload the licentious Rory McBryde (John Castle). A series of encounters, belonging to a tradition of farce reaching back centuries, embraces a history of sexual games in which frustration is the prominent condition. Captain Fyans (Trevor Howard) uses his power in a vain attempt to satisfy his homosexual lust for

his "orderly", the convict Bracefelt (John Waters), who escapes under the cover of darkness and ends up in Eliza's bed, before seeking refuge under it as first McBryde and then Captain Fraser make their play for Eliza's graces.

The importance of the passage lies in the way it draws together, at this point, the three strands of the narrative (connected with McBryde's misadventures, the Frasers' loveless marriage, and the penal colony's repressive world) and points to an underlying sexual tension as the key motivating force for the narrative history of the film. Significantly, the two characters who achieve satisfaction, a convict and a married woman, are those who have the least social power. They are also the ones best able to come to terms with the alien world of the Aboriginals — Bracefelt later adapting himself without difficulty to a life in the exile of the wilderness, Eliza gradually relaxing in the company of the Aboriginal women, both assuming the outward appearance of Aboriginals.

The place of sexuality in the film's construction of a history is further emphasized in a sequence near the end when Eliza delivers an

Eliza during her period of assimilation with the Aboriginals. **Eliza Fraser**.

oral history of her adventures, according to a script prepared by McBryde, to an eager carnival audience. With appropriate embellishments, "to heighten the drama", she presents a titillating, reconstructed version of the Aboriginal elder's marriage preparations: a frightened white woman threatened by a "huge, black, powerful, menacing" creature, a production directed at the fears of the white psyche rather than based on any historical reality. A female voice from the crowd asks eagerly, "Was he naked, miss?" and the point of the sequence is abundantly clear.

The intelligence which has been invested in the structure of **Eliza Fraser** (and I have merely skimmed the surface of its beguiling narrative complexities) owes little to any recorded history. It could be argued that its treatment of Australia's past presents a provocative insight into the relationships between white and black, but, before such an observation can be made, it would be necessary to explore the way it is working as a narrative

fiction, instead of demanding that it first adhere to some simplistic notion of historical accuracy.

For narrative filmmakers to try "to tell it the way it really was", and for commentators to expect that they should achieve that, is to misunderstand the processes of history and fiction. While structurally both might have much in common, there is no reason to demand that, in the interest of some myth of truth, narrative films should bind themselves to the prevailing whim of what is historically accurate. What ought to be focal points for those expressing some concern for narrative film are exactly what are ignored whenever the question of fidelity to recorded history is raised. And these are the patterns of each of the narratives under consideration and the visual forms which contain them. While these do signify a history, it is one that has to do primarily with the cinema as an institution of representation.

Narrative Historical Films

The periods of history represented by films which can be classified as historical are revealing in themselves — from the birth pangs of the colony, through settlement, to the 20th Century with its two world wars, its confrontations between the values of rural and urban environments, its social and political turmoils, and, finally, Vietnam. While the point at which the films are no longer considered to offer representations of history is an arbitrary one, it is significant that there is no narrative film which is set before the occurrence of the European invasion into Australia. Since the production of any film is a question of choice — however complex the procedure of that choice might be (questions of marketability constantly hovering in the background of any screenplay in preparation and endorsed by the machinery of the Australian Film Commission) — then it becomes clear how partial the construction of history has been.

The historical films generally fall into three major categories:

i. Those whose narrative is set in the past, but which employ the historical settings primarily as locations for the particular drama they create — e.g., **The Child, The True Story of Eskimo Nell, Inn of the Damned, The Devil's Playground, Caddie, Raw Deal, My Brilliant Career**.

A fight on the goldfields. Richard Franklin's **The True Story of Eskimo Nell**.

Edward Trenbow (Corin Redgrave) and his wife Deborah (Judy Morris). Michael Thornhill's **Between Wars**.

Jim Allen and Rhys Jones land at the spot where Captain Cook first saw Tasmanian Aboriginals. Tom Haydon's **The Last Tasmanian**.

ii. Those whose particular dramas and settings are merged in such a way as to encourage their being read as representing symbolic as well as concrete worlds — that is, the development of character and narrative, and the specific moment of history in which the fiction is located evoke an abstract portrait of Australia's past as well as a particular drama about particular characters — e.g., **Between Wars**, **Sunday Too Far Away**, **Picnic at Hanging Rock** (1975), **Eliza Fraser**, **The Last Wave** (1977), **The Irishman**, and the television series, **Luke's Kingdom**, **Against The Wind**, **Twenty Good Years**, and **The Sullivans**.

iii. Those whose form and structure indicate precise attempts to recreate a moment of the past, and, in some cases, to analyse that moment: the documentary films. This type of film creates a special example in the context of this argument — its language is that of film, perhaps even narrative film, but its distinct procedure makes clear that it should be read as a historical record or as an interpretation of history: e.g., **Menace** (1977), **The Last Tasmanian** (1978), **Woolloomooloo** (1978).

Perhaps the most significant recurring narrative pattern is that which locates the characters in a position of powerlessness in relation to the movement of the historical periods in which they are placed. In contrast, say, to American narratives which are "typically stories of strength and energy expended in the pursuit and acquisition of or extension of control over geographic areas or political enterprises"[6], these Australian narratives decline the option of stories tracing characters' rises to power. It is not that the Australian films should place their characters in positions of power, in the interest of the assertion of "national identity" and similar nonsense, it is simply that they do not. Films as different as **Between Wars**, **Mad Dog Morgan**, **Caddie**, **Break of Day**, **The Irishman**, **Newsfront**, **Dawn!**, **The Odd Angry Shot** and **My Brilliant Career** have narratives peopled by characters who are governed by forces beyond their control, and who are shown in a position of defeat at the close of the film.

This is not to say that these characters are all totally repressed, completely submerged by the broader flow of history or failing to survive

Michael (Simon Burke) leads the "team", while his father (Michael Craig) and mother (Robyn Nevin) follow. Donald Crombie's **The Irishman**.

its challenges to their security. The impulse of some of these narratives is to qualify this sense of the characters' historical irrelevance. This is achieved by constructing a context of personal drama in which individual achievements (e.g., the reconstruction of the family unit in **Caddie**, the camaraderie of the Australian soldiers in **The Odd Angry Shot** and the publication of Sybylla's novel in **My Brilliant Career**) and the assertion of the energy of a particular morality or spirit courageously defy the individuals' irrelevance by their very survival.

In most cases, the condition of defeat is precisely linked to an historical moment, or to a series of moments. For example, in **The Irishman**, Paddy's (Michael Craig) refusal to change with the times ("I'll stick to what I'm good at") is an expression of his individual dignity ("I've got me wind and a strong back and the best little wife in all the world — that's me fortune"). But it is set against a clear recog-

nition of the irrelevance of such sentiments to the coming of the new order which is presented literally in the arrival of the motor car and the emphasis of the importance of education, and symbolically in the deaths which occur throughout the film and which culminate in Paddy's.

Yet this defeat of the values of an uncompromising past at the hands of the future is qualified by the film's structure. Though Paddy's demise is its focal point, it is his son, Michael (Simon Burke), who mediates this and whose own moral education occupies the foreground at the opening and the closing of the narrative. His final reassertion of the values of his father points to the filmmakers' romantic sensibilities, but it also works as an uneasy celebration in the context of what has preceded it.

Similarly, the narratives of **Caddie**, **Newsfront**, **Dawn!** and **My Brilliant Career** engineer the helplessness of their central characters while working to shift attention from it, by placing emphasis upon their defiance. Caddie (Helen Morse) enters the narrative at the point when she and her two children are in the process of leaving their well-to-do home in a Sydney suburb in the autumn of 1925. The cause of the family breakdown is her husband's infidelity, a fact established in a series of brief flashbacks intercut with images of her departure. The film's strategy is then to take her through a succession of hardships to do with the absence of a man, the crudities of the working classes and the trials of the depression.

Its perspectives throughout coincide with those of its heroine, and so the milieu through which she passes becomes less important than her response to it. The final sequence encapsulates the point when, with the trials she has faced throughout the narrative still unresolved, exhausted by her day's work, she returns home and seeks rest, only to be interrupted by her children. Her exasperation turns to pleasure as she is forced to engage in their play, the camera slowly closing on her before the end titles announce the return to Australia of her Greek lover (Takis Emmanuel), his death in a motor accident before they could be married, and then hers in 1960.

Newsfront also celebrates the indomitable spirit of its central character, Len Maguire (Bill Hunter), whose occupation as a film news cameraman has been rendered out of date by the coming of television. After he has turned down an offer from his brother, Frank (Gerard Kennedy), of $50,000 for some choice news footage, he is described alternately as "galloping towards a precipice with his eyes wide open" (by Frank) and "just a bit old-fashioned, that's all" (by his girlfriend Amy, played by Wendy Hughes). Assured of his identity, he walks away from the group towards the camera until the frame freezes in the film's proclamation of his honor.

While **Dawn!** charts the rise and fall of the career of swimming star Dawn Fraser (Bronwyn Mackay-Payne), it locates this within a flashback structure, with the result that her eventual defeat at the hands of the Australian swimming bureaucracies, as well as her moments of triumph, are framed by the effect of the film's present tense. Here she is presented as an ordinary Australian, resigned to her frustrated potential, her matter-of-fact manner allowing her to be at one with those whom she greets in the opening and closing pub sequences.

Sybylla Melvyn (Judy Davis) in **My Brilliant Career** continually asserts, with her every action, her independence from the world which she finds oppressive (her family, her suitors, the role she is expected to play as a member of her class and as a woman). Nowhere is this better illustrated than in the splendid opening sequence in which a series of shots stresses her separation from the activity outdoors as she remains enclosed within her dreams of "culture and elegance", her domestic responsibilities being the furthest thing from her mind. But, while she is shown to have won a battle at the end of the film — the completion of her novel also suggests that she has gained a clearer sense of her identity — nothing has changed. The forces that have repressed her may have receded to the background in the presentation of her drama, but, having been so forcefully depicted, they are not so easily forgotten.

In all these narratives, the central characters play no effective part in the history of the time they occupy. They are forced to live through their personal dramas according to the constraints of the time, subject to the growth of technology, the social order, the Depression, the bureaucracies set up around them, and so on. The implications of this narrative pattern

Dawn (Bronwyn Mackay-Payne) confronts the police over a speeding charge. Ken Hannam's **Dawn!**

Above: One of the flashbacks showing the break-up between Caddie (Helen Morse) and her unfaithful husband (Phillip Hinton). Donald Crombie's **Caddie**. Below: Sybylla (Judy Davis) cocooned in her own 'world'. Gillian Armstrong's **My Brilliant Career.**

are clear: that the individual, and those with whom he/she is likely to come into contact, can play no part in the construction of history. Its course is in the hands of the powerful institutions which often exist outside the framework of the narratives, but whose presence is felt in the shifting fortunes of the characters who reside within them. There are numerous examples: the faceless powers which withdraw the shearers' bonus prosperity payment in **Sunday Too Far Away**; the government which exploits its soldiers in Vietnam and earns their wrath but not their resistance in **The Odd Angry Shot**; history itself in **The Irishman**; and the intolerance of the sporting authorities in **Dawn!**. Sometimes, mainly in the films whose drama is located before or around the turn of the century, the institutions of power, often with direct links to the Mother Country, find direct representation: in the form of officers of the law in **Mad Dog Morgan**; white Australia in **The Chant of Jimmie Blacksmith**; an Australian bourgeoisie in **Break of Day** and **My Brilliant Career**; the far-reaching forces of government in **Between Wars**; the church in **The Devil's Playground** and the schools in **Picnic at Hanging Rock** and **The Getting of Wisdom**. All impose institutionalized codes of behaviour.

There are many conclusions one could draw from these recurring patterns. In contrast with the American narratives, they are far more modest, preferring to define the individual as a battler against overwhelming odds which cannot be defeated even if they are confronted head-on, but which will allow survival if he/she suffers the indignities without asserting resentment. This individual is a victim, a consumer of history rather than a participant in its course. The American narratives, on the other hand, are filled with bravura performances by individuals capable of taking on these odds and winning through — from Mr Smith's visit to Washington to Bob Woodward and Carl Bernstein's shattering of an administration.

Another view is to see this general thrust of Australian and American narratives as two perspectives on the same *politique* — both dealing with national stereotypes. Against the 'great man' who dominates a significant portion of American narratives, there is the Australian 'little man' or 'little woman' (I should stress here that the reference is to a place in history, rather than to domestic habit). Both styles of narrative, in form and effect,

My Brilliant Career.

deny the possibility of any kind of collective struggle, presenting classes as irrelevant to the movement of history. The American populist hero and the alienated Australian hero and heroine are reactionary creations: the former are set apart from the people by their stature as individuals, the latter are isolated from power and from most of their fellow Australians. Both separate 'the people' from the processes of history and though, as I have argued, the history contained within the narrative film is under no compulsion to attend to some faithful representation of a particular era, the position it takes on the relationship between its characters and the particular history it represents cannot be seen to be an innocent one. Its ordering of characters and events signifies a particular way of seeing the world, and it is in such terms that the Australian historical narrative film is best understood.

The Documentary

Like narrative fictions, documentary films are the constructions of histories. However, documentary realism differs markedly from narrative realism: the former attempts to create the sense that it is directly mediating the events of the real world; the latter endeavors to eliminate anything which might interrupt the flow of its fictional world. The documentary's style of address to the viewer, whether direct, with a verbal commentary linking the images, or indirect, allowing the images to speak for themselves, is one of authority. Their subject matter — whether it is the fall of Idi Amin or the drug culture — is immediately seen to be more serious because it is about real people and real situations. Yet, whether the documentary is directly concerned with the contemporary world or with some past era, its impulse is to create a narrative — though that narrative might take different forms from the one customarily found in narrative fiction films.

Its narrative is not always concerned with individuals and their intimate dramas. Nor are the events it presents always staged especially for the making of the film — as they are for the narrative films I have discussed to this point. Nevertheless it does, as a general tendency, construct a coherent pattern for the history it is presenting — individuals are shown or interviewed, events are included, or collected newsreel footage is used, because they have something to contribute to that pattern. Like

the history confronted earlier in this chapter, whatever is present in a documentary is there because it has a purpose, one that is to do with the coherence of the viewpoint from which the documentary is constructed.

There is a tendency to view the documentary film as somehow truthful, to see it as offering some window on the world, to mistake its 'realism' for some unmediated reality. Such a position cannot be supported, for just as the history book and the narrative film establish their meanings through their structure and the forms of their languages, so does the documentary. Its method and style work to conceal the marks of its language, submerging them beneath its references to the real world. As Colin McArthur argues in *Television and History*, "The central ideological function of the narration (i.e., that perspective inscribed in the work) is to confer authority on, and to elide contradictions in, the discourse."[7]

The documentary film structures its material to support its viewpoint, and "its continuity and its attendant realism is of an imaginary order"[8]. The intelligence which might or might not be conveyed in that construction is not at question here: the concern is with the language it uses, and the rules by which it is bound, one of which is that it should entertain. No more or less than narrative fiction, it is, given the demands now being made of production and distribution, obliged to present itself in a way that will command general audience interest, attention and, usually, sympathy.

Surprisingly few Australian documentaries appear outside the context of television. **The Last Tasmanian**[9] and **Menace** are two which have won commercial release in recent years, and both attempt a rewriting of a period of Australian history. **The Last Tasmanian** provides an account of the annihilation of the Tasmanian Aboriginal by those bearing the authority of 19th Century British colonial rule — "the most complete example of genocide on record". The subject of **Menace** is the more recent, unsuccessful attempt by the Menzies Liberal government to outlaw the Communist Party in Australia by means of a referendum.

The makers of the two films expended a considerable effort in their research: **The Last Tasmanian** makes extensive use of the findings of two archaeologists, Rhys Jones and Jim Allen, from the Australian National University, while **Menace** relies on available newsreel

Opposite: Jim Allen in **The Last Tasmanian**.

Rhys Jones (left) studies drawings done of Tasmanian Aboriginals in 1802 with Le Havre museum curator André Maury. **The Last Tasmanian**.

Historian Sir William Crowther who unearthed the bodies of Tasmanian Aboriginals "in the cause of science". **The Last Tasmanian**.

footage and the personal accounts of members of the Communist Party. Both films are committed to a reconstruction of "how it was". **The Last Tasmanian** shares the Tasmanian government's desire (expressed in the film) "to right the wrong that was allowed to occur back in 1878", and endeavoring to make public a neglected aspect of Australian history. **Menace** uses a voice of the dominant ideology, that of the newsreels, to challenge it and its perspective, and to present another view of the historical events. Both films attempt to produce, from their research, a narrative record of the times, generally adhering to a chronological order of events, though not remaining confined by it.

Where the two films differ markedly is in their formal presentation of their material. Rhys Jones has declared that **The Last Tasmanian** "attempts to present its data in a cold, dispassionate way"[10], a view which points to good intentions, but is contradicted by the construction of the film. Its coherence emerges from the voice-over commentary, from the views expressed to the camera by Rhys Jones, and from the interview material. The voice-over, spoken by Leo McKern, is the major linking force in the film, and works to raise the soundtrack to a position of dominance. That is, the viewer is asked to read the images of the film — which range from shots of anthropologist Francois Peron's burial place, to

Tasmanian landscapes, to Jones and Allen fossicking about, to interview subjects, to the closing, moving record of Truganini's state funeral — according to the meaning given them by the imposed verbal exposition. However, the image is not so easily done away with.

At question here is not the need for a rewriting of Australian history, but the form that such an enterprise ought to take. Instead of challenging the way in which that history has been written, **The Last Tasmanian** endorses it — and worse. While the conventional voice of authority, embodied in McKern's theatrical delivery, presents its heavily-structured information in what is too often mistaken for an impartial account, it is difficult to see why most of the images are there at all, for only rarely do they add anything to the historical project of the film. However, they *are* there, and their general effect is to subvert the filmmakers' intentions by trivializing that which they are, as the soundtrack indicates, concerned to expose.

Pertinent here is the celebratory account of the processes of historical research: Jones and his colleagues become the stars of the film, the usefulness of their work remaining unquestioned as the images record their Tasmanian adventure. For example, the commentary tells that their work, based on drawings held at Le Havre, "exactly reproduced the hut where Francois Peron first met the natives", while the synchronized sound carries whispers of

Opposite: **My Brilliant Career**.

The Tasmanian Aboriginals as drawn by Charles Lesueur in 1802. **The Last Tasmanian**.

wonder ("It is a true record? ... Yes!"). The lesson grasped by the historian, Sir William Crowther, expressing his shame ("I disgraced myself") at having exhumed Aboriginal remains for a paper for Melbourne University, is worth repeating: "You can do almost anything when you can plead science as your excuse."

The lesson which can be learned from **The Last Tasmanian** is not some historical truth about the monstrous slaughter that has scarred Tasmania's past, or even some understanding of the way in which white Australia has assumed a position of moral superiority over black Australia. It is that the documentary film-maker, like any other kind of filmmaker, needs to understand his or her work as the product of language rather than as some ready-made reality upon which a reserve of moral indignation can be unleashed.

Menace, though only to a degree, does give attention to some of these issues. In part it can be seen to fall into the same category as **The Last Tasmanian**: McKern is replaced by Paul Lyneham (uncredited), the resonance of McKern's stage and film work by that of Lyneham's connection with the Australian Broadcasting Commission's current affairs program, **Four Corners**.

Lyneham's commentary quite properly challenges the historical perspective of the newsreel footage from the late 1940s and early 1950s, but it also unambiguously imposes an alternative coherence on to the events of the time. However, while it is clear that the film gives its sanction to this particular coherence, the presentation of its original footage — the interview material and the segments from the Pram Factory's production of *Golden Holden* demonstrate an awareness of the processes of historical analysis quite unique in Australian cinema.

Unnamed men and women, and some of their children, recount their experiences during and after the period, their views coinciding, contradicting, or simply varying, all identifying their communist allegiances as the film identifies their different backgrounds. Their point of departure is clearly seen as the distant present, the locations surrounding them as they speak establishing them as they are today. There is no ambiguity about the fact that they are looking back, yet the film insists on the importance of "voices" apart from its own, demanding that we recognize the place of "popular memory" (albeit that of members of a select group) in the construction of the present.

It is worth quoting at length from an interview published originally in *Cahiers du Cinema* in which French philosopher Michel Foucault sees it as essential that an alternative form of history — that of "popular memory" — should confront the dominant modes of the production of history:

"There's a real fight going on ... over what we can roughly describe as 'popular memory'. It's an actual fact that people —

A cartoon from the Melbourne *Guardian* (April 22, 1949) satirizing ex-communist Eric Sharpley. John Hughes' **Menace**.

Advertisement for film on Sharpley's anti-communist tirades. **Menace**.

I'm talking about those who are barred from writing, from producing their books themselves, from drawing up their own historical accounts — that these people nevertheless do have a way of recording history, or remembering it, of keeping it fresh and using it. This popular history was, to a certain extent, even more alive, more clearly formulated in the 19th Century where, for instance, there was a whole tradition of struggle which was transmitted orally, or in writing or songs, etc. A whole number of apparatuses were set up ('popular literature', cheap books, and the stuff that's taught in schools as well) to obstruct the flow of this popular memory ...

"Today, cheap books aren't enough. There are much more effective means, like television and the cinema ... Since memory is actually a very important factor in struggle (really, in fact, struggles develop in a kind of conscious moving forward of history), if one controls people's memories, one controls their dynamism ..., their experience, their knowledge of previous struggles ..."[11]

The function of this "popular memory" is not to propose an alternative truth about the past, or to attempt to set multiple accounts against each other to establish some democratic facade of truth by popular vote. It is, rather, to provide the individual with a sense of his/her place in history, to validate the voices of those who are usually excluded from most of the major channels of communication: the history text books, the popular media, the narrative fictions.

Menace is best understood in this context. Although it bears some residues of conventional histories, its underlying strength is in its understanding that history is not a reconstruction of things as they were, but that it is the production of an attitude. Its attitude lies in its formal qualities which encapsulate its view of historical struggle as one for control of the means by which history is produced.

It remains to draw attention to that factor which is concealed when one chooses to examine films made over a brief period — in this case, the Australian historical films between 1973 (**Libido**) and 1979 (**My Brilliant Career**). And that is that while the fact of representation remains constant from 1897 to 1979, the styles of representation do not. One needs little film education to recognize the level of sophistication which has been achieved in both visual and narrative construction in films during the last decade, and to appreciate that the way in which an historical period is represented today differs markedly from methods employed in the past. This is not the place to embark upon a comparative analysis of, for example, the representations of **Robbery Under Arms** (1958) and **Mad Dog Morgan**. But it is a precondition for an understanding of these and other Australian historical films that they should not be separated from their context as films; i.e., from their context within the history of representations.

Erotic desirability in the world of a girls' school. Peter
Weir's **Picnic at Hanging Rock**.

with warmth, sensuality and independence of
mind, but political integrity.

These dramas of adultery do not assume a
moral dimension; their driving interest once
again is a social one. The marriages of Australian films are not made in heaven, or even
under the stars, but with a worldly eye to comfort and security, emotional as well as material.
The dramatic problem then becomes one of
finding excitement elsewhere, and keeping up
a minimum of acceptable behaviour to maintain the status quo at home. The open recogni-

Personal Relationships and Sexuality

tion of the ritual pretence involved in such
situations lends a depressing air to the films,
which create a world of impossible and
impoverished choices: men are either lovers or
husbands; women are mistresses or wives.
This is intensified by a style of filmmaking
which tends towards comedy of manners, to
clinically observing how people behave, rather
than how they feel. Only in **Petersen** does the
choice between wife and mistress assume the
status of a genuine and complex emotional
conflict not entirely ruled by cynicism, if not
entirely free of self-interest on Petersen's part.

Petersen is one of the few characters in
Australian cinema to create an effect of
individual personality, as well as social type;
where other characters call for recognition —
sympathetic or otherwise — of their behaviour
and situation, Petersen demands empathy.
However, this is achieved in part by a corresponding reduction of all the other characters in
the film to stereotypes of great abstraction: the
'dumb' working-class wife (Jacki Weaver),
who is wise, as well as sweet and patient; the
cowardly, hypocritical academic Kent (Arthur
Dignam); the exploitative mistress Patricia;
the snobbish girl on the make (Helen Morse);
the Women's Liberationists. Petersen's personality is privileged, because he is indeed
surrounded by ciphers.

Don's Party, too, dissects the social rituals
of sexuality in ruthless detail; but this time the
emphasis is on the ritual language of sexual
adventure. Among all the brash and bragging
men at the party, only Cooley (Harold Hopkins) acts almost as much as he talks. For Don
(John Hargreaves) and Mal (Ray Barrett), the
outer limit of stifling but safe suburban
marriage is a drunken conversation about wife-
swapping. The wives snipe on the side-
lines until a certain limit is reached. The
mistress figure, Susan (Clare Binney), and
Simon's wife, Jody (Veronica Lang), hope for
experiences that are not forthcoming.

All the characters show signs of going
beyond the familiar roles of the game, and the
brittle exchange of insult and innuendo which
passes for social intercourse; but each of them
is controlled by an edge of ridicule in the film.
Kerry (Candy Raymond) insists on her right to
an openly independent existence, but she is
also vain and bitchy; her husband Evan (Kit
Taylor) demands recognition of his feelings,
but he is brutal and pig-headed; Simon
(Graeme Blundell) recoils from the prevailing

141

grossness and crudity of the occasion, but he is foolish, effete, and rejected even by his wife.

At the centre of the representation of sexual relationships in Australian cinema is the mark of an impossibility of some kind: in the study of the ways of the tribe, personal difference and individual emotion have very little place. Whether the films explore a milieu that might claim to represent a majority way of life by virtue of being lower-middle-class (**Don's Party**, **The Family Man**), or are explicitly concerned with a sizeable sub-culture, like **The FJ Holden**, the overriding theme is the mechanism of conformity to group norms which dictates down to the last detail the acceptable forms of taking freedoms.

Unritualized male speech in this context assumes a kind of awkward preciousness. In **Don's Party**, Don has a few affectionate moments with a distressed Jenny (Pat Bishop), but the moment is soon overwhelmed with embarrassment. Clyde (John Wood) in **The Office Picnic** tries to talk to Mara (Kate Fitzpatrick), whom he has ingloriously screwed briefly against a car after a long seduction of rudeness and hostility, but his fear and sexual repression show up much too clearly and she is no longer interested. In **The FJ Holden**, Kevin (Paul Couzens) drunkenly tries to express his feelings to the mate whose constant presence has cost him his girlfriend, but receives, in return, defensive reaffirmations of the male sharing ethos which have caused the problem in the first place.

Speech between women, however, flows

freely when permitted. This often takes the form of an exchange of common wisdom (usually about men) which is silenced when the sexes meet: Anne (Eva Dickinson) briefly shares her pain and anger with a girlfriend at the party in **The FJ Holden**, before Kevin bursts in and starts swearing; the women in **Don's Party** begin a conversation about sexuality, which is verging on the topic of lesbianism, when the men drift back and it stops.

These films are concerned with an essentially segregated society; men and women have separate worlds, and an encounter between them is fraught with difficulty. In films with a different orientation — **Caddie**, **Promised Woman**, **Mouth to Mouth** — moments of intimacy between women are warmer, more developed and less constrained by a definition in terms of a simple opposition to male bonding. But before looking at the films, which to some extent relieve the gloom surrounding relationships, there is another group which

Mara (Kate Fitzpatrick) and Clyde (John Wood). Tom Cowan's **The Office Picnic**.

insists on the conflict of opposites and on a certain social impossibility: those which look to the mysteries of nature, and project a resolution of sexual antagonism which is outside the confines of realist space and time.

In Tom Cowan's **The Office Picnic**, nature provides a means of escape for the two lovers: in the picnic ground they find the possibility of disappearing from the world of rigid social codes and hostile segregation which leaves no place for their affection. In his next film, **Journey Among Women**, the bush is a place which allows the escaped convict women to invent a female culture with a sexuality, language and group ritual which opposes, term for term, the male world of the coastal settlement. Nature nourishes a transcendence of the confinements imposed on women by 'masculine' civilization, which is impossible within them. **Picnic at Hanging Rock** also uses the

Escaped convicts in the bush forge a new, female culture. **Journey Among Women**.

theme of women who vanish into the embrace of nature, although its imagery of 'femininity' is quite different. The women of Cowan's film are strong and openly sexual; the girls in **Picnic** are fragile and delicate blossoms, and the bare hint of a certain eroticism in their embraces is absorbed in a worship of the beauties of 'intact' maidenhood.

However, each film makes poetry out of sexual polarization. **Picnic** is full of oppositions (masculine/feminine, Australian/European, vulgarity/cultivation) and stereotypes (the fat girl, the orphan, the Olympian headmistress, the lovely French mistress). Their banality is rescued by the beauty of the images, which at the same time intensifies their rigidity. There is a kind of sexual hierarchy in **Picnic**, with a form of happy animality being the province of the lower classes. The sensual and already worldly charms of the dark-haired Irma (Jane Vallis) are of a higher order; but it is the ethereal loveliness of blonde Miranda (Anne Lambert) that is the pinnacle of desirability. Miranda, however, is the chosen one of the rock, reserved for a meeting with a strange and phallic force of nature which takes her beyond the impure physicality of this world. **Picnic** is the positive and lyrical expression of the devaluation of a realized female sexuality which dominates the men of **The Office Picnic**.

In Colin Eggleston's **Long Weekend** (1978), there is a deadly conflict between perverse and urban human beings and the natural world. The couple (John Hargreaves and

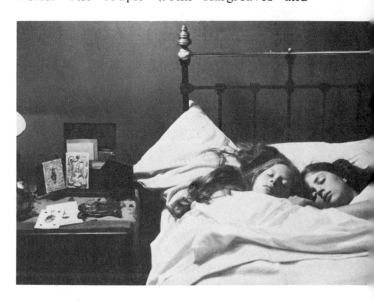

Two delicate blossoms. **Picnic at Hanging Rock**.

Above: Kevin (Paul Couzens) with his girlfriend Anne (Eva Dickinson) in her bedroom. **The FJ Holden**. Below: Tentative lovers: Tim (Ian Gilmour) and Carrie (Kim Krejus). John Duigan's **Mouth to Mouth**.

Briony Behets) are carelessly destructive of natural things and viciously destructive in their relationships to one another. In the centre of this film is an identification of abortion as the ultimate crime against nature; what is worse, the abortion is the outcome of an infidelity. In the dunes of a strange seaside wasteland, nature rises up in revenge.

It is interesting that three foreign films made in Australia all use images of a nature to set up studies in polarization. The most trivial of these, Michael Powell's **Age of Consent** (1969), based on a novel by Norman Lindsay, uses Australia as a tropical paradise in which painter and urban refugee Brad (James Mason) meets innocent and apple-munching nature girl Cora (Helen Mirren); male artist meets female life force and the inevitable happens.

Nicolas Roeg's **Walkabout** (1971) and Ted Kotcheff's **Wake in Fright** look to the more austere image of the interior. In **Walkabout**, the desert is a surreal meeting place of two races: two ways of ordering relationships to other people and the land. The young Aboriginal (Gulpilil) saves the white children (Jenny Agutter and Lucien John) from a desert of monotony and death, and teaches them to find in it a place of variety and life. But the communication he establishes with the little boy is not so easily sustained with the girl, who is wiser in the ways of her race, and death is the outcome for the black man from white (female) presence on his territory.

Wake in Fright places its harrowing vision of ruthless sexual segregation and violent repression in the context of an industrialized desert hell. The environment is a brutalizing one; but there is a difference between the lethal monotony of the tiny settlement at the beginning of the film, and the crazed violence of the mining town, which is purely man-made — the cruel conditions of labor which underlie the town's sense of amusement.

There is a certain gendering of nature in some of these films: nature is in firm affinity with the feminine in **Age of Consent** and **Journey Among Women**, for example, and with phallic force in **Picnic at Hanging Rock**. More intense, however, is a sense of 'here' and 'there', of the possibilities provided by a place which is other and elsewhere. The park in **The Office Picnic**, the bush refuge in **Journey Among Women**, the changing interior landscapes known to the Aboriginal in **Walkabout** and the rock in **Picnic at Hanging Rock**, all

continue to lure those who remain behind — or to leave their trace on those who, like Lizzy (Jeune Pritchard) in **Journey Among Women** and the white girl in **Walkabout**, went 'there' and returned.

Oppositions of place set up important shifts of definition between those who in some sense belong — to a group, a culture, a particular way of life — and those who don't. The young teacher (Gary Bond) in **Wake in Fright** is marked by his outsider status, which brings upon him a fearful education in the ways of the 'here' of the mining town. Otherness can be a source of both attraction — offering something which cannot be realized in a here and now — or a source of repulsion, an occasion for persecution.

The concern with 'placing' is not restricted to the films explicitly drawing upon an imagery of natural landscape in their portrayal of sexual and social relations; it plays an essential part in the way sexuality has been linked to a problem of social identity in Australian films. So pervasive is the tendency to stereotype (which places characters and their environments in a special way) and to organize types into relationships which highlight opposition — from the extreme, schematic simplicity of **Jack and Jill** to the complex arrangements of **Picnic** — that

Lovers in a bush retreat: Gay Steele and Phillip Deamer in **The Office Picnic**.

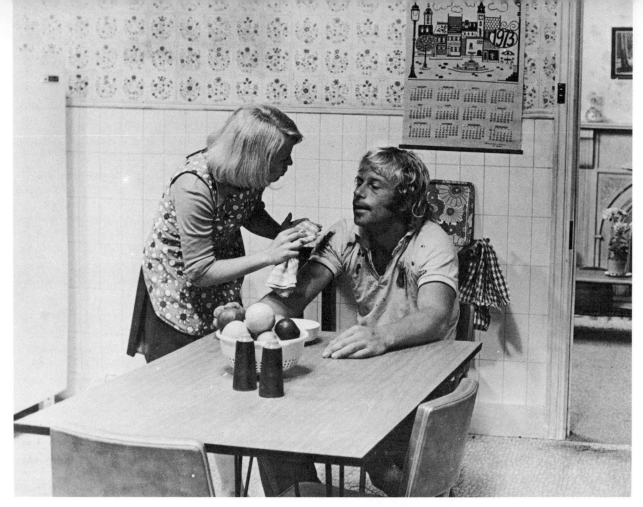

Petersen (Jack Thompson) with his wife (Jacki Weaver) in their working-class world. **Petersen**.

one wonders what function this serves for the films.

It is worth insisting that stereotyping is a highly formalized way of defining a figure by a few essential characteristics sanctified as typical by convention; it is not a debased or inferior form of art beside the greater refinement of something else. It depends on a cultivation of the precise things which characterize a person, a place or an object in an immediately convincing way. Stereotyping, in fact, is an art of identification and recognition; in a sense, it makes it possible to control difference by making it easily interpretable. Petersen, for example, is muscular because he is working-class and a footballer; Kent is slender and ascetic because he is an academic.

Within **Petersen** these details bring out the exact contours of their antagonism; it is of no consequence that in reality, and in other films, tradesmen can be weedy and academics athletic. What matters is the contribution of these details to the coherence of the film; in this case, the contrasting of Petersen's physicality with the insidious emotional violence wreaked by middle-class academia.

This technique calls for a kind of bonding response from the audience. The film demands a reaction of recognition and consent, an acceptance that the images are in conformity with a shared mythology of the typical — the typically masculine, feminine, working-class, middle-class Australian. In **The FJ Holden**, leaving aside the image of the car, an entire way of life can be summoned by a close-up of a garden gnome, or by a man's hand popping a can out of the window of a car. In Thornhill's first feature, **Between Wars** (1974), the difference of Marguerite (Patricia Leehy) from the others is conveyed by her dress and make-up; her sexuality (nymphomania) is defined in her startling emeralds and scarlets, which stand out flamboyantly in the cramped little world of the country town.

These movements towards generalization bond things together, although in an oddly ambiguous way. There is a process of holding figures up to be surveyed and identified, which places them at a distance, and virtually calls upon the audience to play anthropologist to their own culture. At the same time, however, the shared recognition of the typical feeds a sense that a unity and identity of some kind actually exists. This responds, perhaps, to the

146

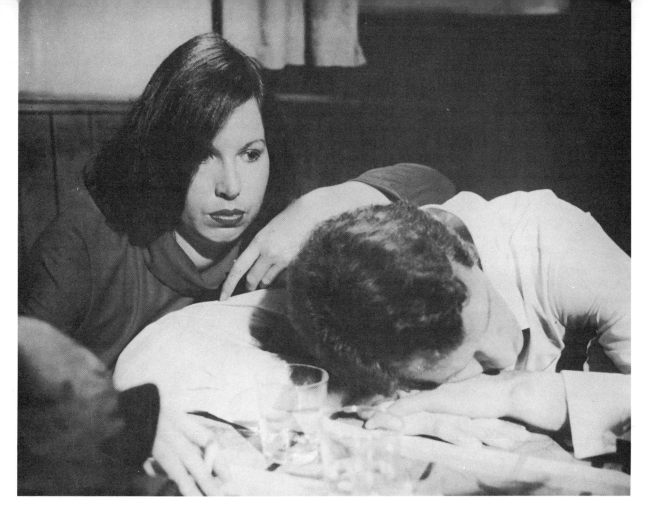

Image of nymphomania: Patricia Leehy as Marguerite (with Corin Redgrave as Dr Trenbow). Michael Thornhill's **Between Wars**.

same problem which is present as a theme in many of the films — the need for a conformity of some kind in a small world full of antagonisms and incompatibilities.

In films which emphasize mateship, and group cohesion among men, one of the functions of women — like foreigners and homosexuals — is to establish an alien difference that assures the group of its identity. Difference can be menacing when it exposes a real vulnerability, as it does for the young soldier Bill (John Jarratt) in 'The Odd Angry Shot, whose dream fuses the girlfriend who has deserted him with the image of the frightening alien statue outside a Vietnamese temple. Another example occurs in the strenuously competitive, all-male working world of Ken Hannam's **Sunday Too Far Away** when one of the shearers (Sean Scully) writes to his wife and finds himself treated as a queer. Difference can also provoke complacent hilarity: the boys in **The FJ Holden** have their harmless fun terrorizing a "wog" in his car; and the men interviewed in a pub in **The Naked Bunyip** sway together in aggressive laughter when questioned about homosexuality.

It is the function of the bonding ritual that counts, and any argument about the rationality or rightness of its content is quite irrelevant. Participation in a ritual of this kind is very much the pleasure offered by films like **Stork, Alvin Purple, Barry McKenzie, Petersen, The Odd Angry Shot** — precisely those films most often taken to task for their sexism — and also by the more clinical perspective set up in **Don's Party** and **Libido**.

It is curious that when such films represent people who are outsiders or marginal in some way — the bikies in **Petersen**, the feminists in **Stork** and **Petersen**, the feeble Simon in **Don's Party** — the characterization can move towards caricature in the negative sense, to weakness and implausibility. In **The Family Man**, for example, the women whom the boys pick up on their night out are given a 'liberated', sub-cultural aura, and one is left with a sense of incredulity that women from that sub-culture would ever go anywhere with those men.

This may only be striking, however, for filmgoers who are bikies, feminists, or feeble; and for whom the film suddenly functions as the instrument of a polarization, breaking up

147

the process of cultural identification invited by the prospect of an 'Australian' film. Canadian Ted Kotcheff's **Wake in Fright** has become a curious touchstone of Australian cinema, perhaps for this reason. For those who can make the fascinated horror of the outsider's perception their own, **Wake in Fright** is one of the most powerful films about that distinctive blend of repression, violence and segregation which is one of the conditions of sexuality in Australian society. For those who do not respond to that vision, it is, at best, a passable fantasy of a 'foreigner'.

Yet the strength of **Wake in Fright** is that it does not pretend to represent a national culture in any sense; and those films which show some signs of treating relationships with a degree of emotional depth and compassion are precisely those that admit to a fragmented and diverse Australia, and which refrain from imposing the weight of generality too heavily upon their characters: **The Office Picnic**, **Promised Woman**, **Caddie**, **The FJ Holden**, **Third Person Plural** and **Mouth to Mouth**. This is not to say they are the best films in some sense, or to argue that none share the attraction for dualisms and stereotypes in other films, but rather that in their move away from cultural centralizing they allow for relationships to become one of their real subjects.

Each of these films is concerned with a particular social group, and sometimes they place

Mates, some beer and a car: images of an Australian male stereotype. Carl Stever and Kevin Couzens in **The FJ Holden**.

the audience in the position of observing and recognizing characteristic behaviour. **The Office Picnic**, and particularly **The FJ Holden**, depict office workers and Bankstown youth respectively in this kind of way. But, at the same time, they show people responding to the social constraints of their lives, rather than simply acting out and demonstrating them for the audience. These films go behind group rituals, and show the strain they place on individuals bound by them, as well as the curious pleasures they provide.

In the pain and confusion of Clyde in **The Office Picnic**, left behind for reasons that he cannot understand, coldly keeping his new girlfriend at a distance as he looks for an answer to his loneliness and abandonment, there is something which does not find an expression in the fleeting, serious moments of mateship or the awkward moments of intimacy with women. In **The FJ Holden**, also, few words are 'wasted' on emotion; Anne carries out her drudgery at home with her father and brothers in a silence broken only by greetings and orders — information necessary for the basic movements of everyday life. Her revolt against the painful absurdity of her relationship with Kevin is sudden and sharp; and the failure of Kevin's attempt at the reconciliation that Anne too might desire — if only things could be different — is a failure born out of a way of life where the language of directly and simply expressed emotion is almost non-existent. But the film manages to make the reality of that emotion all the more strongly felt. In one scene, Anne tells her girlfriend how rarely they were alone together, and how often Kevin and his mates were drunk. And as Kevin gets drunk with his mate, before staggering in to find Anne, one follows through a kind of social inevitability, but it is not just an observation of a set of animated social abstractions in operation. Both characters demand understanding from the audience, and neither is a caricature. If the film makes no suggestions that a different future or a different life is likely to follow, **The FJ Holden** does allow for the aspect of human relations which depends not *only* on social determination, but on chance, uncertainty and poor timing.

James Ricketson's **Third Person Plural** is not set in the world of silent suburban family dinners; its four characters, drawn together by the pleasures of boating, do very little but talk about relationships and the meaning of life.

Opposite: **Mouth to Mouth**.

Wide-eyed Beth (Margaret Cameron) and world-wise Terry (George Shevtsov). James Ricketson's **Third Person Plural**.

Much of this talk is trite and silly, but the film does achieve something rare in Australian cinema: it creates a group of characters, each with his or her own obsessions and eccentricities. Mark (Bryan Brown), for example, is straight, clean-cut and serious, and it is hard to think of another filmmaker who would allow such a potentially conventional character to have a passion for ants and miracles. So, although the film remains mostly on the level of debate about the desirable, rather than that of desire itself, the small and unsensational developments become engaging. One relationship — that between Mark and Danny (Linden Wilkinson) — comes rather painfully to nothing; the other one has some promise when the wide-eyed Beth (Margaret Cameron) accepts the greater wisdom of the view of the world held by Terry (George Shevtsov).

Of the films predominantly concerned with relationships, those which constantly generate a sense of warmth for all their characters are **Caddie**, **Promised Woman** and **Mouth to Mouth**. This is not necessarily a virtue, but in the context of Australian cinema it is certainly a relief. Although **Caddie** is based on an autobiography, and **Promised Woman** details some of the day-to-day experiences of a migrant woman arriving in Sydney, these two films have the charm of unabashed fiction films; they have little of the sense of dramatized documentary that is present in most other films, to a greater or lesser degree. Caddie (Helen Morse) floats through the passage from comfortable gentility to barmaiding, and on through the Depression, always surrounded by an aura of "class"; she remains, at all times, a heroine. While **Caddie** is episodic, **Promised Woman** has a strongly developed story; Antigone (Yelena Zigon) arrives for an arranged marriage with a difficult past behind her and an awkward future, since her age has been hidden from her proposed husband (Nikos Gerissimou). In the developments there is actually an element of psychological suspense.

Mouth to Mouth combines narrative and character development with a firm commitment to social observation: the four young people — two girls having escaped from a home; two boys drifting around unemployed — setting up a home in an abandoned power

Carrie drifts into prostitution, in the 'male' world of the pub. **Mouth to Mouth**.

station have a complexity which is as imaginative as it is plausible. There is a certain schematization at work: the boys are distinguished partly in terms of their origin — Serge (Sergio Frazzeto) is Italian and exuberant, and Tim (Ian Gilmour) is a timid country boy; the girls in terms of their future — Jeannie (Sonia Peat) is recaptured, but has managed to establish a warm relationship with Serge, while Carrie (Kim Krejus) drifts into the city and her beginnings as a prostitute. Nevertheless, the delicate balance between showing the remorseless constraints of the economic situation they are in, and creating a sense of identification with the individual characters, gives **Mouth to Mouth** a subtlety and an openness which takes it well beyond sociological generalization.

These three films, in their different ways, place sexual relationships off-centre in their dramatic development. For the Greek woman absorbed in her past and trying to adapt to a new society, for the barmaid trying to feed her children, and for the young people staying one step ahead of the police, work and money are of pressing importance. But, and perhaps for that reason, sexual relationships are not symbolic of other problems, although they can be inextricable from them. At the same time, the various characters have differences of personality — they do not simply illustrate the range of behaviour acceptable in their given social milieu — and the main characters, at least, can be changeable, have moods, seem unaccountable or inaccessible to others, be inconsistent, and transform their wishes and desires during the development of the film.

They also have a variety of feelings for others: in Caddie's interactions with her children, and her friendships with Josie (Jacki Weaver) and Leslie (Melissa Jaffer), in Antigone's contacts with the other boarders as well as in her shifting relations with the two brothers, and between all the characters of **Mouth to Mouth**, there is a sense of the emotional shading of small moments. There are nuances of affection, understanding, anxiety or distance which can come into being, without being raised and abstracted to the status of an immutable collision of opposing forces. These films stand out as distinctive,

Len (Bryan Brown) with his estranged wife, Barbara (Kris McQuade). Stephen Wallace's **Love Letters from Teralba Road**.

perhaps because Australian mainstream cinema has so far been largely concerned with other things.

The films so far discussed in this chapter are full-length features, all directed by men. There are different treatments of sexuality and relationships in a number of short films — many of them, like Margot Nash's **We Aim to Please** (1977), and Jeni Thornley's **Maidens** (1976), were made explicitly to provide an alternative image of female sexuality and of women's relationships to other women. In a broader context, **Mouth to Mouth**, for example, seems less unusual if compared with Stephen Wallace's **Love Letters from Teralba Road** (1977), James Ricketson's **Drifting** (1976), and Gillian Armstrong's **The Singer and the Dancer** (1977).

While these short films — like **Mouth to Mouth** and **Promised Woman** — are still seen by comparatively few people, they do point to new possibilities which Australian films have rarely taken up so far; and, without them, one might be obliged to conclude that despite a certain emphasis on sexuality as a form of social behaviour, a representation of personal relationships in Australian cinema has been so far virtually non-existent.

9 LONELINESS AND ALIENATION

Rod Bishop and Fiona Mackie

Australian cinema has only tentatively examined the complex forms of alienation and loneliness found in Australian culture. Alienation exists between classes, between generations and between sexes. There is evidence of our alienation from nature, from history and, at times, from our own personalities.

The monotony most Australians experience in their routine lives points to an inner alienation, a separation from their own perceptions. They accept the image bestowed on them by society and ignore the chances to create their own from the abundance of raw material around them. Barraged by pressures and numbed by habit, they become more easily manipulated, losing their spontaneity, creativity and, eventually, their hope.

Nearly a decade separates **2000 Weeks** (1969) and **Newsfront** (1978). During those intervening years, Australia experienced the Vietnam war, conscription, five federal elections, six prime ministers, inflation, recession, soaring unemployment, the sacking of the Whitlam government, cynical manipulations of electoral and government processes, and the emergence of more than 100 feature films. By contrast, Australian social and political history in the two decades before 1969 was one of safe, dormant, conservative rule, sustained by intense economic expansion.

2000 Weeks courageously tackled themes of cultural nationalism and personal politics, but found little sympathy from critics or the box-office. **Newsfront** incorporated the same themes, and found local and international acclaim from critics and public. While **Newsfront** is clearly the superior film, both treat their subjects with the same verisimilitude, use similar narrative development and, at times, identical situations.

The main characters in **Newsfront** and **2000 Weeks** are media functionaries — reporters, writers, news cameramen, artistes, television producers — professional careerists whose personal relationships are treated with the same honesty as their public lives. Both films climax with their protagonists violently rejecting old friends who have sold out to international and commercial interests.

In **Newsfront**, Len (Bill Hunter), a news cameraman, confronts his brother Frank (Gerard Kennedy), an expatriate television producer, and knocks back his offer to work for a lucrative American television company. In the concluding sequence from **2000 Weeks**, Will (Mark McManus), a young writer, brawls with his oldest childhood friend Noel (David Turnbull), an expatriate television producer, refusing any notion of compromise with British television. In both films the women in their lives witness the final breakdown of the men's lifelong friendships, and watch Len and Will stride away from the confrontation, a sense of national dignity swelling within them.

As 'heroes', Len and Will are 'little battlers', aware of British and American control of the Australian media, and resisting this pressure with nationalistic fervor and moral dignity. Both films are consciously set within historical epochs, **2000 Weeks** defiantly summing up the isolationist attitudes and parochial values that masqueraded as national sentiment in the 1960s. When Noel returns from England, Will is close to a breakdown, his career in crisis and his lover (Jeanie Drynan) leaving for the 'old country'.

Noel taunts Will with his competitive drive: "Expatriates come back to plunder Australia, like commandoes on a raid." He is the ultimate destroyer of Will's life, taking Will's girlfriend and writing off his one chance to collaborate on a television drama series: "No one's ever heard of you in England", he says. "Why should they", retorts Will, "I work in Australia."

At the end of **Newsfront**, Len's final response to Frank is a short and succinct: "Get stuffed, mate." In **2000 Weeks**, this sentiment

Opposite: Phillip Adams and Brian Robinson's **Jack and Jill: A Postscript**.

153

Above: Will (Noel McManus) with girlfriend Jacky (Jeanie Drynan). Right: Will and Noel (David Turnbull) during a university lecture. Tim Burstall's **2000 Weeks**.

is given a more explicit form. Before Will comes to blows with Noel, he delivers a final verbal barrage: "You are morally corrupt. Sold out your principles. Gone over to the other side."

The entire drama of **2000 Weeks** is seen through Will's eyes; his personal anxiety is the main focus of action. Surrounded by lost opportunities and second chances, he represents the consciousness of the film, a middle-class careerist striving for national recognition and meaning in his personal life. Will achieves neither, but finds limited salvation in his own sense of personal dignity. People and events only enter his life when he can't keep them out. Unable to express himself, Will is a helpless witness to the collapse of his personal relationships.

Yet the sympathy generated by writer-director Tim Burstall is somehow misplaced. Will's passivity is too intimate and too solitary to be entirely convincing. Will is alienated from his culture, and some historical analysis is suggested, but the promise of more deeply ingrained reasons for his malaise are left unfulfilled. Noel, with his inconsiderate, cruel expatriatism, is too easily cast as the dark force. By contrast, Len's heroic exit in **Newsfront** is set in a wider historical context, generating greater sympathy for a character who has weathered many crises and identified the genuine social and political forces that have 'conspired' to entrench his inherent conservatism.

Newsfront touches on many seemingly

154

unrelated issues: British and American control of Australian culture, immigration, Australian combat heroism, the Communist Referendum, women's oppression, the introduction of television and the hardening of American media control, and the influence of Catholicism on personal and political morality.

The film opens with a kaleidoscope of 1950s images, ending on a group of immigrants coming to the promised land. Work opportunities and higher standards of living have drawn these people to Australia, but the structure of the international workforce has pulled their families apart, broken down traditional bonds and developed a new form of class structure.

While the migrants have a better than even chance of becoming 'factory fodder' for Australian secondary industry, the media workers of **Newsfront** are similarly drawn into the international market. Geoff (Bryan Brown), the editor of Cinetone, leaves Australia for England, believing it the "best place for ageing radicals". Frank returns to Australia, treating Len as a country bumpkin and Australia as a naive and exploitable market. Frank and Geoff become increasingly alienated from their cultural roots. Documentary footage of a migrant renouncing his country at a naturalization ceremony becomes an image of what Frank has done to himself. The introduction of television increases American domination of Australian media. Competition for media coverage gets fiercer. Len's footage is doctored. News must be spectacular; therefore, it must be manipulated. Distorted news becomes distorted history.

Frank (Gerard Kennedy) with Amy (Wendy Hughes). Phillip Noyce's **Newsfront**.

155

Len (Bill Hunter), the company man, with Amy. **Newsfront**.

Accepted power structures serve as another alienating force. The director of Newsco, the newsreel company Len works for, is the archetypal, patriarchal authority; as he is to his men, so they are to their families. Sexual roles alienate husband and wife, and woman from woman. Fay's (Angela Punch) unswerving loyalty to Catholicism and her children help mould her as a candidate for the housewife neurosis of the 1950s. Increased competition for media positions erodes personal friendships, and the tightly-knit group who helped build their friends' houses in 1948 become increasingly isolated from each other. Len admits, "I'm 50 years-old and I'm lonely", only to be told, "You suffer from an excess of hope."

When Frank offers Len the final sell-out, Len's rebuttal embodies the film's strongest sentiment: moral dignity as the last cultural defence. Amy (Wendy Hughes) explains it in the only way Frank can understand: "He's just a bit old-fashioned." In fact, Len is much more. A company man who defends Newsco for "the little blokes it helped during the depression", a Labor voter with no apparent radical sentiments, his personal code of ethics is that of a self-centred patriarch. Len's fundamentalism is a thin disguise for his true reactionary nature. He clings to his nationalist sentiments for their sense of dignity and positive emotive qualities.

Newsfront shows the social, political and personal pressures that mould Len, and if the film has a succinct political point to make, it is that cultural imperialism trivializes and demoralizes a culture. **Newsfront** counters this with waves of parochial nationalism, striking a nerve with audiences and critics. But as an essentially reactionary proposition, it deserves considerable critical attention.

If **Newsfront** and **2000 Weeks** dwell on questionable nationalist sentiments to achieve a sense of optimism and dignity, the central characters of Esben Storm's **27A** (1973) and Jim Sharman's **The Night The Prowler** (1978) are trapped within closed environments, their dignity destroyed by an overwhelming feeling of irrelevance to a world beyond their reach.

Billy (Robert McDarra), the protagonist of **27A**, leaves skid row for the confines of a mental institution, his alcohol problem being more than he can bear. Felicity (Kerry Walker), the focal point of **The Night The Prowler**, is young, and born at the top of the scale where all the benefits of upper-middle-class status define her inevitable future. Laws and locked doors keep Billy in a concrete prison, and Storm uses stark realism to convey Billy's experience, while Sharman uses exaggerated surrealism to show how Felicity is trapped by the insulation and false values of the middle class. Each film focuses on a character, but there is a strong sense of all characters being trapped.

Billy, self-interned to get treatment for his alcoholism, is subjected to institutional demoralization. Marched down to a communal washroom, he is undressed and shamed by a sadistic male nurse. Billy's outrage is interpreted as an inability to co-operate. His visitors

Robert McDarra (left) as Billy, interned in a mental institution as a 'cure' for his alcoholism. Esben Storm's **27A**.

Felicity (Kerry Walker) in her virginal, middle-class bedroom. Jim Sharman's **The Night The Prowler**.

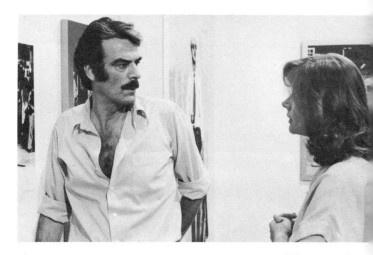

A clash of cultures: Greek taxi-driver Kostas (Takis Emmanuel) at the art exhibition organized by Carol (Wendy Hughes). Paul Cox's **Kostas**.

are stopped. Isolated, he communicates by tapping on the wall. His light is turned on and off by a guard outside his room. Billy has lost control over the simplest decisions of his life. Purposeless bodies sit staring into space. Four men hold down an inmate and inject him. Billy stages a fit, runs away and gets back on the drink. He is found on a park bench and returned to the institution. Sitting again before the middle-class psychiatrist he says: "You're the doctor and I'm the patient. But you've never been there. You've only got the postcards somebody sent you." The gulf between 'custodian' and 'inmate' is built into the system.

When Billy tries to reach "The Authority" he finds only a bureaucracy. He gets no treatment for his alcohol problem. He tries to get discharged, but "The Committee" only meets once a year. He then learns his wife is dying and escapes once again. He finds her in a coma, now part of the same sterilized institutional atmosphere that confined him. Eighteen months later he is still interned. Esben Storm has highlighted the alienation inherent in such institutions. Billy, as 'inmate', is a powerless victim of bureaucracy. Branded as misfits and problems, inmates are prime targets for inhuman manipulation.

In **The Night The Prowler** a different prison is explored. Felicity is caught in the web of upper-middle-class respectability, with its hypocrisy and petty values. Since childhood, her parents have treated her like a doll. Felicity, protected from any real contact with life, is caught in a private drama. She acts out

her neuroses and stages the loss of her virginity, winning release from her parents' preoccupation and the hold it gives them over her. Romantically, she searches for meaning among the down-and-outs in the park at night.

Felicity's attempts to break out unfold as further reflections of her vacuum. Surrounded by trivia and artificiality, she has no sense of meaning. Her parents want a delicate girl whom they can wrap up like a chocolate box and present, intact, to a worthy husband with appropriate status. And status means money — to the parents, the neighbors, to everyone.

Billy and Felicity are at opposite ends of the class spectrum, fighting the same stultifying pressures: a lack of control over their destiny; an immense sense of loneliness; and a belief that "the better things of life" lie beyond the divisions of class. **The Night The Prowler** highlights the process of alienation by caricature, more symbolic than realistic.

The caricature in films with migrant themes more often seems an unintended consequence of the filmmaker's distance from a different culture. The migrant experience is fraught with alienation — through the stigma of cultural difference and the pressures on the margins between cultures. Paul Cox's **Kostas** (1979) caricatures these pressures. The formal, old-fashioned passion of Kostas (Takis Emmanuel), the Greek taxi-driver, for an independent middle-class Australian woman, Carol (Wendy Hughes), comes across as a stereotype, while the situation gives a smug perspective on the unassailability of the barriers of class and culture. Kostas' audacity in pressing himself

157

Cathy (Michele Fawdon) waits as Dick (Alan Cassell), the journalist who is helping her find her child, talks to a Greek contact. Donald Crombie's **Cathy's Child**.

forward becomes acceptable in the light of his professional journalistic past, cut short by political resistance (presumably against the Greek junta). But this is left unclear and reflects the indifference of the Australian film-maker to a seminal political experience. Paul Cox is only interested in establishing Kostas' credentials as a worthy partner for Carol. Since he is not above his station, the romance gains our blessing and the bulk of working-class Greeks are thereby obliquely put down; for them, presumably, the barriers remain invincible.

Considerably more empathy with Greek culture is shown in **Cathy's Child** (1979) and **Promised Woman** (1975). In **Cathy's Child**, sensitive performances by Alan Cassell (Dick) and Michele Fawdon (Cathy) portray the growth of understanding between a hard-bitten Australian journalist and a lonely Maltese woman fighting to retrieve a daughter

abducted by her Greek husband. When Cathy first goes to the press for help, the busy newspaper office seems alien and sinister, offering a view of Australian culture through a migrant's eyes. As the journalists brush her aside, one feels Cathy's exhausted familiarity with their typical misunderstanding. When they investigate her story, the endless anomalies of Australian bureaucracy and law are revealed. These pressures have left her unprotected against exploitation by her husband and his friends, their prejudices licensed by the male orientation so deeply ingrained in Greek culture.

This is also the theme of **Promised Woman**. A marriage arranged through letters brings Antigone (Yelena Zigon) to Sydney. But Telis (Nikos Gerissimou), the prospective husband, finds Antigone older and more experienced than the pliant bride he expected, and is no longer interested in marriage. As Antigone moves from job to job, the film hovers be-

Antigone (Yelena Zigon), the Greek 'bride' who comes to Australia but is left unwed when her husband-to-be decides she is too old. Tom Cowan's **Promised Woman**.

tween empathy and stereotype. Telis' mother (Thea Sevastos) haunts Antigone as the caricatured black Greek widow, reduced to irrelevance by her son's adjustment to Australia. Antigone grapples with her memory, and the old culture loses its hold, giving the film an assimilationist perspective that would be a flaw without the critique embodied in the character of Telis. His denial of life and commitment to work as the price of success are contrasted with Antigone's determined attempts to maintain the spirit of her culture while finding a personal liberation.

In **Caddie** (1976), a similar theme is set in a historical context. Caddie (Helen Morse) is separated from her husband and forced away from the comforts of middle-class security. She is divested of the only socially-acceptable role available for women: that of wife and mother. Sydney, during the 1920s and 1930s, presents her with little alternative. When married, she had an acceptable status, though she was isolated from the struggles of the world and from the development of her personality.

Confronting the realities of working-class life, she finds herself naive and unprepared. Nobody is interested in renting a house to a single mother and children, and what accommodation she does find is flea-infested. Baby-sitters treat the children with contempt and they become seriously ill. A barmaid's job introduces Caddie to the bluntness of working-class life, and her friendship with Josie (Jacki Weaver) breaks down some of the distance and competition forced on women through divisions in the class structure. But they are still alienated from control over their lives; even their own reproduction. A pregnancy is only terminated by an illegal backyard abortion.

Caddie's journey from the security of married life becomes a battle to survive in a world organized by men. Being seen as a sex object is a central alienation which haunts her. As a wife she was protected, but as a single mother Caddie faces all the constraints on her independence that society can muster. Her delayed divorce and custody of the children are final legal wedges that separate Caddie from her Greek lover, Peter (Takis Emmanuel). This time, law and bureaucracy take control of her life. Having supported her children and fought for independence, she remains legally confined and entangled by her marriage. But Caddie's children and her working-class friends provide the warmth and honesty missing from her middle-class marriage.

Caddie (Helen Morse) with her Greek lover, Peter (Takis Emmanuel). Donald Crombie's **Caddie**.

The monotonous pressure of everyday routine helps stifle the emotional lives of the central characters in **Caddie**, **27A** and **The Night The Prowler**. Yet these routines are often the only means of survival. The *angst* of this double-bind is reflected in the low-budget cinema that emerged after 1968.

The three intersecting stories of **Palm Beach** (1979) are set in the hedonistic world of the Barrenjoey Peninsula. The characters relate to this flagrant display of wealth in different ways, and their stories are presented as different faces of the same prism. The mother grieving for her runaway daughter, the unemployed neurotic surfie, the cryptic drug undercover agent and the searching detective are equally authentic, and audiences can watch the negative chemistry produced as the characters intersect. At every possible chance, they exploit each other without realizing they are exploiting themselves. Commercialism is consuming the surf scene, once an escape and a viable alternative lifestyle. A continuous radio soundtrack preys on their lifestyle, reminding the characters of their obligation to the dominant culture. The mass media moulds the commercial 'hype', effectively eroding meaningful personal relationships.

The human texture of **Love Letters From Teralba Road** (1977) arises from the real love letters from which the film drew its inspiration. Trapped by mechanical factory work, Len (Bryan Brown) struggles to express his genuine emotions. But the sexual barriers that mould and imprison are the basis of Barbara's (Kris McQuade) determined attempts to reject Len's unconscious pressure to restrain and confine her. The boredom of their daily routine tests the strength of their love and their capacity to resist the pressures of industrialism that threaten to erode it.

A less assured, but equally significant, attempt to identify these forces is found in **Jack and Jill: A Postscript** (1970) — an attempt to probe a union between Jack (Anthony Ward), a working-class bikie, and Jill (Judy Leech), an affluent, middle-class girl struggling against her mother's protectiveness. Their relationship is a conflict of class cultures; Jack's inner torment being an inability to communicate with Jill's desire to cross a class barrier.

The fantasy of escape from oppressive working-class conditions is an equally dominant theme. In **Queensland** (1976), two ageing factory workers summon their last reserves, determined to leave industrial Melbourne for the sun and easy life of Queensland. But extricating themselves from family and friends is an emotional wrench, and the film builds to a painful confrontation. The final image of Doug (John Flaus) pushing his broken-down car along a Collingwood street, underscores his manic determination to make the final psychological break.

Similarly, **Pure S . . .** (1975) concludes with a car full of desperate heroin junkies heading for a new life in Queensland. Their FJ might take them 3000 km, but their drug habits will travel with them. In **Out of It** (1976), three working-class youths botch a warehouse robbery and head for Queensland to escape the police. Their car breaks down, and is eventually stolen. They run out of

Paul (Bryan Brown) holds up a supermarket in Albie Thoms' **Palm Beach**.

Len (Bryan Brown) and Barbara (Kris McQuade). Steven Wallace's **Love Letters From Teralba Road**.

The beach scene in Phillip Adams and Brian Robinson's **Jack and Jill: A Postscript**.

money and enthusiasm, finally returning to Sydney and their old habits.

This struggle to break from oppressive conditions is the undercurrent to **Mouth to Mouth** (1978) as it follows the lives of four unemployed youths scratching out a living from dole cheques, theft, menial shopwork and eventually prostitution. The desperate working-class whites and shanty-town blacks in **Backroads** (1977) use a more attacking strategy to fight their environment, tearing apart every social convention holding them under. Their spirit is fierce, but the mission suicidal; a tragic bloodbath ending their flight from oppression.

The FJ Holden (1977) deals with subtler resistance: the day-to-day boredom of working-class teenagers in Bankstown as they roam suburban streets in hot cars and alcoholic stupors. Their life is an endless competition. The boys compete for the girls and use their cars as coin — the price of mobility and the status that goes with it. Kevin (Paul Couzens) and Ann (Eva Dickinson) grab their moments together and fend off endless bouts with their "oldies", the cops and their jobs. This lifestyle

is eventually strained to breaking point; their relationship collapses and Kevin runs foul of the law.

A uniformly pessimistic mood pervades these low-budget films. Their characters are shown as depressed, bored and drug dependent. They fight against oppressive environments and dream of escape, but are emotionally and economically unequipped to win the battle. They go through the motions, and audiences admire the antics of these 'little battlers', secure in the knowledge that working-class heroes never win — they merely assume heroic dimensions during the fight.

The image of the 'little battler' is the myth of perseverance, a begrudging admiration from the middle class for people whose life has been a constant fight against oppressive conditions.

In **Picnic at Hanging Rock** (1975) and **The Getting of Wisdom** (1977), the experience of a girls' boarding school shows how female education moulded the appropriate passive personality, cocooning girls in the isolating middle-class morality that ensured their insulation, as women, from socially-relevant issues. The parallel process at a boys' boarding school is explored in **The Devil's Playground** (1976).

In **Picnic** one can see how cultural alienation goes deeper. Cut off from nature and the powers of imagination, one cannot perceive or enter a dimension of Australia that was familiar to Aboriginal culture. A psychic alienation is uncovered. Weir approaches this theme more directly in **The Last Wave** (1977). Neither film, however, quite manages to convey it.

Walkabout (1971) comes much closer, using its structure to orchestrate a transition

The schoolgirls of Bruce Beresford's **The Getting of Wisdom**.

161

Cathy waits at a restaurant for Dick. **Cathy's Child**.

between worlds; it conveys, through dramatic and surreal images, the story of a father and his children marooned in a desert world of altered reality and perception. The father immolates himself in his car, and the rest of the film portrays the exploding perception of the children's experience. Saved by an Aboriginal, they are taken on a journey through his world with its intimate knowledge of nature and its wider sense of perception. The erosion of black culture is contrasted with concrete cities and their ultimate product, concrete minds.

Australian films which explore the experience of people trying to escape from this prison of the senses include the avant-garde. The stream of consciousness dialogue in **Third Person Plural** (1978) and **Apostasy** (1979) underpins a psychological alienation of the most extreme intellectual form. In both films, the relationships between characters are predominantly verbal. Every subject, from the humblest household routine to the metaphysical and cosmic concerns of duality, is talked out until the sheer force of inquiry causes the language to break under its weight. The central characters in **Third Person Plural** stretch their perceptual and experiential boundaries to the limit. Nothing short of a "new language" can salvage the situation.

In the first sequence of **Apostasy**, history is retold as a gangster story. Classicism and romance are rejected as mystification, and the central characters squabble themselves into intellectual cul-de-sacs as the television in the corner spews out a coverage of the political machinations of November 11, 1975. Trapped like wild animals by the *realpolitik* of the day, and the intellectual contortions of their own minds, they occasionally stumble across abstract truths, only to rediscover them as flakes at the bottom of the ashtray. The characters reflect a numbed and narrow consciousness, locked in the forms that condition and imprison. In **Apostasy**, one is asked to reflect on fevers, drugs, dreams, drunkenness — altered states of consciousness one cannot hold onto without risking permanent madness. In **Sunshine City** (1973), Brett Whiteley articulates this potential, "I always feel there are bags in the brain that have never been opened."

Although these films are examples of an

Above: Outside the church, the priest (John Flaus) hands out pamphlets supporting the outlawing of the Communist Party. **Newsfront**. Below: The boat leaves port, taking Frank to the U.S. and fortune. **Newsfront**.

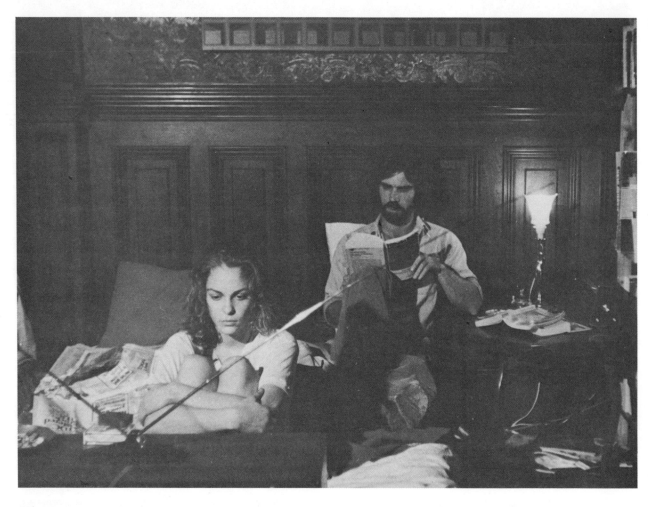

The woman (Juliet Backsai) and the filmmaker (Rod McNicol). Zbigniew Friedrichs' **Apostasy**.

avant-garde film culture in Australia, their directors have not benefited from the historical movements one associates with similar European filmmakers. Cinematic styles like German Expressionism or Italian Futurism were searches for a new language; by attacking the routine narrative, these avant-garde filmmakers hoped to reconstitute the child-like exploration of the film, thereby altering audience perception and producing a new order in cinematic language. A few Australian films have followed in this avant-garde tradition: **Harry Hooton** (1970), the Cantrills' homage to the local anarchist poet from the 1940s, and Albie Thoms' **Marinetti** (1969), an exploration of Italian Futurist theory in a complex, poetic work.

Although most of the films mentioned in this chapter reflect different states of alienation and loneliness, only a handful have tackled these themes directly and set them in an appropriate social context. **Newsfront** touched on the media's prominent role in Australian culture and the paramount influence of foreign control over mass communications. The persona of **Newsfront** are victims of history,

People trying to escape the "prison of the senses": Terry (George Shevtsov), Danny (Linden Wilkinson) and Mark (Bryan Brown). James Ricketson's **Third Person Plural**.

autonomous in their personal relationships but bound to the social and political attitudes of their time. The "Greek" films are pointedly assimilationist and based on traditional liberal sentiments for ethnic minorities.

The low-budget cinema of the period has achieved some success in exploring the social mores of working-class life, and the avant-garde has tackled the psychological alienation of paralysed perception and experience. However, the low-budget cinema has barely survived the massive government funding which still remains the key to the Australian film industry.

The economic, cultural and aesthetic influence of government intervention in the industry is expressed by the dominant commercial criteria used in the funding process. Private investment and commercial "viability" define the acceptability of a product which cannot depart from established formula, safe topics and recognizable themes. Yet the vast majority of Australian films have been commercial disasters. Only a handful have returned their investments or survived the crippling battle with foreign-owned exhibition and distribution chains. About $30 million has been spent in the past 10 years making so-called commercial features, and at most $3 million making so-called experimental films.[1] Ironically, on a cost-to-return basis, the low-budget cinema of the 1970s has been more financially successful.

The future for Australian films lies with the attitudes of government film funds. In the past they have leant towards middle-of-the-road

Frame enlargement from Arthur and Corinne Cantrill's **Harry Hooton**.

formula films in the hope of achieving box-office success and recognition in the *realpolitik* of the international industry. But the cards are stacked against the Australian producer. This country's population is too small to sustain a free enterprise industry through private investment, and the foreign ownership of exhibition and distribution chains severely limits potential returns to the producer. Government funds have restricted and confined Australian films within this false image of the market place. Should this continue, the funds will reduce the potential of their films to break through the economic and aesthetic restrictions imposed by Australian culture and, worse still, solidify the alienation found in the films by including it as an integral part of the film-funding structure.

10 CHILDREN'S FILMS

Virginia Duigan

There is a perfectly understandable tendency to think of children's films as in some way inferior to adult entertainment. After all, one's subconscious probably reasons that people grow out of children's films. In order to grow up, people put away childish things; and when they are adults, they don't rush off to the holiday matinee to see young Greg Rowe's latest film. Or if they do, they don't tell their friends.

Yet children's cinema stands or falls by roughly the same criteria as those applied to adults' films. If one accepts that a film aimed at children need not talk down to its audience, need not compromise artistic standards and can encompass many, if not most, of the subtleties, ironies and sophistication that adults value in their own entertainment, a children's film need not fall into a separate category.

There is one major difference, however: books, plays and films designed to appeal to a young audience almost invariably involve children. As a rule, adults don't greatly interest them; they are more intrigued by other children. They want to see themselves on the screen and identify with the action. Their own world, away from mortgages, parenthood and responsibility, appears infinitely more alluring.

Between 1969 and 1978, 13 feature films for young people were made in Australia. Although they encompass a variety of styles, they constitute a resounding reinforcement of some hoary Australian myths which should by rights be defunct. Most of the films have a country or semi-rural setting, and there is almost no acknowledgment that migrants (or Aboriginals) exist, let alone that they are a significant and influential force in society. The majority (nine films) have boys as the main characters; **Blue Fire Lady** (1977) and the animated **Dot and the Kangaroo** (1977) have a girl; **Ride a Wild Pony** (1975) and the semi-documentary **Lost in the Bush** (1973) have shared heroes/heroines.

An observer at a festival of Australian children's cinema might assume that most people are native English speakers, living in the country or by the sea in a tranquil landscape away from such 20th Century city phenomena as pollution and traffic congestion, broken families and overcrowded schools. He would conclude that Australia is a male-dominated country in which women are vague domestic figures who wait patiently at home while the men and boys go out in the boats, ride the wild ponies or avenge the reefs. The picture that emerges is strangely old-fashioned and especially curious when one compares it with children's literature, where the modern trend is towards extreme realism and the close documentation of social situations with which many children are familiar.

The almost complete absence of urban references in these 13 films separates the stories from the direct experience of most of their audience. The average Australian child has never sat on a horse, and **Blue Fire Lady** is the only film with much city footage. This would be largely irrelevant if there were some attempt at balance. Anyone, adult or child, enjoys the unfamiliar if it is imaginatively and provocatively presented. The city child knows there is an Australian bush where children fish and ride and do country-type things; this is neither foreign nor unexpected. And for a city child there is a particular excitement in watching Snook (Greg Rowe) among the tuna fishermen in **Blue Fin** (1978), or Teddy (Robert Bettles) winning the trotting race in **Born to Run** (1979).

It wouldn't matter if there were also the occasional acknowledgment that a lot of us are being brought up in housing commission towers, rather than sprawling farms. And the housing commission child has just as urgent a need to come to grips with his own environment, to discover the possibilities of an imaginative inner life, to identify with a few credible heroes and to get his life into perspective less clumsily than by such, often cruel, direct cinematic comparisons.

Being pragmatic, sensible creatures, child-

Opposite: Charles Schultz's **Blue Fin**.

Scene from Mende Brown's **Strange Holiday**.

ren tend to like their fiction clearly defined. Entertainment should be either reasonably realistic or pure fantasy. They distrust things in between, or which veer from realism to the foolishly far-fetched. They enjoy a joke, but they like to know when someone is joking. Directors who ignore this do so at their peril.

There is a tendency to cut corners in children's films. One such example is **Strange Holiday** (1970), made in Australia by American director Mende Brown. Jules Verne is given a credit for the story, but what unfolds is such a patronising and tedious saga that his ghost can be absolved confidently from any responsibility.

The film begins with a shipwreck that wouldn't convince a five year-old. In the next scene, the children – all boys, and far too many for this director to control — wake up on a deserted island. From then on the film is an amalgam of the worst features of *The Swiss Family Robinson*, *Lord of the Flies* and *Huckle-*

berry Finn. The examples of cheating are numerous. The boys quickly form equal teams with none of the usual spirited squabbling and jockeying for position. "Go and make a raft,

The jungle boy explores the big city in Mende Brown's **Little Jungle Boy**.

The crippled Josie (Eva Griffith), with the pony Taff, which she is given by her father. Don Chaffey's **Ride a Wild Pony**.

you guys'', orders the head boy, and in the next scene a well-constructed raft appears, as impeccable as a production-line Holden. This is plain stupidity: children love to see how things

Scotty (Robert Bettles) is dragged away from a reunion with his beloved pony by Josie's father (Michael Craig). **Ride a Wild Pony**.

are made, especially something as romantic as a raft. They should have seen the wood gathered, the logs nailed and the structure lowered gingerly into the water for its maiden voyage.

In another example, a boy tosses a rope to scale a cliff. The audience does not see the loop of the rope connect. The boy shins up and gazes round in amazement, but the audience doesn't see anything of his panoramic view.

Because children have real and often tortuous problems in their social orbits, they like to see other children grappling with difficulties and surmounting them. They like to see processes, developments, beginnings, middles and ends. In Mende Brown's world the children have only to ask and all is given: raft, a cave to live in, lamps (that miraculously survived the storm), loaded guns, plenty of water, ship's stores. There are no real quarrels, or tensions, no suspense and no interest. The director does his best with Australian fauna

("Crazy ostrich!" yells one boy at a fleeing emu), but one senses his growing unease.

Strange Holiday illustrates some of the unforgiveable sins in children's filmmaking. Mende Brown makes a similarly cynical job out of a film inaccurately called **Little Jungle Boy** (1970); but at least he has a tame elephant to provide some visual relief. But even here the audience is short-changed. It doesn't see nearly enough of the elephant and far too much of several distinctly unappetizing adults. Children have unerring judgment where grown-ups are concerned; they do not need over-made-up ladies, smooth men with matinee idol looks or romancing couples.

Little Jungle Boy purports to deal with a promising Mowgli-like character who emerges from the wilds on his elephant. Instead, it is largely concerned with adults' tiresome affairs: a missionary padre rebelling against the church, a misfit medico, a courting couple. There is far too much dialogue, and what little happens is often talked about, rather than acted out. Because children's experience of the world is necessarily limited, it is essential to see a story unfold. The audience is effectively forbidden any imaginative participation. Even the dialogue is stilted and banal: "So one morning he came to see me, in all his childish splendour, to say goodbye", intones the padre, after a monologue lasting five minutes and underscored by wistful violins.

One American director who does understand that children want fast, robust action laced with humour, not interminable, sentimental hogwash, is Don Chaffey. Beside the cynical amateurishness of **Jungle Boy** and **Strange Holiday**, his **Ride A Wild Pony** and **Born to Run** supply a refreshing counterpoint. Neither is an especially memorable film, but from the brisk openings and stirring music one feels in reassuringly professional hands. There is a lot to be said for Disney productions. Large budgets ensure that essential corners are not cut, and the audience is treated with due respect. When there is a fire in the stables (**Born to Run**), the audience sees it take hold. When a horse escapes from the blaze, they see it pick its way out. When the audience needs a convincing historical atmosphere (**Wild Pony** is set in 1911), settings and costumes are colorfully in period.

Both films centre on horses, and both star the same young actor, Robert Bettles, who is also used by Oliver Howes in **Let the Balloon**

Right: Henri Safran's **Storm Boy**.

Climbing trees instead of jumping puddles: Robert Bettles in Oliver Howes' **Let the Balloon Go**.

Go (1976). He is a lively boy with a handy Churchillian scowl and an engaging grin. More importantly, he has the kind of independent, faintly insolent air to which children respond.

In **Wild Pony** he is matched against a girl; and after watching these films one starts to think of girls in the "Just William" sense. The film sets up a situation of some complexity and subtlety: the boy, son of a struggling bush farmer, has his beloved pony. taken, unwittingly, by a neighboring rich family for their crippled daughter (Eva Griffith). The audience is torn between the rival claims, both of which have emotional and rational support. The two youngsters are equally spirited and determined; one is disabled by economic hardship, the other by physical injury. It is a tricky moral predicament, approached sensitively in the screenplay by Rosemary Anne Sisson and intelligently in the performances, particularly by John Meillon as the sympathetic local lawyer.

Wild Pony illustrates the truism that there are no easy answers to the real questions of life, and justice is neither automatic nor guaranteed. Life is not necessarily fair. Even the ending has an appropriately contrived flavor.

Let the Balloon Go, on the other hand, after a story by Ivan Southall, is a yarn of Alan Marshall-type simplicity. But this time the crippled hero climbs a tall tree instead of jumping puddles. The film has speed, child-oriented humour and a healthy scorn for pathos, and, like **Wild Pony**, engages the audience mentally and imaginatively. These two films, together with **Storm Boy** (1976) and, to a lesser extent, **Blue Fire Lady**, have an authority that comes from not shirking the problem of whether to give moral directives to children. Adults are often unnecessarily cautious about this; children, like most people, need values to which they can aspire, as well as heroes to believe in. The best children's films don't preach; neither are they remotely pious. They work by implication, giving the audience a framework in which to make up their mind.

Wild Pony illustrates a story from the school of hard knocks, and **Storm Boy** is a poetic fable from a similar source. But much of **Storm Boy**'s impact lies in constructive implication. All men are not senseless destroyers; therefore, it is possible to imagine a better world in which no men are destroyers. From a child's point of view it is a very hopeful film.

On this level, **Storm Boy** is deeply in tune with the natural optimism of children, one of their best and most fragile characteristics. It has a beauty and simplicity that strike a responsive chord, and it also has in Fingerbone Bill (Gulpilil), the Aboriginal, a hero approaching mythical stature. It is a quietly provocative

story on an unusually profound level, and, unlike most children's films, has no surplus fat.

There are few principal characters in **Storm Boy**: the boy Mike (Greg Rowe), his taciturn father (Peter Cummins) and Mr Percival, the pelican. In each of the most successful children's films made in Australia, animals (or birds) are an essential ingredient. In **Storm Boy**, the teasing, show-off pelican is really the central character, and for an audience of any age he is a winner. Like **Wild Pony**, with its lyrical shots of boy galloping pony through the Australian countryside, **Storm Boy** uses the gaunt, enigmatic wastes of the Coorong to great effect. Bleak, with windswept grasses and lonely shores, the landscape forms a trinity with the boy and pelican. Fingerbone springs naturally out of this impassive land, teaching the white boy its secrets and unlocking undreamt-of imaginative powers.

The film does not shirk reality, in the same way that reality has few qualms about wound-

Mike (Greg Rowe) and Fingerbone Bill (Gulpilil), a hero approaching mythical stature. **Storm Boy**.

ing the susceptibilities of children. By flying out against the buffeting gale with a life-saving line, Mr Percival saves a ship foundering in a storm. But, in life, heroism guarantees nothing except nobility of spirit: the free and beautiful Mr Percival is shot down by a party of hunters.

The climax of the film illustrates the fine line between showing everything and letting the imagination provide detail that is too personal, too intrusive for the camera to record. Mike's grief over the death of his pelican is not dwelt upon. He buries the bird in a sand grave, but its death is a devastating moment, more poignant because each watching child has been allowed to tailor the scene in his own way, making the experience individual and memorable. It is this kind of artistic reticence that stretches perceptions and develops imagination — an essential role of the best of childhood entertainment. A film that involves its audience, that makes demands, is satisfying in a way that passive enjoyment can never be. A child who goes from **Storm Boy** to a television pap series will know the difference, even if he doesn't articulate it.

Blue Fin is a film that is often linked with **Storm Boy** because it stars Greg Rowe, was written by the same scriptwriter (Sonia Borg) and made by the South Australian Film Corporation. Again, **Blue Fin** has few central characters and isn't fussily scrupulous about the facts of death; again there is a rural setting, although this time it is a small fishing community; and there is a rather faltering relationship between the boy, Snook, and his father, played with teutonic sternness by Hardy Kruger. But this time the director is Carl Schultz, instead of Henri Safran, and Schultz doesn't have the same finesse and finely-orchestrated verve. Nevertheless, **Blue Fin** is popular with its target audience, and it has some scenes of gutsy, almost swashbuckling action, particularly the sequences among the swarming school of tuna.

Up to this point there isn't much story, just a boy whose father thinks he doesn't have it in him to be a fisherman; the boy, of course, is determined to prove his father wrong. Later, after a spectacular storm which makes the one in **Strange Holiday** look like the fake it is, Snook gets his chance to prove himself. With the rest of the crew washed overboard and lost, the ship a shattered wreck and his father severely injured, the boy uses every ounce of ingenuity and courage to get the two of them back to shore.

Here is a classic situation that must be every child's dream: to take on the adult world and win. It is the very basis of childhood romance, and not surprisingly it crops up again in **Born to Run**. The climax of that film is a series of trotting races on which the family has wagered its future. In a series of exciting, well-shot scenes (at times reminding one disconcertingly of **Ben Hur**), the horse-drawn traps hurtle around a dusty circuit. Fortunes fluctuate predictably, tension mounts — Chaffey is a master at building suspense on an elementary "Will they or won't they?" level — and then the family's star driver, Teddy's older brother, is hurt. For a moment it seems the family must face bankruptcy and disgrace. But wait, who could step in for the final, decisive race? Who else but Teddy: small, slight,

Jenny (Cathryn Harrison) with her horse, and with Barry (Mark Holden). Ross Dimsey's **Blue Fire Lady**.

Above: Braving the storm, Marco journeys to the fabled city of Xanadu. Eric Porter's **Marco Polo Junior Versus the Red Dragon**. Below: Dot and the snake from Yoram Gross' **Dot and the Kangaroo**.

Tension in a faltering father/son relationship: Snook (Greg Rowe) and Pasco (Hardy Kruger). **Blue Fin**. Below: The windswept Coorong, a boy and a pelican. **Storm Boy**.

vulnerable and full of guts. And Teddy, driving against grown men and fighting against overwhelming odds for his family honor, triumphs — of course. Of such brave deeds, dreams and more prosaic games are made.

In an altogether different class is David Waddington's **Barney** (1976), a film which, on the surface, would seem to have certain important similarities. **Barney** tells the story of a 12 year-old boy, shipwrecked on the Australian coast in the 1800s. Again, boy against the elements, both natural and man-made, but here the comparisons end. The film chronicles the adventures of a rather stodgy young hero (Brett Maxworthy) who teams up with a singularly charmless Irish convict (Sean Kramer) after both survive yet another unconvincing shipwreck. The period is the gold rush, with uncomfortably-drawn quasi-Wild-West characters (the Irishman changes from calculating opportunist to reformed reprobate under Barney's purifying influence) and thoroughly unlikely things go on. All of which wouldn't matter much were it not compounded by constant evidence of cost-cutting, blatant plot holes, inept editing and graceless, fumbling humour. The film is a sanitized, fairyland 'Austramerica', written and directed with an airy disregard for children's intelligence and discrimination.

A measure of the achievement of a successful children's film can be its reception by an adult audience. A feature like **Storm Boy** can be just as enthralling if you are eight or 80, or 30 and cynical. **Barney**, on the other hand, while fairly well received by children, leaves an adult distinctly cold, and by this criterion alone is an inferior film. The obvious danger in all this, where adults control the purse strings and select the options, particularly for the under-10s, is for grown-ups to take children only to films they think are good (i.e., films they think *they* would enjoy too) rather than letting the children wallow in sub-standard rubbish now and again. Just as Enid Blyton never did anyone any harm until interfering oldies decided she was shallow and, therefore, bad, a foolish film like **Barney** isn't going to warp any aspiring young Peter Weir or Gillian Armstrong. Unfortunately, there are too many other children's films like it. Where children's rights are concerned, adults are often cynical; never more so than with their rights to entertainment that doesn't treat them like undersized morons.

Avengers of the Reef (1973), directed by Christopher McCullough, and starring Noel Ferrier and Gary McDonald, is a marginally less patronizing effort than **Barney**. With two fine comic names one would have thought it couldn't go wrong; but the film scarcely uses them. It takes an inordinately long time to get the story going, and treats its audience with breathtaking disdain. Once again, there is a castaway situation. After the bad man has dispatched Timothy's scientist father, young Tim (Tim Elliot) is seen drifting in a disabled motor boat. In the next scene, Tim appears miraculously washed up in Fiji, yet another idyllic, palm-fringed island paradise. Luckily, he meets a local boy of his own age, with whom he teams up. Much later, when the boys have reached civilization, Tim's Fijian friend fortuitously bursts on Tim and the villain during their confrontation in a hotel room. Surely it is not unreasonable for children to want to know how and why Tim's friend arrived just at the right moment; a director who thinks his audience should just grin and bear it doesn't deserve his job.

The script is shoddy and leaves too many fundamental questions unanswered. At the end Tim is reunited with his father, but we don't see anything of their meeting. Obviously McCullough wanted to avoid a mawkish scene, but he did so by avoiding the scene altogether. In a film where everything leads logically to this point, it is selling the audience short to gloss over it with an embarrassed hiccough. Certainly there is some superb Fijian scenery

Tim and his Fijian friend in Christopher McCullough's **Avengers of the Reef**.

The evil magician in **Marco Polo Junior Versus the Red Dragon**.

to keep the audience quiet, and a promising chase sequence, but these scenes, with the villain tracking down the two boys on the run, are long drawn out, handled without any snap or crackle and, finally, ennui-inducing.

At this point it is worth examining a film in a different category — one which manages to avoid such pitfalls and also to be a considerable artistic tour de force. **Marco Polo Junior Versus the Red Dragon** (1972) is a stylish and ambitious animated feature, produced and directed by Eric Porter. It is the tale of young Marco's journey to the fabled city of Xanadu and his hair-raising adventures. A witty, imaginative extravaganza, it combines elements of musical comedy, magic, pantomime, fantasy and suspense. Visually it is often stunning, like a series of paintings, and it uses vivid, dramatic colors. Many of the sequences are sufficiently evocative to stay in the memory: Marco's tiny sailboat adrift on a vast ocean; the storm at sea, the turreted fairytale city of Xanadu.

Porter recognizes the first two laws of dynamics in children's films: never be boring, and include a strong vein of humour. **Marco Polo** is ingenious in its use of humour, maintaining a deft balance between high drama and light relief. Much of the fun is quite sophisticated and pitched equally at adults — including some in-jokes for the grown-ups: "This is a ship of fools", growls a Long John Silver character; there is a long wrangle among the

A combination of animation and filmed backgrounds of the Australian bush. **Dot and the Kangaroo**.

Scene from Peter Dodds' **Lost in the Bush**.

drunken crew over whether one can say "man overboard" when it's a boy; and there is a limp-pawed camp dinosaur. The adult jokes also amuse the children, but for different reasons.

The film has much humour: verbal and visual jokes; eastern mystic, Popeye, and Gilbert and Sullivan jokes. There is a delicious moustachioed villain who finishes up hanging by his britches from the tower, and a princess who displays some Women's Lib resource. Voices are in the "fe, fi, fo, fum" tradition, exuberantly delineating characters. Accents — another aural joke — are an eclectic mixture of continents: American, Indian, Oxbridge and North Country. Almost the only accent missing, curiously, is the Australian.

The film is fast and furious, with one trick after another, and never succumbs to the temptation to linger, or even exploit to the full. It is a rich, multi-faceted entertainment, illustrating the immense advantages animation has over low-budget action. There are monsters, floods, giant waterfalls, dinosaurs, rampaging elephants, and villains who bounce back from unmentionable catastrophes. There is no illusion (apart from the central suspension of disbelief), and no feeling of having been sold short. It is even mildly instructive — the signs of the zodiac, the eastern star, Middle-East lifestyles, etc.

Dot and the Kangaroo, another animated film which could scarcely be more different — it is rather unfair to compare them — is gentler

and less frenetic than **Marco Polo**. Produced and directed by Yoram Gross, it is also aimed at a very much younger audience. Dot (a heroine for once) is a simpering, traditional little girl who is lost in the bush, and is befriended by the animals and birds. The film humanizes the wild creatures and gives them distinct personalities: a platypus, a dingo, kookaburras, snakes — even an imaginative bunyip.

At the opposite end of the scale, the most realistic of the films is the semi-documentary **Lost in the Bush**. Made on a shoestring budget by Peter Dodds, the film is based on a story by Les Blake, and set in the Wimmera district of Victoria in 1864. Of all the films this is the most emphatically Australian, with the children in their broad hats under the burning sun, the white-haired little boy, the leathery honest bush faces of the farmers in the search party. The scrubby bush is also unmistakeable, and one regrets that this was chosen rather than Frederick McCubbin's tall timber country.

Dodds wins fine performances from the three children, painful in their accuracy. It is a harrowing story; not so much a film for children as an Australian morality tale about the dangers of wandering unaccompanied into the bush.

Blue Fire Lady is the only other film that has a heroine. It is a realistic, compact and intelligent effort that avoids talking down and can be enjoyed by adults. The film also utilizes rural settings (with horses), and some excellent performances, from Cathryn Harrison as Jenny, Marion Edward as the buxom, heart-of-gold Italian landlady, Peter Cummins as the irascible racehorse trainer ("Animal lovers will

Father and daughter: Lloyd Cunnington and Cathryn Harrison. **Blue Fire Lady**.

Mrs G. (Marion Edward), Jenny and Barry (Mark Holden). **Blue Fire Lady**.

be the death of me''), and pop singer Mark Holden as Barry.

Jenny goes to Melbourne to find work in a racing stable, against the wishes of her father, whose wife was killed in a riding accident. There she has to contend with hostility from a stablemate and ill-treatment of the horse that is her special charge. The climax of the film is not a horse race but a sale.

Had **Blue Fire Lady** been an American film, it would probably have been unable to resist indulging in some teenage romance. As it is, the friendship between Jenny and Barry is handled with sensitivity and tact. The audience, a susceptible age group of widely varying maturity, is free to indulge in whatever pleasurable flights of fancy it chooses; there is nothing overt, and the film is the better for it.

Blue Fire Lady, together with the best of the titles under discussion (including, for that matter, the animated **Marco Polo**), demonstrates the value of using good actors. Lacklustre performances in **Little Jungle Boy** and **Barney** result in tired, unconvincing products that no amount of special effects can rectify.

Used in connection with cinema, integrity is one of those fashionable and pretentious words that put one's back up; but it is hard to avoid here. Defined as the belief that a project is intrinsically worthwhile, and the desire to reach the same level of artistic standards as one would aim for with a discriminating, informed audience, this kind of integrity is detectable in the best children's films. One responds to great cinema with a certain exhilaration and enhanced self-esteem, with the feeling that a film has evoked a personal response and willing participation, and the agreeable impression that one's experience of the world has been somehow expanded. It was worth the time.

The best children's cinema is no exception, and young people ultimately react against having their time wasted. The products of this accumulated resentment are apparent in every Australian city and country town. The great untouched area waiting to be tackled by the makers of children's cinema is the predicament of the city child, and the real implications of growing up in this society in the closing years of the 20th Century.

11 AVANT-GARDE

Sam Rohdie

It is not the avant-garde film that film theory has worked upon, but the narrative film. A consequence of this has been the development of grammars of narrative as rules for the production of narrative texts: i.e., general theories of narrative, and specific theories of narrative film.[1]

Despite the work by avant-garde filmmakers on film language — on the particularity of filmic signifiers, and on their material substances — theories for the production of avant-garde film exist only in the most adumbrated forms. A consequence of this situation has been the discussion of avant-garde film outside the terms of general film debate, as if "on its own terms". In practice, "on its own terms" has meant a discussion of avant-garde film in relation to artistic modernism and work in the traditional arts (however avant-garde), rather than to narrative cinema which theorists of the avant-garde film have rejected as foundering in traditional concerns of realism, illusion, representation and narrative exegesis.[2]

This essay is no more than a modest attempt to place avant-garde film within a more general context of film theory. At first, I found myself caught in the task of defining a particular Australian avant-garde film as distinct from other national film avant-gardes. Despite the obvious specificity of Australian conditions (from the most general cultural ones to detailed aspects of film production, distribution and exhibition), a specific Australian avant-garde film failed to appear to which I could assign a peculiar set of names, beyond that of their filmmakers, or the exotic nomenclature of Australian locations: Bouddi, Chauritichi, Uluru. The preoccupations of the Australian film avant-garde seemed not to be merely local, but to be related to the preoccupations of film avant-gardes elsewhere.[3]

What I shall do here is to provide terms for a discussion of avant-garde film and then begin to sort out Australian avant-garde films in relation to these terms.[4] I have tried to avoid giving these films names, other than, somewhat reluctantly, that of "avant-garde". The categories offered are more fields of practice, or relations between terms, than an absolute fixed ground.

I shall take an initial set of terms from a 1967 *Manifesto on the Hand Made Film* written by Albie Thoms of the Sydney Ubu School, one of the first groups of Australian avant-garde filmmakers: Dave Perry, Aggy Read, Albie Thoms.[5] The *Manifesto* insists on the absolute non-registration of external reality: i.e., the complete suppression of the camera, of its capacity to reproduce or to make images of things outside itself: "Let photography be no longer essential to filmmaking — hand-made films are made without cameras."

Complementary to the rejection of a mediated, recorded image is the demand for a wholly constructed, directly-made image, an absolute intervention upon the celluloid and the material substances of film: "They can be scratched, scraped, drawn, inked, colored, dyed, painted, pissed-on, black and white, bitten, chewed, filed, rasped, punctured, ripped, burned, burred, or bloodied with any technique imaginable."

Lynsey Martin describes his hand-made film **Whitewash** (1973):

"Horizontal movements, cross-hatching, holes punched, strobing with groups of lines, interweaving verticals, looping swirls, bushy forests of meshes (created with steel wool) and trapped (by spray fixative) images of sprayed-on water, and like bubbles in some dream, like *white* ocean, they *wash* over the screen."[6]

In 'pure' hand-made films it is the intervention as such which *is* the image in the form of scratches, incisions, paints, dyes. The means of image production coincide with the image produced — the films are 'about' scratch, incision, paint and dye.

So, in the founding gesture of the Australian film avant-garde, a manifesto appeared insisting on absolute non-registration on film/ absolute intervention upon the image. The terms imply their contradictory instances: absolute registration on film/absolute non-intervention on the image. In fact, implied are the terms of an ideal realism.

As if filling a negative space constructed by the Ubu *Manifesto* are the writings, more than a decade earlier, of French film theorist Andre Bazin:

"The objective nature of photography confers on it a quality of credibility absent from all other picture-making . . . we are forced to accept as real the existence of the object reproduced, actually re-presented . . . this transference of reality from the thing to its reproduction."

And, ". . . in photography . . . between the originating object and its reproduction there intervenes only the instrumentality of a non-living agent. For the first time an image of the world is formed automatically, without the creative intervention of man."

The *Manifesto* and Bazin's ontological realism are in a relation of recto and verso as contradictory idealisms. Realism seeks the presence of the very thing which the image denotes as absent; the reality no longer *there*, and therefore requiring that recourse to the image as a sign of a former presence; the exact, precise absence which it re-produces, re-turns. The Ubu *Manifesto* insists on the full presence of the image without reference to any externality, objects, or time.

In a realist film, the signifying image has a signified 'reality' to which it refers, which is not the image (the image contains it). In the hand-made film, the signifying image is itself the signified; the image *is* its own object. The ideal sign in the hand-made film is sign of itself, not of anything *else*. Says Lynsey Martin: "**Whitewash** has nothing much to say other than itself."

The terms, registration and intervention, and their contradictory instance, non-registration and non-intervention, form a logical grid of paired contradictions (⟷), oppositions (⟷̸), and simple implications (⟵----⟶), which may be represented:

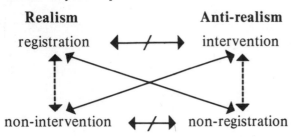

Realism		**Anti-realism**
registration		intervention
non-intervention		non-registration

A total then of six possible combinations may be calculated on the basis of the three sets of logical relations. It is in terms of these relationships between the poles of contradictory idealisms — one, a realism, the other, the extreme of a traditional modernism[7] — that I wish to discuss strategies of the Australian avant-garde film.

Non-registration and Intervention

In a recent interview in *Cinema Papers*, Corinne Cantrill said: "In looking at hand-made films there is nothing to involve one other than the quality of the image itself and its inherent qualities of movement, form, etc."[8]

The suppression of the camera and the rejection of photographic registration, combined with a direct involvement with the film material, establish a symmetrical *loss* of exterior-reproduced reality to be fixed on the image to a *gain* in reality by the image itself. The hand-made film asserts the reality of film against the reality of a referred-to world represented on film. The image is restored as object, not as means for the restoration of objects (illusionism).

The Ubu *Manifesto* stresses a self-contained, self-referring art object and has, as a consequence, the centring of the material substances of film (emulsion, celluloid, light and movement) as the defining specific character of film. Film is 'about' film. It is its very subject. Says Lynsey Martin (on **Whitewash**): "Its realization as pure hand-made film is that it is created purely with incising and sanding instruments on perfectly transparent colorless film. No color or black ink (with the exception of the inked titles) has been used. It harnesses completely the essence of scratch and light . . ."

Such marking of film may be structured, or not — at least not structured in the sense of a strictly ordered patterning of marks. If film material can function as a sign of itself, the structuring of such material can also be, tautologically, a sign of itself; that is, structure may be 'about' itself in much the same manner as incision or scratching is 'about' incision or scratching.

In Australia, hand-made film has been concerned with a seemingly spontaneous, not structured marking of film with a consequent emphasis on intuition, creativity, expression of self. The lack of apparent structure is a sign of an immediate, often unconscious, non-rational

Albie Thoms in his own **Marinetti**.

perception. The Ubu *Manifesto* specifically poses spontaneity, sensuality, visual intuition against intellection, understanding, knowledge: "... hand-made films are created spontaneously ... not to be absorbed intellectually, but by all the senses". And, Corinne Cantrill says: "These are the films which do act on our

essential beings, for which we have an immediate visual intuition".[9]

In the hand-made films, or sequences of hand-making — by Dave Perry: **Mad Mesh** (1968), **Album** (1970); by Aggy Read: **A Random Walk to Classical Ruin** (1971); by Albie Thoms: **Dave Perry** (1968), **Marinetti** (1968),

Two scenes from Albie Thoms' 1973 feature, **Sunshine City**.

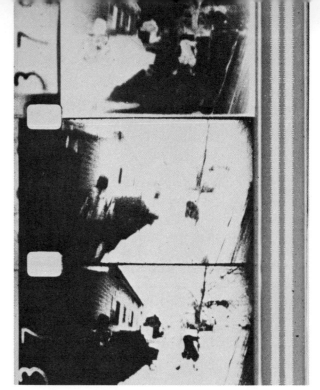

Dirk de Bruyn's **Running**.

Dirk de Bruyn's **Running**.

Sunshine City (1973) — the scratches, rubbings, tears, punched holes, cut-outs on the films have no discernible pattern or reference beyond their own presence. On the other hand, in Dirk de Bruyn's **Running** (1976), Read's **Far Be It Me From It** (1972), as well as certain sections of Thoms' **Marinetti** and **Sunshine City**, a precise structure is established but, to prevent any intellection by the audience, they bombard the senses so as to force the audience into a purely visual, immediate, and not rational 'response' to the film.

In what reads as a parody of behaviourist experimentation, Read describes an aspect of the structure of his **Far Be It Me From It**:

"I got a 100 feet of alpha rhythm film from a psychology department in the U. S. ... the flicker rate is one white frame and one black frame alternating ... It's interesting, because when you look at it the white frames are totally clear but the black frames have slightly curved edges ... so over two frames it would be about 55 per cent white and 45 per cent black. This is because the actual alpha rhythm in the brain, which they can plot on an ence[pha]lograph, is not a square wave tube pattern, which a simple black and white flicker is; in fact, it's got curves in it, and they determined that the way to create these curves in a visual form on film was to continue some of the clear frame into the next frame."

The editing of **Far Be It Me From It** involves a structuring of hand-made and photographic material, but in a manner which accords with the Ubu School ideology of hand-making. Structure in Read's film serves to oppose perception against understanding, as if to deliver the audience wholly within a visual and emotive sensual surround, an ambition not confined simply to the hand-made film, but implicit in the ideology generally of Australian avant-garde film. Writing of his film **Running**, which structures a flicker effect over a solarized 100 ft of looped film of a couple walking that has been printed to achieve a high contrast positive/negative version of the original image, De Bruyn says:

"Having four frames of negative and four frames of positive for 1300 feet is very hard on the eyes, but on some strange level they adjust and you are then in *an almost trance-like state in which you are just watching* on the screen. But it does take a lot out of your eyes. They take a lot of very systematic beating." [My italics.]

Registration and Intervention

Intervention to Bazin was a matter primarily of structures of narrative which threatened to destroy the integrity, fullness and uniqueness of the photographic image and its representation. In a conventional narrative each image functions as a sign for another image in a linear progression: an image is never there for itself but always as one in a chain of images. To restore, not simply the presence of things represented but the full presence of their representation, Bazin posed photographic registration in an opposition to intervention — intervention conceived as a variety of devices for the construction of illusory fictions: fragmentation of space, disruption of time, ellipsis, compression, summary.[10]

Bazin has been misrepresented as an apologist for illusionism. Rather, he was an apostle of a realism which sought somehow to break the illusory connections constructed by conventional narrative devices.

Bazin supported the 'new' narratives of Bresson and Rossellini, narratives which, however strange and in an ordinary sense not realist, sought to create 'objective' films in a manner not dissimilar to the 'objective' literature of Alain Robbe-Grillet and the French New Novel, where the object, event and person represented are freed from the continuous linear time of narrative destinies and spaces, the object and the event for the first

time *there*, present in their own rights, in their own duration, literally dislocated from a narrative stream.[11]

Bazin's stress on non-intervention is to be taken perhaps less literally than the contrary stress on intervention in hand-made film. In the desire for objectivity, Bazin wished to exclude from representation marks of personal expression, feeling, interpretation — all additions to the image and the 'reality' it reproduced. His aesthetic is specifically impersonal, quite other than an extreme avant-garde foregrounding of the person of the artist as origin, creator, source of film and of film language, an illusionism more staggering than anything ever proposed by Bazin.

Most films can be placed somewhere between registration and intervention, whether narrative or non-narrative film, realist or avant-garde. In the case of narrative film, intervention is most often subordinate to registration, maintaining the reality of the represented scene against the material reality of the image which has constructed it. In avant-garde film the relationship tends to be reversed: the image and its processes are privileged in relation to photographic registration.

Arthur and Corinne Cantrill have been making films together since 1960. At first their films were conventional documentary shorts, then from 1969, with **Home Movie** (1969), **Eikon** (1969), **White-Orange-Green** (1969), **Bouddi** (1970), **4000 Frames** (1970), **Earth Message** (1970) and **Harry Hooton** (1970), began an activity of avant-garde filmmaking which, along with the works of James Clayden, most equally blends what in their terms are

Two images from Arthur and Corinne Cantrill's **Home Movie**.

subject matter and film process, as if to conjoin a documentary past (record, registration) and a modernist present (process, intervention).[12]

Most of their films have the Australian bush landscape as a subject, but one subjected to concerns with light, color, camera movement, the concrete activities of photography, editing, and film manipulation. In the *Cinema Papers* interview Corinne Cantrill said:

"All the landscape work is to do with process, too! **At Eltham** (1973), for example, isn't that to do with a cinematic process? **Ocean at Point Lookout** (1977) is also very much to do with cinematic process. In landscape, there is this question of what sort of images you want to have in your head. And one of the images we want to get into more and more people's heads is landscape, so that they can perhaps be more aware of it, or think about it ... We have been trying to create a relationship between a cinematic process, or maybe two, depending on the film, and a particular landscape."

In the same interview, Arthur Cantrill said: ... "we have chosen certain techniques or processes which very often seem to be related to that landscape. Not so much to depict the landscape as it exists out there, but to reflect our response to it at a given time. It's not as if we are attempting to record the landscape to make people feel good about the fact that landscape exists. Our other landscape material is the three-color separation material, which is very process orientated, and to that extent gets right back to what are almost still photographic images of certain aspects of the landscapes."

Intervention for the Cantrills is less a mark

Above: A superimposition of landscapes. Arthur and Corinne Cantrill's **Earth Message**. Left: Arthur and Corinne Cantrill's documentary short, **Eikon**.

of person than it is of the film process, as if to foreground film against a background of the reality of a landscape. The landscape is there as part of the image to provoke a certain film process ("our response") with which the landscape is in some formal and aesthetic harmonious accord. If subject matter to the Cantrills is thought of as some kind of content, and process as its formation, what they institute ideologically is a notion of coherence as a mutual unity of content and form. It is expressed not only as a harmony of landscape and film process in terms of qualities such as light and movement that these both share, but as a harmony between the 'form' of the film and its 'content' expressed as meanings of hope, death, energy, and despair. The films, in their particular formations, are believed to function as metaphors of distinct ideas: "liberated rapid animation" in **Bouddi** as evocative of "life energies at work in a serene landscape ... ceaseless life rhythms"; **At Eltham**, "a metaphor of death"; **Earth Message**, "a film of oceanic consciousness"; **Harry Hooton**, "an expression of hope in time of turmoil".

Arthur Cantrill said: "... we have links with romanticism, and we don't try to block that in our work. We find it possible to deal with themes that are not considered by other avant-garde filmmakers, and at the same time use techniques which have very much to do with the processes of film: the act of photography; the act of editing; the action of light upon the film. The common denominator of a metaphor for life or energy is light. We see no difficulty in using this as a common metaphor for what might be regarded as somewhat romantic ideals, and combining these with

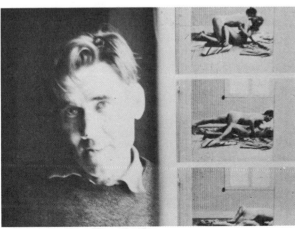

Above: Harry Hooton (left) and stills from **I'm Curious**. Arthur and Corinne Cantrill's **Harry Hooton**. Right: "Liberated, rapid animation" in Arthur and Corinne Cantrill's **Bouddi**.

Frame enlargements from Arthur and Corinne Cantrill's **Ocean at Point Lookout**.

physical material approaches to the filmmaking question.''

It is less that 'content' (the registration of a landscape) is disrupted by 'form' (the intervention of the film process) in the work of the Cantrills than that both aspects are used to construct a harmony in which neither the one nor the other is subject to a disruption, a displacement, or an analysis. The conventional divisions of form and content are posed, then conventionally resolved and smoothed out into a homogeneity, a compressed whole — the illusion of unity, rather than an awareness of (productive) difference.[13]

Registration and Non-registration

In Paul Winkler's **Bark Rind** (1977), a registered 'reality' (trees, leaves, bark, grass) is subjected to a radical reworking by means of single-frame shooting; multiple superimpositions of the same object in combinations of close-up, medium-shot and long-shot; the wearing down of the emulsion; rapid pans; a pulsating zoom; sound distortion of the 'natural' sounds of bees buzzing, of birds and crickets. Recorded nature, as objects and as sounds, disintegrates and fragments before a massive assault by the film against an initially-posed registration. The assault is not simply on the represented and recorded, but on the audience. Flickers, zooms, accelerated movement and rapid pans combine to disrupt simultaneously the place of the object and the place of the subject filmgoer, as all perspective and position are destroyed.

In **Scars** (1972), the film moves against isolated objects — trees, people, buildings — by an alternation of slow and rapid pans, by forward and reverse zooms, by the build-up of staccato camera movements, and an acceleration and intensification of sound somewhere between machine-gun and pneumatic drill, pulsating, intrusive, unyielding and unavoidable.

In **Chants** (1975), a multiple image of a gold cross is further multiplied, combined, bunched, dissolved and superimposed until the cross disappears, and becomes an abstract pattern of film. In **Red Church** (1976), an image of a church altar and its stained glass windows disintegrate into relations of light and color, reds, yellows and white.

Films by Winkler textualize and filmicize represented reality, forcing a loss of external

Timber workers 'attack' a tree in Paul Winkler's **Scars**.

The texture of a tree. Paul Winkler's **Bark Rind**.

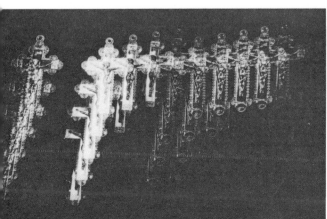

Multiple images of a gold cross. Paul Winkler's **Chants**.

Disintegrated image of an altar. Paul Winkler's **Red Church**.

193

reference by an aggressive fragmentation and dispersal of the filmed object, as if the object, lost to the 'world', is gained for the 'film'; the reality of the photographed world ('nature') replaced by the material reality of the film (the nature of film). More than other Australian avant-garde films, his films work within an extreme contradictory relation of registration to non-registration. Despite a certain metaphoric set of meanings which his films produce and to which the audience might more securely relate (the aggression of the zooms in **Scars** as analogues of aggression in the urban environment; the kinetic energy of the camera in **Bark Rind**, a sign of 'eternal growth'; the abstracted liturgical imagery of **Chants**, "a spiritual experience, a long prayer"), the assault upon the audience and the severe dislocation of position, place, perspective and viewpoint by the superimpositions of conflicting camera movements and camera scales serve to disrupt any security of messages which the films may otherwise be thought to put forward.

Intervention and Non-intervention

In an utterly opposed position to that of the films of Winkler, but as sharply contradictory are those of John Dunkley-Smith. In Dunkley-Smith's work, recorded images of external reality function as terms within an abstract and formal structure concerned primarily with the relationship of pattern to indeterminacy.

Pedestrians at a set of traffic lights. John Dunkley-Smith's **Down by the Station**.

Images of passing trains. John Dunkley-Smith's **Train Fixation**.

Events and objects represented in his films, before any reworking of these, are of a strictly determined yet random movement: e.g., pedestrians at a traffic light-controlled street crossing in **Down by the Station** (1977); traffic flow along an arterial urban roadway in **Hoddle Street Suite** (1977); the scheduled crossing of trains along parallel tracks in **Train Fixation** (1977).

The external reference of represented events is lost since the events appear as being without significance: nothing but traffic. The image of things is direct, undecorated, banal, without a rhetoric, 'styleless', and seemingly non-authored. Objects presented lack all intention: the camera in **Hoddle Street Suite** pans in patterns across the traffic, independent (as if oblivious) of the content of what is being 'taken'. There is only the brute, dull, denotative fact of cars, lorries, roadways and streets. 'Reality' is a purely structural term within the structure of the film; a structure organized around a play between determined orders and indeterminate relations.

In the films the registration, the taking of an exterior reality (e.g., views of a street from a second storey window in **Windows** — 1979), is predetermined. A mathematical order dictates shot patterns whatever these may be: a repeated panning shot, a circular camera movement, an alternating movement back and forth, a vertical-patterned movement. The author has no particular stake or responsibility in the sight shown, which in the case of **Windows** is literally what turns up randomly as the camera moves in a pre-arranged vertical pattern across the window frame. The window frames movement in the street; what is framed is whatever happens to appear from the window at the moment when its frame is within the mechanical (impersonal) frame of the camera which moves without reference to any 'events' which might occur. Structure, not person, marks out spaces in which things take place, in which (a) sight is constructed and deconstructed.

Imposed upon the structure of the shooting is another layer of structure equally subject to an impersonal mathematical genesis: variously, a pattern of masks upon the represented events, the imposition of a regulated flicker as masking, or, in certain films, the use of 'natural' masks of the passing of trains, or of wall-to-wall window masks constructed by means of vertical pans as in **Windows**. None of these structures bear any 'intrinsic' (i.e., natural, motivated) relation to the filmed sub-

Van as "moving object". John Dunkley-Smith's **Back in Bedford**.

jects. Again, relations are arbitrary, indeterminate, a further reading out of intention, of an originating author-subject source, and the contrary privileging of structure.

Since **Hoddle Street Suite**, most of Dunkley-Smith's films have been made to be screened in a variety of multiple projection relations involving one, two, or three screens (there is not *a* film). Multiple projection of more than a single film further serves to establish indeterminate structural patterns between multiple images formed in the actual concrete activity of projection. The works either superimpose multiple images on a single screen, as in **Bus Stop** (1978), or place images parallel on two or three screens, engaging relations of positive versus negative, black and white versus color, sound versus silence, etc.

Three films made by Dunkley-Smith in London in 1976 (**Back**, **Bedford's Back**, **Back in Bedford**) have been re-combined into a multiple projection triptych 'film', **Bedford**. The three films have been set side by side on three screens. On the left-hand screen: black and white, no sound, a non-moving object (house), and a non-moving camera. On the centre screen: color, natural sound (of a moving van), a moving object (the van going around the street), and a non-moving camera. On the right-hand screen: black and white, no sound, a moving object (the street 'moves' as it is seen through the moving van which crosses it), a moving camera (more precisely a still camera within a moving van, a tracking).[14]

Each film in the triptych is subject to a

An arterial urban roadway. John Dunkley-Smith's **Hoddle Street Suite**.

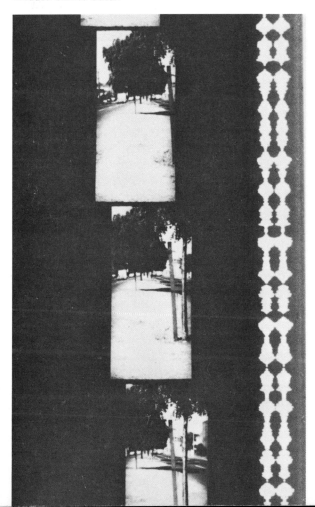

195

flicker mask pattern which begins with a single frame alternation of mask to image and, after a gradual running down, ends with a 'normal', unmasked, uninterrupted sight projected at 24 frames per second. Each film of the 'film' begins and ends at a different time though the duration of each is 23 minutes.

The three projectors are simply turned on in arbitrary sequence and at arbitrary intervals, so that even the flickers, calibrated in the separate films at the same rate of diminution, appear on the screen(s) at different rates in relation to one another. Images are looped-printed and systematically replayed in each film to a pattern on which the continuously diminishing flicker is laid down. No projection of the triptych is likely to be the same. The structure of relations between images will alter at each screening despite the 'permanence' of pattern within each film.

In **Bedford**, structures generate structures which produce further structures, without end or hierarchy. Structure, in the words of Dunkley-Smith, is an activity of structuring, not a thing to be named, had, fixed, or possessed. The film produces itself from within a play of differential patterns, contradictory codes, multiple intersecting systems: e.g., in **Bedford** relations of movement/not movement, framed/not framed, determined/not determined, presence/absence, positive/negative, subject/object, repetition/difference. Such relations do not end at a secure goal or purpose. They have no definite place to proceed, no particular structure to form, no definite origin or precise beginning from which they originate.

Dunkley-Smith's films realize a Bazinian ideal of non-intervention more completely than in any realism and by a radically contrary route. Structure, not person, produces the film; and structure operates independently, not only of human intention, but of exterior reality. In a precise sense nothing is registered in the films; rather, the films are a play of relations where events, objects and persons constitute only terms in a structural play, in which 'reality' is, from the beginning, part of language.

Non-registration and Non-intervention

The relation between non-registration and non-intervention, though logically possible, is not actual in Australian film practice, though it has been realized elsewhere, particularly in the work of Anthony MacColl in the U.S. In MacColl's **Line Describing a Cone** (1975), four projectors are set up at the corners of a large darkened space, each with a loop of film composed of black and clear leader so that the light from the projectors describes a cone shape as the loops run through the projector.[15] The projectors are turned on and the continuous loops project intersecting lines of light by their direct three-dimensional relation with its projection and with each other.

No image is registered. No screen is gazed upon. No three-dimensional illusion is constructed upon a two-dimensional surface. The concrete facts of light, of projection, of real duration, of real space, and of the literal production of the film by the audience most radically foregrounds the material means of film production. At the same time, film negates the most conventional aspects of registration and intervention, realism and expression, film and audience, product and consumer.

Registration and Non-intervention

As in the early films of Andy Warhol, it is possible to have a realist, almost Bazinian, relation of registration and non-intervention but with very opposite consequences. In **Empire** (1964) and **Eat** (1963), the camera is turned on an object or event from a fixed position and simply records what is there before it, but in a manner so extreme (a 12-hour sight of the Empire State Building; a 45-minute film of the 45-minute action of eating a single mushroom) as to overstress the fact of registration and non-intervention, so that it is these terms of the image production that became privileged and not the image produced.[16] An extreme pursuit of realism, in its very extremity, produces its exact contradiction.

Mike Parr and Tim Burns relate simultaneously to an extreme realism and to conceptual performance art. Their films are primarily documentaries of performance art situations and, therefore, outside the usual practices of most Australian avant-garde filmmakers.

Most of Parr's work has involved live performances of self-inflicted pain, some of which have been recorded and used in his films: **Idea Demonstrations** (1972), **Rules and Displacement of Activities, Part I** (1974), **Part II** (1976)[17]. Parr presents his 'own' body, which has only one arm, as incomplete, deformed, alien, impersonal and a site of work. He exhibits his dismemberment. The unity of his body, already fragmented in an act of disfigurement, is further disrupted by burning, exploding, tearing, cutting, mutilating, ripping open — his wounds and his pain made a spectacle. The entrances of the body are multiplied and re-marked as new bodily sites are constructed and constituted.

Parr's actions are aggressive, asocial, antisocial, and specifically revolting. He establishes a series of sensual material conflicts which are scandalous, socially outrageous, and culturally nauseating, disrupting not only his body, but a body of thought, of convention, and of conventional representations. In **Part II** the naked body (the classical nude) is smeared with dead fish, molasses, honey, ice cubes, fresh chicken blood, animal carcasses, feathers. The body is desecrated, humiliated, celebrated, deconstructed, and remade between terminological differences of warm/cold, death/flesh, smooth/sticky, classical/not classical,

illusion/performance. The body made totem becomes good to think by; its nature is transformed into the culture of a language.

Tim Burns' films, **CARnage** (1977), and **Against the Brain** (1979), unlike the films of Mike Parr, are less a working of concepts than diaries of fictional performances — in the case of **Against the Brain** the assassination of the general manager of the multi-national Utah Corporation. For both filmmakers, work on film is more a matter of manipulating what is there to be filmed (the pre-filmic event) than manipulating in the actual filming or in the editing. Most of the editing is done in the camera. Entire sequences are simply cut in series end to end.

Two kinds of performances take place in Parr's and Burns' works: one before the camera, and the other of the camera.[18] Both kinds are marked as performances. Neither of these means for the production of the image ever become transparent or hidden from view; on the contrary, it is these means that are precisely placed at the centre of the film.

Tim Burns' **Against the Brain**.

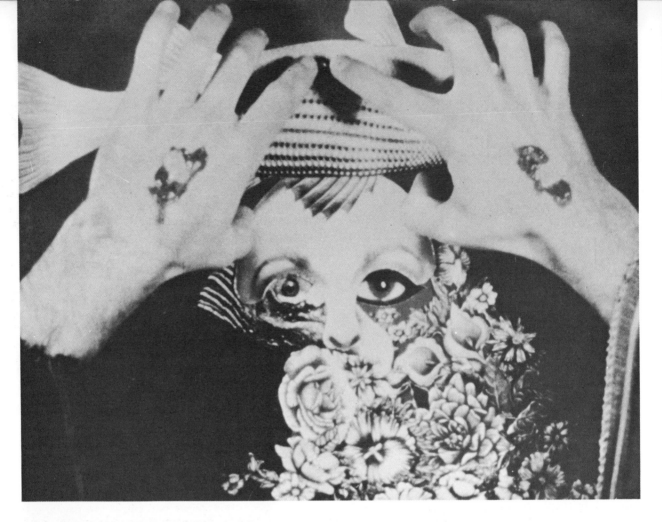

Above and below: Michael Lee's **Mystical Rose**.

In the work of other Australian avant-garde filmmakers, this foregrounding of the signifiers of the film is self-sufficient, the film becoming its own subject. In the works of Parr and Burns, however, what is of concern is the relation between the signifiers as means of production of meanings and the signified meanings. In **Part II** the killing of the rooster is significant in many ways, a single signifier but a plurality of signifieds: phallus, castration, dismemberment, father, Marx, Freud, asocial politics. Similarly, signified meanings — e.g., self-aggression versus social political action — are spread along a range of performance signifiers involving self-mutilation, group sexuality, group voyeurism, and group exhibitionism; these in turn involving differential relations between video and film, seeing and seen, subject and object.

For a realism, representation displaces the instance of its production. For an extreme modernism, the sign displaces all representation to become a sign simply of itself. In the performance films of Parr and Burns, the relation of object to sign is restored, not for one or the other term, or in an effacing harmony of both, but in their mutual difference and contradictory activity.

A great number of avant-garde films were made in Australia in the late 1960s. Only a few of these have been discussed. Many filmmakers have not been even mentioned: Bill Anderson, Jonas Balsaites, Phil Brophy, Mike Glasheen, Peter Kingston, Michael Lee, Dusan Marek, Tom Psomotragos and Garry Shead. It is not that the films which have not been discussed are without interest. Certainly were this essay a descriptive survey of the Australian film avant-garde they necessarily would have to be included, particularly the hand-

Tim Burns' **CAR**nage.

made work of Graeme Cutts and Lynsey Martin which combine the earlier hand-making concerns of the Ubu School with later, more structural interests; also the structural plays of pattern and perceptual space devised in the films of Jonas Balsaites; and the work of Michael Lee, including his **Mystical Rose** (1976), involving relations of process and representation which link him to the Cantrills (as well as to the concern of Parr and Burns with social meanings).[19] But what I have done instead is to see a number of emphases and tendencies in the filmmaking practices of the Australian avant-garde as these relate to issues of realism, representation, person and language. I have discussed films and filmmakers which either typify certain positions or have attempted a somewhat radical departure from a conventional avant-garde modernism, as is the case I believe with the works of Burns, Parr, Dunkley-Smith and Winkler.

FEATURE CHECKLIST 1970~79

The following checklist covers all dramatic features made in Australia since 1970. (A feature is defined as a film made on 35mm or 16mm, and 60 minutes or longer in duration.) The director's name is given under the title.

The date given for a film is that of its Australian commercial release. The only exceptions are films premiered at overseas festivals and awaiting release in Australia.

1970
Jack and Jill: A Postscript
Phillip Adams, Brian Robinson
Three to Go
Brian Hannant, Oliver Howes, Peter Weir
Adam's Woman
Phillip Leacock
Beyond Reason
Giorgio Mangiamele
Strange Holiday
Mende Brown
Little Jungle Boy
Mende Brown
Color Me Dead
Eddie Davis
Squeeze a Flower
Marc Daniels
The Set
Frank Brittain
Ned Kelly
Tony Richardson
That Lady From Peking
Eddie Davis
The Naked Bunyip
John B. Murray
Harry Hooton
Arthur and Corinne Cantrill

1971
A City's Child
Brian Kavanagh
Wake In Fright
Ted Kotcheff
Walkabout
Nicolas Roeg
Country Town
Peter Maxwell
Nickel Queen
John McCallum
Stockade
Hans Pomeranz
Stork
Tim Burstall
And the Word Was Made Flesh
Dusan Marek
Shirley Thompson versus the Aliens
Jim Sharman

Demonstrator
Warwick Freeman
Bello onesto emigrato Australia sposerebbe compaesana illibata (Girl in Australia)
Luigi Zampa
Sympathy in Summer
Antony I. Ginnane
Bonjour Balwyn
Nigel Buesst

1972
Marco Polo Junior Versus The Red Dragon
Eric Porter
Sunstruck
James Gilbert
The Adventures of Barry McKenzie
Bruce Beresford
806/The Beginning
Chris Lofven
Private Collection
Keith Salvat
The Office Picnic
Tom Cowan

1973
Alvin Purple
Tim Burstall
Sunshine City
Albie Thoms
Don Quixote
Rudolph Nureyev, Robert Helpmann
An Essay on Pornography
Chris Carey
Skin of Your Eye
Arthur and Corinne Cantrill
Lost in the Bush
Peter Dodds
Libido
John B. Murray, Tim Burstall, Fred Schepisi, David Baker
Sabbat of the Black Cat
Ralph Marsden
Crystal Voyager
Franz Falzon, George Greenough
27A
Esben Storm
Avengers of the Reef
Chris McCullugh
Dalmas
Bert Deling

1974
Yaketty Yak
David Jones

Alvin Rides Again
  David Bilcock, Robin Copping
Stone
  Sandy Harbutt
Number 96
  Peter Bernardos
Petersen
  Tim Burstall
The Cars That Ate Paris
  Peter Weir
Between Wars
  Michael Thornhill
Wokabout Bilong Tonten
  Oliver Howes
Rolling Home
  Paul Witzig
Children of the Moon
  Bob Weis
Barry McKenzie Holds His Own
  Bruce Beresford

1975
The True Story of Eskimo Nell
  Richard Franklin
Made in Australia
  Zbigniew Friedrichs
Picnic at Hanging Rock
  Peter Weir
The Love Epidemic
  Brian Trenchard Smith
Sunday Too Far Away
  Ken Hannam
The Great MacArthy
  David Baker
The Removalists
  Tom Jeffrey
Inn of the Damned
  Terry Bourke
End Play
  Tim Burstall
Scobie Malone
  Terry Ohlsson
Plugg
  Terry Bourke
The Man From Hong Kong
  Brian Trenchard Smith
The Golden Cage
  Ayten Kuyululu
The Box
  Paul Eddy
Ride a Wild Pony
  Don Chaffey
The Lost Islands
  Bill Hughes
Sidecar Racers
  Earl Bellamy
Solo Flight
  Ian Mills
Pure S . . .
  Bert Deling
Australia After Dark
  John Lamond
How Willingly You Sing
  Gary Patterson
Nuts, Bolts and Bedroom Springs
  Gary Young

Promised Woman
  Tom Cowan
Down the Wind
  Kim McKenzie, Scott Hicks
The Firm Man
  John Duigan

1976
Don's Party
  Bruce Beresford
Fantasm
  Richard Bruce (alias for Richard Franklin)
Oz
  Chris Lofven
Mad Dog Morgan
  Philippe Mora
Storm Boy
  Henri Safran
The Devil's Playground
  Fred Schepisi
Summer of Secrets
  Jim Sharman
Barney
  David S. Waddington
Eliza Fraser
  Tim Burstall
Caddie
  Don Crombie
Break of Day
  Ken Hannam
The Fourth Wish
  Don Chaffey
The Trespassers
  John Duigan
Surrender in Paradise
  Peter Cox
The Olive Tree
  Edgar Metcalfe
Deathcheaters
  Brian Trenchard Smith
Illuminations
  Paul Cox
Let the Balloon Go
  Oliver Howes
Betty Blokk-buster Follies
  Peter Batey

1977
High Rolling
  Igor Auzins
The Getting of Wisdom
  Bruce Beresford
The Mango Tree
  Kevin Dobson
Journey Among Women
  Tom Cowan
Inside Looking Out
  Paul Cox
Fantasm Comes Again
  Eric Ram (alias for Colin Eggleston)
Summerfield
  Ken Hannam
Raw Deal
  Russell Hagg
Highway One
  Steve Otton

The New Australian Cinema

The Picture Show Man
John Power
The FJ Holden
Michael Thornhill
The Last Wave
Peter Weir
Cosy Cool
Gary Young
Summer City
Chris Fraser
Blue Fire Lady
Ross Dimsey
Backroads
Phil Noyce
Dot and the Kangaroo
Yoram Gross
At Uluru
Arthur and Corinne Cantrill

1978
The Irishman
Don Crombie
Mouth to Mouth
John Duigan
The Chant of Jimmie Blacksmith
Fred Schepisi
Newsfront
Phil Noyce
Weekend of Shadows
Tom Jeffrey
The Last Tasmanian
Tom Haydon
The Night The Prowler
Jim Sharman
Patrick
Richard Franklin
Long Weekend
Colin Eggleston
Solo
Tony Williams
Blue Fin
Charles Schultz
Little Boy Lost
Terry Bourke
ABC of Love and Sex — Australia Style
John Lamond
Third Person Plural
James Ricketson

The Reef
John Hayer

1979
Dawn!
Ken Hannam
Felicity
John Lamond
Snapshot
Simon Wincer
Thirst
Rod Hardy
Dimboola
John Duigan
My Brilliant Career
Gillian Armstrong
The Odd Angry Shot
Tom Jeffrey
Money Movers
Bruce Beresford
Mad Max
George Miller
Kostas
Paul Cox
Cathy's Child
Don Crombie
Tim
Michael Pate
The Last of the Knucklemen
Tim Burstall
The Journalist
Michael Thornhill
Apostasy
Zbigniew Friedrichs
Palm Beach
Albie Thoms
In Search of Anna
Esben Storm
Born to Run*
Don Chaffey

---

* Made in 1976 and originally titled **Harness Fever**, this film was not released theatrically in Australia. It was, however, shown under the title **Born to Run** as two consecutive episodes of **The Wonderful World of Disney** on television.

CONTRIBUTORS AND ACKNOWLEDGMENTS

Rod Bishop: Senior tutor in film at the Preston Institute of Technology. Writer and director of several short films and documentaries.

Keith Connolly: Film critic and arts editor of *The Herald*, Melbourne.

Susan Dermody: Lecturer in film at the New South Wales Institute of Technology. Presently co-editing a book on Australian cultural history.

Virginia Duigan: Freelance journalist and frequent contributor to national magazines and newspapers.

Fiona Mackie: Lecturer in sociology at La Trobe University and novelist. Recently completed a PhD on critical phenomenology. Has also worked on several independent films.

Adrian Martin: Assistant teacher in film studies at the Melbourne State College, and freelance writer on film.

Geoff Mayer: Lecturer in English at the State College of Victoria at Coburg, and previously method tutor in film at La Trobe University.

Brian McFarlane: Head of the Department of English and Common Languages at the State College of Victoria at Frankston. Edited several books of literary essays and author of *Martin Boyd's Langton Novels*.

Meaghan Morris: Film critic for *The Sydney Morning Herald*. Part-time lecturer in semiotics at the New South Wales Institute of Technology.

Andrew Pike: Research fellow in the Research School of Pacific Studies at the Australian National University, Canberra. Co-author with Ross Cooper of *Australian Films 1900-1977*.

Sam Rohdie: Lecturer in cinema studies at La Trobe University.

Tom Ryan: Lecturer in film studies at the Melbourne State College. Presently co-authoring a book with Michael Walker on melodrama in the cinema. Contributor to *Movie* and *Film Comment*.

The Editor would like to thank the following individuals and organizations for their assistance in making available prints of films, or providing screening facilities: Phillip Adams; Australasian Film Hire (John Politzer, Barry Hall); Australian Film Commission (Alan Wardrope, Geoff Gardiner, Murray Brown); Australian Film Institute (John Foster, Sue Murray, Kevin Morrison); Harold Baigent; Jenny Barty; Terry Bourke; Mende Brown; Mal Bryning; Tony Buckley; Arthur and Corinne Cantrill; Joy Cavill; Tom Cowan; Paul Cox; John Duigan; Bernard Eddy; David Elfick; Richard Franklin; Noel Ferrier; Filmways (Ian Williams); Fox-Columbia (Frank Henley); Antony I. Ginnane; Gordon Glenn; Garry Gray; Greater Union Organization (Doug O'Brien, Joyce Dowling-Smith); Greater Union Film Distributors (Keith Milroy); Yoram Gross; GTV-9 (Ross Plapp); Russell Hagg; Tom Haydon; HSV-7 (Wendy Brock, Marg Young); Lyn Hyem; Tom Jeffrey; Byron Kennedy; John Lamond; Chris Lofven; Pat Lovell; Giorgio Mangiamele; George Miller; Natalie Miller; Sue Milliken; Betty McDowell, McElroy and McElroy (Jim McElroy, Hal McElroy, Fiona Gosse); National Library, Films Division (Ray Edmondson, Karen Foley, Jennifer Sabine); New South Wales Film Corporation; Steve Otton; Michael Pate; Eric Porter; Mike Reid; Roadshow Distributors; Jim Sharman; South Australian Film Corporation (Paul Davies, David Sabine); State Film Centre; David Stratton; Sydney Filmmaker's Co-operative (Peter Page); Michael Thornhill; Twentieth Century-Fox; United Artists (Geoff Hamilton); Victorian Film Corporation (Colin James); John Weiley; Bob Weis; Paul Witzig.

The Editor would like to thank the following individuals and organizations for their assistance in providing stills and/or clearances: Australian Film Commission (Rea Francis); Australian Film Institute (Matthew Percival); Australian Television Program Sales (Ron Booker); Brooks White Organization (Kevin Brooks, David White); Tony Buckley; Tim Burns; Tim Burstall; Arthur and Corinne Cantrill; Elsa Chauvel; Cinesound (W. Stratton); Noel Ferrier; Filmhouse (Robert Le Tet); Tom Jeffrey; Antony I. Ginnane; Greater Union Organization (Joyce Dowling-Smith); Ian Hannah; Viccy Harper; Hoyts (John Mitchell, John Thornhill); Chris Lofven; Pat Lovell; Natalie Miller; Sue Milliken; McElroy and McElroy (Jim McElroy, Fiona Gosse); National Library (Glenys McIver); Andrew Pike; James Ricketson; Roadshow Distributors (Alan Finney, Ian Kerr, Marilyn Greig); South Australian Film Corporation (David Sabine); Jeanine Seawell; Mark Strizic; Chris Suli; Sydney Filmmakers' Co-operative (Peter Page); Victorian Film Corporation (Andrew Knight, Colin James); Paul Winkler.

Special thanks to Keith Connolly for his editorial advice.

NOTES

1 The Past: boom and bust

1 In 1931, Union Theatres was restructured and re-named as Greater Union Theatres. Later it became the core of the present Greater Union Organization.
2 *Daily Telegraph*, Sydney, November 9, 1946.

2 Social Realism

1 *Fontana Dictionary of Modern Thought*, London, 1977.
2 *Cinema Papers*, No. 8, p. 347, 1976.
3 *Who Needs Shakespeare?*, International Publishers, New York, 1973.

3 Comedy

1 *Movie Comedy*, ed. Stuart Byron and Elizabeth Weis, Grossman, New York, 1977, p. 284.
2 *The Age*, March 1, 1979.
3 Russel Ward compares the frontier tradition in both countries in *The Australian Legend*, Oxford University Press, 1958. See particularly pp. 222-235.
4 T. Inglis Moore, *Social Patterns In Australian Literature*, Angus and Robertson, 1971, p. 174.
5 G. Blainey, *The Tyranny of Distance*, Sun Books, 1966, p. 172.
6 Ibid.
7 R.Ward, Op cit.
8 Ibid, pp. 1-2.
9 The other basic screen comic modes are situation comedy, which is common today, particularly on television; and the man/woman screwball comedy, which reached its high point in Hollywood in the late 1930s (e.g., **The Awful Truth**, **His Girl Friday**, **Bringing Up Baby**), and revived in more recent years with **What's Up Doc**, **A Touch of Class**, etc. This mode is noticeably absent in the 1970s Australian cinema. The third broad mode is parody and this forms the basis of the comedy from people such as Norman Gunston and Paul Hogan, and in such television shows as **The Naked Vicar Show**.
10 Barry's anachronistic qualities are easily established by his dress — broad-brimmed 'cocky's' hat, double-breasted pin-stripe suit with stove-pipe pants of the late 1940s — together with his attitude to such matters as motherhood, royalty and sex.
11 *The Age*, April 28, 1979.
12 D. Williamson, *Don's Party*, Currency Press, 1973, pp. 8-9.
13 The party takes place on Saturday evening, October 25, 1969, as the election results for the 27th Parliament begin to emerge.
14 *The Age*, April 28, 1979.
15 Will Wright, *Six Guns and Society*, University of California Press, 1975.
16 Ibid, Ch. 7.
17 The top shearer in the shed.
18 **The Picture Show Man**, with its anachronistic hero facing difficulties because of social and technological change, is similar in this respect to Sam Peckinpah's **The Ballad of Cable Hogue** (1970).

19 Another film in this tradition is the lunatic **Yaketty Yak** (1974) which jettisons narrative, reality and coherence.

4 Horror and Suspense

1 One is reminded of the opening remark of James Agee's 1945 review of **Uncle Harry**: "It may be unforgivably decadent of me, but I cannot get much excited about incest." *Agee on Film*, McDowell and Obolensky, New York, 1958.
2 My review of **Patrick** in *Cinema Papers*, No. 18, pp. 141-2, develops this idea more fully.
3 Casey's numerous screenplays include the remarkable Bette Davis films, **Dark Victory**, **The Old Maid** and **Now Voyager**, Sam Wood's **King's Row** and Fritz Lang's **While the City Sleeps**.
4 *Cinema Papers*, No. 15, p. 259.
5 *Cinema Papers*, No. 15, p. 244.

7 Historical Films

1 Stephen Heath, "Questions of Property: Film and Nationhood", *Cinetracts*, No. 4, p. 10.
2 Christian Metz, "History/Discourse: Notes on Two Voyeurisms", *Edinburgh '76 Magazine*, p. 21.
3 Raymond Williams' tracing of the meaning of the word "history" might be of particular interest here. See *Keywords*, Fontana, 1976, pp. 119-120.
4 Keith Connolly, **Eliza Fraser** (review), *Cinema Papers*, No. 12, p. 362.
5 Of particular relevance here is the exchange which occurred in the pages of *The Age* Green Guide (November 16, 30, and December 7, 1978) between Bronwyn Binns, the creator of **Against the Wind**, and a collection of historians and others critical of the television series.
6 Robert L. Carringer, "**Citizen Kane, The Great Gatsby**, and some Conventions of American Narrative", *Critical Inquiry*, Winter, 1975, p. 320. Carringer also comments of **Citizen Kane** that "Kane's is . . . a story of the possession of America".
7 Colin McArthur, *Television and History*, British Film Institute Television Monograph, No. 8, London, 1978, p. 22.
8 Bill Nichols, "Fred Wiseman's Documentaries: Theory and Structure", *Film Quarterly*, Spring, 1978.
9 **The Last Tasmanian** was screened on Australian television shortly after its cinema release.
10 The Australian Logie awards, 1979.
11 "Michel Foucault: Interview", translated in *Edinburgh '77 Magazine*, pp. 21-22.

8 Personal Relationships and Sexuality

1 Examples of such criticism addressed to American and European cinema are:
M. Haskell, *From Reverence to Rape*, New York, Penguin, 1974.
J. Mellen, *Women and their Sexuality in the New Film*, New York, Horizon Press, 1973.

2 The filmmaker who came in for most criticism was Tim Burstall: cf John Tittensor's review of **Alvin Purple** in *Cinema Papers*, No. 2, p. 179, and Burstall's response to this and other criticisms in "What's it like on the receiving end of Australian film criticism?", *Cinema Papers*, No. 7, pp. 214-215.

3 **Fantasm** was made by Richard Franklin using the alias of Richard Bruce.

Suggested reading:

1 *A Catalogue of Independent Women's Films*, ed. Sydney Women's Film Group, Sydney Filmmakers' Co-operative Ltd, 1979.

2 D. Baker, "In Search of **The Goodbye Girl**", *Cinema Papers*, No. 17, pp. 24-27.

3 B. Hodson, "A State of False Consciousness — Australian Film", *Cinema Papers*, No. 2, pp. 125-127.

4 N. Purdon, "Under Western Eyes", *Cinema Papers*, No. 7, pp. 217-219, 286.

5 "David Williamson Interviewed", *Cinema Papers*, No. 1, pp. 6-11, 93.

9 Loneliness and Alienation

1 Taken from an interview with Albie Thoms, *Cinema Papers*, No. 22, p. 472.

11 Avant-garde

1 *Screen*, the leading journal of film theory in English, devotes itself almost exclusively to the investigation of narrative codes in film. Since narrativity is not a particular preserve on film, much of the major theoretical work on narrative has come from outside the area of film, specifically in studies of narrative by Bakhtin, Barthes, Genette, Greimas, Levi-Strauss and Propp. Much of Christain Metz's cinema semiotics turns on narrative systems as at the centre of film structures.

2 If film theory has tended to neglect avant-garde film, theorists of the avant-garde film have equally tended to neglect a relation between the avant-garde film and narrative film, particularly in the U.S. in the writings of A. Michelson and P. Adams Sitney. For an important critique of their positions see Peter Wollen's " 'Ontology' and 'Materialism in Film' ", *Screen*, Vol. 17, No. 1, Spring, 1976.

3 Two specific conditions of the Australian avant-garde film may be noticed, though I am reluctant to speculate on their aesthetic significance or consequences: the Australian avant-garde film begins some half-century after its beginnings in Europe, an entire generation after its post-war appearance in the U.S.; Australian avant-garde film-makers tend to be more isolated from each other, from filmmakers, abroad, an audience, and official recognition and support than their overseas counter-parts. In Melbourne, there is no regular venue for the screening of avant-garde films, Australian or not; in Sydney, the Filmmakers' Co-operative gives primary attention to short political documentaries and independent short narratives, while its house journal, *Filmnews*, 'reviews' ordinary feature narratives on the circuits in a language not far beneath that of the daily press.

4 Many of the ideas in this essay derive from Peter Wollen's writings, particularly the " 'Ontology'... " article cited above.

5 The artistic context of the Ubu filmmakers seems to have been a traditional, albeit specific, European modernism: Artaud, Jarry, Marinetti, and American Abstract Expressionism, the latter most clear in the hand-making ideology and film practice.

6 Lynsey Martin is a Melbourne-based filmmaker, and though his work is roughly contemporaneous with the Ubu School, he was not a member of it; his hand-made films have a quality of carefully-controlled system and structure that the more self-expressive Ubu School films notably lack.

7 See A. J. Greimas' "Elements of a Narrative Grammar", *Diacritics*, March 1977; also Peter Wollen's "Two Avant-gardes", *Studio International*, 190, No. 978, 1975. The Wollen model sets out a sign-referent relation to distinguish two avant-gardes: one privileging the sign to the seeming negation of all referents, except the self-reference of the sign itself; the other positing a critical relation of sign to referent. I have added to this opposition the privileging of referent to sign in the narrative cinema and computed a series of logical relations of registration and intervention from a model proposed by Greimas for the generation of meaning and of narratives.

8 *Cinema Papers*, No. 21, pp. 359-361, 400, 403.

9 There is a formulaic ontology encased in this unfortunate expression of idealist ideology: essence of man/essence of film/nature of man/nature of film.

10 For a full discussion of these narrative orderings of temporal duration see G. Genette's *Figures III*, Du Seuil, 1972, pp. 122-144; also P. Wollen's "Introduction to **Citizen Kane**", *Film Reader*, No. 1, 1975, pp. 13-14. Wollen derives his categories, un-acknowledged, from Genette. Metz's "Grande Syn-tagmatique" of narrative film seems no more than a transposition of this restricted aspect of narrative temporality.

11 See Roland Barthes' "Objective Literature", "There is No Robbe-Grillet School", "The Last Word on Robbe-Grillet?", *Critical Essays*, Northwestern, 1972; also G. Genette's "Vertige Fixe", *Figures I*, Du Seuil, 1966.

12 See particularly Clayden's films **Back to Back** and **Workstitle**.

13 For what seems to me at least a terminological sorting out of the idealist difference of form and content, see C. Metz's "Methodological Propositions for the Analysis of Film", *Screen*, Vol. 14, Nos. 1 and 2, Spring/Summer 1972.

14 On their own, the films establish expectations of an eventual 'full view' and a wholeness as well as a calculated suspense of arrival/disappearance of the van and objects; the films projected together subvert these easy identifications.

15 I am relying on my memory of the MacColl work; there may have been more than four projectors in the installation, either six or eight.

16 **Empire** in fact elongates 'real' duration since the sight of the building is filmed at 24 frames per second but projected at 16 frames per second so that the eight-hour film takes 12 hours to watch.

17 Peter Kennedy was involved with **Idea Demonstra-tions** and Part 1 of **Rules** as a joint filmmaker with Mike Parr.

18 Or, in other terms, a relation of non-cinematic codes to cinematic codes as Metz defines these.

19 See particularly Balsaites' **Processed Process** (1974) and **Space-Time Structures** (1977); Cutts' **Dots** (1972) and **Luna Lunera** (1973); Lee's **Black Fungus** (1971), **Contemplation of the Rose** (1971), and **National Geographic Magazine** (1971); and Martin's **Approximately Water** (1972) and **Inter-View** (1973).

TITLE INDEX